Entertainment Directory

EDINBURGH
TRAVEL GUIDE
2015

SHOPS, RESTAURANTS, ATTRACTIONS & NIGHTLIFE

The Most Positively
Reviewed and Recommended
by Locals and Travelers

EGP
Editorial

EDINBURGH
TRAVEL GUIDE
2015

SHOPS, *RESTAURANTS, ATTRACTIONS* & *NIGHTLIFE*

EDINBURGH TRAVEL GUIDE 2015
Shops, Restaurants, Attractions & Nightlife

© Jack M. Hirschman, 2015
© E.G.P. Editorial, 2015

Web: http://www.EGPGuides.com/

ISBN-13: 978-1505245080
ISBN-10: 1505245087

INDEX

EDINBURGH TRAVEL GUIDE 2015

Shops, Restaurants, Attractions & Nightlife

*This directory is dedicated to Edinburgh Business Owners and Managers
who provide the experience that the locals and tourists enjoy.
Thanks you very much for all that you do and thank for being the "People Choice".*

*Thanks to everyone that posts their reviews online and
the amazing reviews sites that make our life easier.*

*The places listed in this book are the most positively reviewed
and recommended by locals and travelers from around the world.*

*Thank you for your time and enjoy the directory that is
designed with locals and tourist in mind!*

TOP 500 SHOPS

The Most Recommended by Locals & Trevelers

(From #1 to #500)

#1
Demijohn
Category: Flowers & Gifts
Average price: Modest
Area: Old Town
Address: 32 Victoria Street
Edinburgh EH1 2JW
Phone: 0845 604 8350

#2
Miss Dixiebelle
Category: Women's Clothing,
Makeup Artists, Hairdressers
Average price: Modest
Area: Bruntsfield, The Meadows
Address: 19 Bruntsfield Place
Edinburgh EH10 4HN
Phone: 0131 629 7783

#3
Paper Tiger
Category: Cards & Stationery
Average price: Modest
Area: Old Town
Address: 53 Lothian Road
Edinburgh EH1 2DJ
Phone: 0131 228 2790

#4
Elvis Shakespeare
Category: Music & DVDs, Bookshop
Average price: Modest
Area: Leith
Address: 347 Leith Walk
Edinburgh EH6 8SD
Phone: 0131 561 1363

#5
W. Armstrong & Son
Category: Vintage, Accessories
Average price: Modest
Area: Old Town, Grassmarket
Address: 83 Grassmarket
Edinburgh EH1 2HJ
Phone: 0131 220 5557

#6
Jenners
Category: Department Store,
Beauty & Cosmetics, Local Flavour
Average price: Expensive
Area: New Town
Address: 47 Princes Street
Edinburgh EH2 2YJ
Phone: 0131 225 2442

#7
Oxfam
Category: Charity Shop, Bookshop, Music &
DVDs
Average price: Modest
Area: Newington
Address: 120-122 Nicolson St
Edinburgh EH8 9EJ
Phone: 0131 662 4498

#8
Edinburgh Books
Category: Bookshop
Average price: Modest
Area: Old Town
Address: 145-147 W Port
Edinburgh EH3 9DP
Phone: 0131 229 4431

#9
Scottish National Portrait Gallery
Category: Art Gallery, Landmark, Historical
Building
Average price: Inexpensive
Area: New Town
Address: 1 Queen St
Edinburgh EH2 1JD
Phone: 0131 624 6200

#10
Himalaya Shop
Category: Arts & Crafts, Cafe
Average price: Inexpensive
Area: Newington
Address: 20 South Clerk Street
Edinburgh EH8 9PR
Phone: 07598 936528

#11

**Edinburgh International
Book Festival**
Category: Bookshop, Festival
Average price: Modest
Area: New Town
Address: A 5 Charlotte Sq
Edinburgh EH2 4DR
Phone: 0131 718 5666

#12
Vogue Video
Category: Videos & Video Game Rental
Average price: Inexpensive
Area: Newington
Address: 59 Clerk Street
Edinburgh EH8 9JQ
Phone: 0131 667 2993

#13
Molton Brown Emporium
Category: Beauty & Cosmetics
Average price: Expensive
Area: New Town
Address: 35a George Street
Edinburgh EH2 2HN
Phone: 0870 224 3952

#14
Word Power Books
Category: Bookshop
Average price: Modest
Area: Newington
Address: 43 West Nicolson Street
Edinburgh EH8 9DB
Phone: 0131 662 9112

#15
Armchair Books
Category: Bookshop
Average price: Modest
Area: Old Town, Grassmarket
Address: 72 W Port
Edinburgh EH1 2LE
Phone: 0131 229 5927

#16
Lakeland
Category: Home & Garden
Average price: Exclusive
Area: New Town
Address: 55 Hanover St
Edinburgh EH2 2PJ
Phone: 0131 220 3947

#17
Harvey Nichols
Category: Department Store
Average price: Exclusive
Area: New Town
Address: 30 - 34 St Andrew Square
Edinburgh EH2 2AD
Phone: 0131 524 8388

#18
Analogue Books
Category: Bookshop
Average price: Modest
Area: Old Town, Grassmarket
Address: 39 Candlemaker Row
Edinburgh EH1 2QB
Phone: 0131 220 0601

#19
Run 4 It
Category: Sports Wear
Average price: Expensive
Area: West End
Address: 108 - 110 Lothian Road
Edinburgh EH3 9BE
Phone: 0131 228 3444

#20
Leith Circle Gallery
Category: Art Gallery
Average price: Modest
Area: Leith
Address: 115 Leith Walk
Edinburgh EH6 8NP
Phone: 07564 138768

#21
The Red Door Gallery
Category: Art Gallery,
Cards & Stationery
Average price: Expensive
Area: Old Town, Royal Mile
Address: 42 Victoria Street
Edinburgh EH1 2JW
Phone: 0131 477 3255

#22
Scottish National Gallery
of Modern Art
Category: Art Gallery, Museum
Average price: Modest
Area: West End
Address: 75 Belford Road
Edinburgh EH4 3DR
Phone: 0131 624 6200

#23
Poundland
Category: Pound Shop
Average price: Inexpensive
Area: New Town
Address: St James Ctr
Edinburgh EH1 3SS
Phone: 0131 558 3113

#24
Boots
Category: Beauty & Cosmetics, Pharmacy
Average price: Expensive
Area: New Town
Address: 101-103 Princes Street
Edinburgh EH2 3AD
Phone: 0131 225 8331

#25
Curiouser and Curiouser
Category: Home Decor, Gift Shop
Average price: Modest
Area: New Town
Address: 93 Broughton Street
Edinburgh EH1 3RZ
Phone: 0131 556 1866

#26
20 20
Category: Eyewear & Opticians
Average price: Expensive
Area: New Town
Address: 17 Queen Street
Edinburgh EH2 1JX
Phone: 0131 225 1222

#27
Courtyard Antiques
Category: Antiques
Average price: Modest
Area: Newington
Address: 108a Causewayside
Edinburgh EH9 1PU
Phone: 0131 662 9008

#28
Penhaligon's
Category: Beauty & Cosmetics
Average price: Exclusive
Area: New Town
Address: 33 George Street
Edinburgh EH2 2HN
Phone: 0131 220 3210

#29
John Lewis
Category: Department Store
Average price: Modest
Area: New Town
Address: St James Centre
Edinburgh EH1 3SP
Phone: 0131 556 9121

#30
Paper Tiger
Category: Cards & Stationery
Average price: Modest
Area: West End
Address: 6A/8 Stafford Street
Edinburgh EH3 7AU
Phone: 0131 226 2390

#31
Paperchase
Category: Art Supplies,
Cards & Stationery
Average price: Modest
Area: New Town
Address: 77a George Street
Edinburgh EH2 3ES
Phone: 0131 226 4323

#32
Herman Brown
Category: Vintage, Accessories
Average price: Modest
Area: Old Town
Address: 151 West Port
Edinburgh EH3 9DP
Phone: 0131 228 2589

#33
The Disney Store
Category: Toy Shop
Average price: Expensive
Area: New Town
Address: 18-19 Princes Street
Edinburgh EH2 2AN
Phone: 0131 557 2772

#34
Forbidden Planet
Category: Toy Shop, Comic Books
Average price: Modest
Area: Old Town, Newington
Address: 40-41 Southbridge Street
Edinburgh EH1 1LL
Phone: 0131 558 8226

#35
Mr Woods Fossils
Category: Antiques, Hobby Shop
Average price: Expensive
Area: Old Town, Grassmarket
Address: 5 Cowgatehead
Edinburgh EH1 1JY
Phone: 0131 220 1344

#36
Helios Fountain
Category: Arts & Crafts, Bookshop
Average price: Modest
Area: Old Town, Grassmarket
Address: 7 Grassmarket
Edinburgh EH1 2HY
Phone: 0131 229 7884

#37
Aha Ha Ha Jokes & Novelties
Category: Toy Shop, Fancy Dress
Average price: Modest
Area: Old Town, Grassmarket
Address: 99 West Bow
Edinburgh EH1 2JP
Phone: 0131 220 5252

#38
Rosie Brown
Category: Jewellery
Average price: Expensive
Area: Bruntsfield
Address: 148 Bruntsfield Place
Edinburgh EH10 4ER
Phone: 0131 228 9269

#39
Drum Central
Category: Musical Instruments
Average price: Modest
Area: Newington
Address: 58 Clerk Street
Edinburgh EH8 9JB
Phone: 0131 667 3844

#40
House of Fraser
Category: Department Store
Average price: Expensive
Area: New Town
Address: 145 Princes Street
Edinburgh EH2 4YZ
Phone: 0844 800 3724

#41
Underground Solu'shun
Category: Electronics,
Vinyl Records, DJs
Average price: Modest
Area: Old Town, Royal Mile
Address: 9 Cockburn St
Edinburgh EH1 1BP
Phone: 0131 226 2242

#42
Rock Candy Gallery
Category: Jewellery
Average price: Modest
Area: New Town
Address: 111 Rose Street
Edinburgh EH2 3DT
Phone: 0131 225 4109

#43
Graham Tiso
Category: Outdoor Gear
Average price: Expensive
Area: New Town
Address: 123 Rose Street
Edinburgh EH2 3DT
Phone: 0131 225 9486

#44
Urban Outfitters
Category: Fashion, Home Decor
Average price: Expensive
Area: New Town
Address: 124 Princes Street
Edinburgh EH2 4AD
Phone: 0131 226 4188

#45
Present
Category: Cards & Stationery
Average price: Modest
Area: Old Town, Royal Mile
Address: 18 Saint Marys Street
Edinburgh EH1 1SU
Phone: 0131 556 5050

#46
Steptoes
Category: Furniture Shop, Antiques
Average price: Inexpensive
Area: Newington
Address: 5a East Preston Street
Edinburgh EH8 9QQ
Phone: 07747 064470

#47
Doodles Ceramics Workshop
Category: Arts & Crafts
Average price: Modest
Area: Marchmont
Address: 29 Marchmont Crescent
Edinburgh EH9 1HQ
Phone: 0131 229 1399

#48
Marys Living and Giving
Category: Arts & Crafts, Charity Shop
Average price: Inexpensive
Area: Stockbridge
Address: 34A Raeburn Place
Edinburgh EH4 1HN
Phone: 0131 315 2856

#49
Games Workshop
Category: Hobby Shop
Average price: Expensive
Area: Old Town, Newington, Royal Mile
Address: 136 High Street
Edinburgh EH1 1QS
Phone: 0131 220 6540

#50
Trouvé
Category: Women's Clothing
Average price: Modest
Area: Newington
Address: 77 Newington Road
Edinburgh EH9 1
Phone: 0131 667 0631

#51
Boots
Category: Pharmacy,
Beauty & Cosmetics
Average price: Modest
Area: Leith
Address: Waverley St
Edinburgh EH7 5
Phone: 0131 558 9412

#52
River Island
Category: Accessories,
Men's Clothing, Women's Clothing
Average price: Modest
Area: New Town
Address: 111 Princes Street
Edinburgh EH2 3AA
Phone: 0131 226 3272

#53
K1 Yarns Knitting Boutique Edinburgh
Category: Knitting Supplies
Average price: Modest
Area: Old Town, Grassmarket
Address: 89 W Bow
Edinburgh EH1 2JP
Phone: 0131 226 7472

#54
Deadhead Comics
Category: Comic Books
Average price: Modest
Area: Old Town
Address: 27 Candlemaker Row
Edinburgh EH1 2QG
Phone: 0131 226 2774

#55
Southside Books
Category: Bookshop
Average price: Inexpensive
Area: Old Town, Newington
Address: 58 S Bridge
Edinburgh EH1 1LS
Phone: 0131 558 9009

#56
Swish
Category: Women's Clothing,
Men's Clothing, Children's Clothing
Average price: Expensive
Area: Old Town
Address: 22-24 Victoria Street
Edinburgh EH1 2JW
Phone: 0131 220 0615

#57
Marks & Spencer
Category: Department Store
Average price: Modest
Area: New Town
Address: 54 Princes Street
Edinburgh EH2 2DQ
Phone: 0131 225 2301

#58
Edinburgh Bargain Store
Category: Pound Shop
Average price: Inexpensive
Area: Newington
Address: 5-9 ST Patrick Square
Edinburgh EH8 9EZ
Phone: 0131 662 4318

#59
Till's Bookshop
Category: Bookshop, Comic Books
Average price: Modest
Area: Newington
Address: 1 Hope Park Cres
Edinburgh EH8 9NA
Phone: 0131 667 0895

#60
Ronde Bicycle Outfitters
Category: Sporting Goods
Average price: Expensive
Area: Stockbridge
Address: 68 Hamilton Place
Edinburgh EH3 5AZ
Phone: 0131 260 9888

#61
Ness Scotland
Category: Vintage
Average price: Modest
Area: Old Town, Royal Mile
Address: 336-340 Lawnmarket
Edinburgh EH1 2PH
Phone: 0131 225 8815

#62
Russell & Bromley
Category: Shoe Shop, Accessories
Average price: Expensive
Area: New Town
Address: 106 Princes Street
Edinburgh EH2 3AA
Phone: 0131 225 7444

#63
Unknown Pleasures
Category: Vinyl Records,
Bookshop, Music & DVDs
Average price: Modest
Area: Old Town, Royal Mile
Address: 110 Canongate
Edinburgh EH8 8DD
Phone: 0131 652 3537

#64
Kurt Geiger
Category: Shoe Shop, Accessories
Average price: Expensive
Area: Old Town
Address: St Andrews Square
Edinburgh EH1 3DQ
Phone: 0131 556 1816

#65
The Bead Shop Edinburgh
Category: Accessories,
Haberdashery & Fabrics
Average price: Modest
Area: Stockbridge
Address: 6 Dean Park Street
Edinburgh EH4 1JW
Phone: 0131 343 3222

#66
Laing Edinburgh
Category: Jewellery,
Accessories, Watches
Average price: Modest
Area: New Town
Address: 29 Frederick Street
Edinburgh EH2 2ND
Phone: 0131 225 4513

#67
The Cat's Miaou
Category: Gift Shop
Average price: Modest
Area: Leith
Address: 36 Elm Row
Edinburgh EH7 4AH
Phone: 0131 557 1277

#68
Edinburgh Fabrics
Category: Haberdashery & Fabrics
Average price: Modest
Area: Newington
Address: 12-14 St Patrick Square
Edinburgh EH8 9EZ
Phone: 0131 668 2790

#69
Digger
Category: Flowers & Gifts, Jewellery
Average price: Modest
Area: Newington
Address: 35 West Nicolson Street
Edinburgh EH8 9DB
Phone: 0131 668 1802

#70
Waterstones
Category: Bookshop, Coffee & Tea, Cards
& Stationery
Average price: Modest
Area: New Town
Address: 128 Princes Street
Edinburgh EH2 4AD
Phone: 0131 226 2666

#71
Hijinks
Category: Fancy Dress, Party Supplies
Average price: Inexpensive
Area: Old Town, Grassmarket
Address: 88 Grassmarket
Edinburgh EH1 2JR
Phone: 0131 225 3388

#72
Cult Clothing Co
Category: Fashion
Average price: Expensive
Area: Old Town, Royal Mile
Address: 7 North Bridge
Edinburgh EH1 1SB
Phone: 0131 556 5003

#73
Cath Kidston
Category: Home & Garden,
Jewellery, Fashion
Average price: Expensive
Area: New Town
Address: 58 George Street
Edinburgh EH2 2LR
Phone: 0131 220 1509

#74
Stringers
Category: Musical Instruments
Average price: Exclusive
Area: New Town
Address: 13 York Place
Edinburgh EH1 3EB
Phone: 0131 557 5432

#75
Shelter Shop Edinburgh
Category: Charity Shop, Vintage
Average price: Inexpensive
Area: Newington
Address: 134 Nicolson Street
Edinburgh EH8 9EH
Phone: 0131 662 9585

#76
Joe
Category: Jewellery, Accessories,
Cards & Stationery
Average price: Inexpensive
Area: Old Town
Address: 3 Greyfriars Place
Edinburgh EH1 2QQ
Phone: 0131 225 4881

#77
Eden
Category: Flowers & Gifts,
Furniture Shop
Average price: Modest
Area: Old Town, Royal Mile
Address: 37 Cockburn Street
Edinburgh EH1 1BP
Phone: 0131 220 3372

#78
Transreal Fiction
Category: Bookshop, Hobby Shop
Average price: Modest
Area: Old Town, Grassmarket
Address: 7 Cowgatehead
Edinburgh EH1 1JY
Phone: 0131 226 2822

#79
Miss Selfridge
Category: Women's Clothing, Accessories
Average price: Modest
Area: New Town
Address: 13-21 Hanover Street
Edinburgh EH2 2DL
Phone: 0131 220 1209

#80
L'Occitane
Category: Beauty & Cosmetics,
Flowers & Gifts
Average price: Expensive
Area: New Town
Address: 18b Frederick Street
Edinburgh EH2 2HB
Phone: 0131 226 5350

#81
Barnardo's Books
Category: Charity Shop, Bookshop
Average price: Inexpensive
Area: Newington
Address: 45 Clerk Street
Edinburgh EH8 9JQ
Phone: 0131 668 3142

#82
Greyfriars Art Shop
Category: Arts & Crafts
Average price: Modest
Area: Old Town
Address: 1 Greyfriars Place
Edinburgh EH1 2QQ
Phone: 0131 225 4600

#83
Joy
Category: Women's Clothing, Accessories,
Cards & Stationery
Average price: Modest
Area: Old Town
Address: Princes Street
Edinburgh EH1 1BQ
Phone: 0131 558 9111

#84
Vinyl Villians
Category: Vinyl Records
Average price: Modest
Area: Leith
Address: 5 Elm Row
Edinburgh EH7 4AA
Phone: 0131 558 1170

#85
Aihua Chinese Supermarket
Category: Wholesaler, Ethnic Food
Average price: Exclusive
Area: Newington
Address: 36 W Crosscauseway
Edinburgh EH8 9JP
Phone: 0131 662 8888

#86
Broughton Street Bookshop
Category: Bookshop
Average price: Inexpensive
Area: New Town
Address: 44 Broughton Street
Edinburgh EH1 3
Phone: 0131 5575 67819

#87
Bill Baber
Category: Women's Clothing,
Men's Clothing, Local Flavour
Average price: Expensive
Area: Old Town, Grassmarket
Address: 66 Grassmarket
Edinburgh EH1 2JR
Phone: 0131 225 3249

#88
Bohemia
Category: Women's Clothing
Average price: Exclusive
Area: Marchmont
Address: 17 Roseneath Street
Edinburgh EH9 1JH
Phone: 0131 478 9609

#89
Lush
Category: Beauty & Cosmetics, Beauticians
& Day Spa, Massage
Average price: Modest
Area: New Town
Address: 115 Princes Street
Edinburgh EH2 3AA
Phone: 0131 225 4688

#90
The Old Children's Bookshelf
Category: Bookshop,
Arts & Crafts, Antiques
Average price: Modest
Area: Old Town, Royal Mile
Address: 175 Canongate
Edinburgh EH8 8BN
Phone: 0131 558 3411

#91
The Writers' Museum
Category: Museum, Art Gallery
Average price: Inexpensive
Area: Old Town, Royal Mile
Address: Lady Stairs House Lady Stair's
Close, Edinburgh EH1 2PA
Phone: 0131 529 4901

#92
Black Lion Games
Category: Hobby Shop
Average price: Modest
Area: Newington, The Meadows
Address: 90 Buccleuch Street
Edinburgh EH8 9NH
Phone: 0131 667 2128

#93
Old Town Bookshop
Category: Bookshop
Average price: Modest
Area: Old Town, Grassmarket
Address: 8 Victoria Street
Edinburgh EH1 2HG
Phone: 0131 225 9237

#94
Joey D
Category: Vintage
Average price: Modest
Area: New Town
Address: 54 Broughton Street
Edinburgh EH1 3SA
Phone: 0131 557 6672

#95
International Newsagent
Category: Newsagent
Average price: Inexpensive
Area: Old Town, Royal Mile
Address: 351 High Street
Edinburgh EH1 1PW
Phone: 0131 225 4827

#96
Pie In The Sky
Category: Accessories,
Women's Clothing, Jewellery
Average price: Modest
Area: Old Town, Royal Mile
Address: 21 Cockburn St
Edinburgh EH1 1BP
Phone: 0131 220 1477

#97
Topshop
Category: Women's Clothing, Accessories
Average price: Expensive
Area: New Town
Address: 30 Princes Street
Edinburgh EH2 2BY
Phone: 0131 556 0151

#98
Clementine Home & Gifts
Category: Home Decor
Average price: Modest
Area: Bruntsfield
Address: 141 Bruntsfield Pl
Edinburgh EH10 4EB
Phone: 0131 477 2237

#99
Bravissimo
Category: Lingerie
Average price: Modest
Area: New Town
Address: 20 Multrees Walk
Edinburgh EH1 3DQ
Phone: 0131 550 3620

#100
Fab Hatrix
Category: Fashion
Average price: Expensive
Area: Old Town
Address: 13 Cowgatehead
Edinburgh EH1 1JY
Phone: 0131 225 9222

#101
The White Company
Category: Home Decor
Average price: Expensive
Area: New Town
Address: 52 George Street
Edinburgh EH2 2LE
Phone: 0131 225 2991

#102
Monsoon
Category: Fashion
Average price: Exclusive
Area: New Town
Address: 45-46 Princes Street
Edinburgh EH2 2BY
Phone: 0131 558 3544

#103
Joolz
Category: Women's Clothing, Jewellery
Average price: Expensive
Area: Tollcross
Address: 31 Leven Street
Edinburgh EH3 9LH
Phone: 0131 229 4504

#104
Newington Stationers
Category: Cards & Stationery
Average price: Modest
Area: Newington
Address: 29 South Clerk Street
Edinburgh EH8 9JD
Phone: 0131 667 4967

#105
Meadows Pottery
Category: Arts & Crafts
Average price: Expensive
Area: Newington
Address: 11a Summerhall Place
Edinburgh EH9 1QE
Phone: 0131 662 4064

#106
Rusty Zip
Category: Vintage, Accessories
Average price: Inexpensive
Area: Old Town
Address: 14 Teviot Place
Edinburgh EH1 2QZ
Phone: 0131 226 4634

#107
Lime Blue Diamond Store
Category: Jewellery
Average price: Exclusive
Area: New Town
Address: 107 George Street
Edinburgh EH2 3ES
Phone: 0131 220 2164

#108
Antiques
Category: Antiques
Average price: Expensive
Area: Old Town, Newington, Royal Mile
Address: 11 St Marys Street
Edinburgh EH1 1TA
Phone: 0131 557 0423

#109
The Mutt's Nuts
Category: Home & Garden,
Cards & Stationery, Gift Shop
Average price: Modest
Area: Old Town, Grassmarket
Address: 108 W Bow
Edinburgh EH1 2HH
Phone: 0131 225 7710

#110
Varsity Music
Category: Musical Instruments
Average price: Modest
Area: Newington
Address: 8-10 Nicolson Street
Edinburgh EH8 9DH
Phone: 07831 225551

#111
Waterstones
Category: Bookshop
Average price: Modest
Area: New Town
Address: 83 George Street
Edinburgh EH2 3ES
Phone: 0131 225 3436

#112
Sheila Fleet Gallery
Category: Jewellery
Average price: Expensive
Area: Stockbridge, New Town
Address: 18 St Stephen Street
Edinburgh EH3 5AL
Phone: 0131 225 5939

#113
Hospice of Hope Romania
Category: Charity Shop
Average price: Inexpensive
Area: Stockbridge
Address: 5 Deanhaugh Street
Edinburgh EH4 1
Phone: 0131 332 8625

#114
The Bay Tree Company
Category: Cards & Stationery
Average price: Expensive
Area: Bruntsfield, The Meadows
Address: 110 Bruntsfield Place
Edinburgh EH10 4ES
Phone: 0131 228 6180

#115
Scayles Music
Category: Musical Instruments
Average price: Modest
Area: Newington
Address: 50 Saint Patrick Square
Edinburgh EH8 9EZ
Phone: 0131 667 8241

#116
Flux
Category: Cards & Stationery,
Home Decor, Accessories
Average price: Modest
Area: Leith
Address: 55 Bernard Street
Edinburgh EH6 6SL
Phone: 0131 554 4075

#117
Leith Army Store
Category: Shoe Shop, Outdoor Gear
Average price: Inexpensive
Area: Leith
Address: 7-10 Brunswick Place
Edinburgh EH7 5HW
Phone: 0131 556 8100

#118
Borlands Sports Goods Shop
Category: Sporting Goods, Electronics
Average price: Modest
Area: Leith
Address: 7 Croall Place
Edinburgh EH7 4LT
Phone: 0131 556 4038

#119
Debenhams
Category: Department Store
Average price: Modest
Area: New Town
Address: 109 Princes Street
Edinburgh EH2 4
Phone: 0844 561 6161

#120
The Paper Rack
Category: Newsagent, Tobacconists
Average price: Modest
Area: Old Town
Address: 44-46 George Iv Bridge
Edinburgh EH1 1EJ
Phone: 0131 225 3461

#121
Lokaah
Category: Haberdashery & Fabrics, Cards &
Stationery, Jewellery
Average price: Inexpensive
Area: Newington
Address: 4-6 Nicolson Street
Edinburgh EH8 9DH
Phone: 0131 556 5646

#122
Oxfam
Category: Charity Shop
Average price: Modest
Area: Old Town, Royal Mile
Address: 109 High Street
Edinburgh EH1 1SG
Phone: 0131 557 3539

#123
Zara
Category: Women's Clothing,
Children's Clothing
Average price: Modest
Area: New Town
Address: 104 Princes Street
Edinburgh EH2 3AA
Phone: 0131 240 3230

#124
Boardwise
Category: Sporting Goods
Average price: Inexpensive
Area: Old Town
Address: 4 Lady Lawson Street
Edinburgh EH3 9DS
Phone: 0131 229 5887

#125
Fat Face
Category: Fashion
Average price: Exclusive
Area: New Town
Address: 122-124 Rose Street
Edinburgh EH2 3JF
Phone: 0131 225 5275

#126
Space NK
Category: Beauty & Cosmetics
Average price: Exclusive
Area: New Town
Address: 97 George Street
Edinburgh EH2 3ES
Phone: 0131 225 6371

#127
Goodstead
Category: Men's Clothing,
Women's Clothing
Average price: Expensive
Area: New Town
Address: 76 Rose Street
Edinburgh EH2 2NN
Phone: 0131 228 2846

#128
H&M
Category: Accessories,
Men's Clothing, Women's Clothing
Average price: Modest
Area: New Town
Address: 41-43 Princes Street
Edinburgh EH2 2BY
Phone: 0131 226 0790

#129
Jo Malone
Category: Beauty & Cosmetics
Average price: Expensive
Area: New Town
Address: 93 George Street
Edinburgh EH2 3ES
Phone: 0131 478 8555

#130
Long Tall Sally
Category: Women's Clothing
Average price: Modest
Area: Old Town, Grassmarket
Address: 1 Victoria Street
Edinburgh EH1 2HE
Phone: 0131 225 8330

#131
Narcissus Flowers
Category: Florist
Average price: Modest
Area: New Town
Address: 87 Broughton Street
Edinburgh EH1 3RG
Phone: 0131 478 7447

#132
Iconic Antiques
Category: Antiques
Average price: Expensive
Area: Old Town, Grassmarket
Address: 23 Grassmarket
Edinburgh EH1 2HS
Phone: 07745 299281

#133
Marchbrae
Category: Accessories,
Men's Clothing, Women's Clothing
Average price: Expensive
Area: Old Town, Royal Mile
Address: 375 High Street
Edinburgh EH1 1PW
Phone: 0131 225 8023

#134
Karen Millen
Category: Women's Clothing, Accessories
Average price: Exclusive
Area: New Town
Address: 53 George Street
Edinburgh EH2 2HT
Phone: 0131 220 1589

#135
Newington Pharmacy
Category: Pharmacy
Average price: Inexpensive
Area: Newington
Address: 46-50 Clerk Street
Edinburgh EH8 9JB
Phone: 0131 667 2368

#136
Ocean Jewellery
Category: Jewellery
Average price: Modest
Area: Old Town
Address: 39 Lothian Road
Edinburgh EH1 2DJ
Phone: 0131 229 6767

#137
Pebbles
Category: Jewellery
Average price: Expensive
Area: Old Town, Royal Mile
Address: 9 Jeffrey Street
Edinburgh EH1 1DR
Phone: 0131 557 4908

#138
Robert Graham Cigar Store
Category: Tobacconists
Average price: Modest
Area: Old Town, Royal Mile
Address: 254 Canongate
Edinburgh EH8 8AA
Phone: 0131 556 2791

#139
Pretty Pregnant
Category: Maternity Wear, Accessories
Average price: Modest
Area: New Town
Address: 4 Howe Street
Edinburgh EH3 6TD
Phone: 0131 225 9777

#140
Run and Become
Category: Sporting Goods
Average price: Expensive
Area: New Town, West End
Address: 20 Queensferry Street
Edinburgh EH2 4QW
Phone: 0131 313 5300

#141
Concrete Wardrobe
Category: Arts & Crafts,
Home Decor, Fashion
Average price: Exclusive
Area: New Town
Address: 50a Broughton Street
Edinburgh EH1 3SA
Phone: 0131 558 7130

#142
Organic Pleasures
Category: Adult
Average price: Expensive
Area: New Town
Address: 71 Broughton Street
Edinburgh EH1 3RJ
Phone: 07789 007347

#143
Candle It
Category: Flowers & Gifts
Average price: Modest
Area: Morningside
Address: 318 Morningside Road
Edinburgh EH10 4QH
Phone: 0131 452 8900

#144
Monica Higgins
Category: Florist
Average price: Exclusive
Area: Marchmont
Address: 22 Argyle Place
Edinburgh EH9 1JJ
Phone: 0131 477 2923

#145
Ooh! Ruby Shoes
Category: Shoe Shop
Average price: Modest
Area: Bruntsfield
Address: 117 Bruntsfield Place
Edinburgh EH10 4EQ
Phone: 0131 229 6909

#146
W. Armstrong & Son
Category: Vintage, Accessories
Average price: Modest
Area: Newington
Address: 64-66 Clerk Street
Edinburgh EH8 9JB
Phone: 0131 667 3056

#147
Context Interiors
Category: Home Decor
Average price: Expensive
Area: Morningside
Address: 79 Morningside Road
Edinburgh EH10 4AY
Phone: 0131 447 6384

#148
Bohemia Boutique
Category: Women's Clothing, Accessories
Average price: Expensive
Area: Bruntsfield
Address: 33a Morninngide Road
Edinburgh EH10 4DR
Phone: 0131 447 7701

#149
Cutie House
Category: Cards & Stationery, Toy Shop
Average price: Expensive
Area: Old Town, Royal Mile
Address: 5 Cockburn Street
Edinburgh EH1 1BP
Phone: 0131 220 5258

#150
Office
Category: Shoe Shop, Accessories
Average price: Modest
Area: New Town
Address: 79A Princes St
Edinburgh EH2 2ER
Phone: 0131 220 4296

#151
Antiques and Curious Cabaret
Category: Antiques, Jewellery
Average price: Modest
Area: Old Town
Address: 137 West Port
Edinburgh EH3 9DP
Phone: 0131 229 4100

#152
Hobbs
Category: Fashion
Average price: Expensive
Area: New Town
Address: 47 George Street
Edinburgh EH2 2HT
Phone: 0131 220 5386

#153
Superdrug
Category: Pharmacy,
Beauty & Cosmetics
Average price: Modest
Area: New Town
Address: 83 Princes St
Edinburgh EH2 2ER
Phone: 0131 225 2367

#154
Applejack
Category: Men's Clothing, Women's
Clothing, Jewellery
Average price: Modest
Area: Old Town, Newington
Address: 37 South Bridge
Edinburgh EH1 1LL
Phone: 0131 556 5324

#155
Stampers Grove
Category: Cards & Stationery,
Art Supplies
Average price: Expensive
Area: West End
Address: 92 Grove Street
Edinburgh EH3 8AP
Phone: 0131 221 9440

#156
Cruise Clothing
Category: Accessories,
Men's Clothing, Women's Clothing
Average price: Exclusive
Area: New Town
Address: 94 George St
Edinburgh EH2 3DF
Phone: 0131 226 3524

#157
Totty Rocks
Category: Fashion
Average price: Expensive
Area: Old Town, Grassmarket
Address: 40 Victoria Street
Edinburgh EH1 2JW
Phone: 0131 226 3232

#158
Cigar Box
Category: Tobacconists
Average price: Modest
Area: Old Town, Royal Mile
Address: 361 High Street
Edinburgh EH1 1PW
Phone: 0131 225 3534

#159
Thomas Pink
Category: Fashion
Average price: Exclusive
Area: New Town
Address: 35 Castle Street
Edinburgh EH2 3HT
Phone: 0131 225 4909

#160
Robert Graham
Category: Tobacconists
Average price: Modest
Area: New Town
Address: 194 Rose Street
Edinburgh EH2 4AT
Phone: 0131 226 1874

#161
Crabtree and Evelyn
Category: Beauty & Cosmetics,
Flowers & Gifts
Average price: Expensive
Area: New Town
Address: 4 Hanover Street
Edinburgh EH2 2EN
Phone: 0131 226 2478

#162
Blacks Leisure Group
Category: Outdoor Gear,
Leisure Centre
Average price: Modest
Area: New Town
Address: 24 Frederick Street
Edinburgh EH27 2JR
Phone: 0131 225 8686

#163
Next Retail
Category: Fashion
Average price: Expensive
Area: New Town
Address: 63-67 St James Centre
Edinburgh EH1 3SS
Phone: 0131 558 9590

#164
Covet
Category: Accessories
Average price: Exclusive
Area: New Town
Address: 20 Thistle Street
Edinburgh EH2 1EN
Phone: 0131 220 0026

#165
New Look
Category: Accessories,
Women's Clothing
Average price: Modest
Area: New Town
Address: Princes Mall
Edinburgh EH1 1BQ
Phone: 0131 524 7930

#166
Hogs Head Music
Category: Music & DVDs
Average price: Modest
Area: Newington
Address: 62 S Clerk Street
Edinburgh EH8 9PS
Phone: 0131 667 5274

#167
First XV
Category: Sporting Goods
Average price: Modest
Area: Haymarket, West End
Address: 6-8 Haymarket Ter
Edinburgh EH12 5JZ
Phone: 0131 337 4746

#168
Margiotta Retail
Category: Newsagent
Average price: Expensive
Area: Marchmont
Address: 102-104 Marchmont Road
Edinburgh EH9 1BG
Phone: 0131 452 8584

#169
Footworks
Category: Outdoor Gear
Average price: Expensive
Area: Bruntsfield, The Meadows
Address: 14-15 Bruntsfield Place
Edinburgh EH10 4HN
Phone: 0131 229 2402

#170
Studio One
Category: Flowers & Gifts
Average price: Modest
Area: West End
Address: 10 Stafford Street
Edinburgh EH3 7AU
Phone: 0131 226 5812

#171
Rene Walrus
Category: Bridal, Jewellery
Average price: Modest
Area: Old Town, Royal Mile
Address: 30 St Marys Street
Edinburgh EH1 1SU
Phone: 0131 558 8120

#172
Shelter Shop
Category: Charity Shop, Vintage
Average price: Inexpensive
Area: Stockbridge
Address: 106 Raeburn Place
Edinburgh EH4 1HH
Phone: 0131 315 0221

#173
Canongate Jerseys & Carfts
Category: Arts & Crafts
Average price: Modest
Area: Old Town, Royal Mile
Address: 164-166 Canongate
Edinburgh EH8 8DD
Phone: 0131 557 2967

#174
Barnardos
Category: Bookshop
Average price: Modest
Area: Newington
Address: 45 Clerk Street
Edinburgh EH8 9JQ
Phone: 0131 668 3142

#175
Gramophone Emporium
Category: Vinyl Records, Antiques
Average price: Inexpensive
Area: Stockbridge, New Town
Address: 12 St Stephen Street
Edinburgh EH3 5AL
Phone: 0131 225 1203

#176
The Paper Gallery
Category: Flowers & Gifts
Average price: Expensive
Area: Newington
Address: 49 Clerk Street
Edinburgh EH8 9JQ
Phone: 0131 662 0369

#177
Primark
Category: Department Store
Average price: Inexpensive
Area: New Town
Address: 91 93 Princes Street
Edinburgh EH2 2ER
Phone: 0131 226 3443

#178
The Works
Category: Bookshop, Art Supplies,
Cards & Stationery
Average price: Inexpensive
Area: New Town
Address: 63 Princes St
Edinburgh EH2 2DF
Phone: 0131 225 3192

#179
Drummond
Category: Arts & Crafts
Average price: Modest
Area: Haymarket, West End
Address: 79-81 Haymarket Terrace
Edinburgh EH12 5HD
Phone: 0131 539 7766

#180
Fabrick
Category: Fashion
Average price: Modest
Area: Old Town, Royal Mile
Address: 50 Cockburn St
Edinburgh EH1 1PB
Phone: 0131 226 7020

#181
Next
Category: Fashion, Home Decor
Average price: Modest
Area: New Town
Address: 107-109 Princes Street
Edinburgh EH2 3AA
Phone: 0844 844 5103

#182
Schuh
Category: Shoe Shop
Average price: Expensive
Area: New Town
Address: 6 Frederick Street
Edinburgh EH2 2HB
Phone: 0131 220 0290

#183
Topshop / Topman
Category: Accessories,
Men's Clothing, Women's Clothing
Average price: Modest
Area: New Town
Address: Princes Street
Edinburgh EH2 2BY
Phone: 0131 556 0151

#184
HMV
Category: Music & DVDs,
Electronics, Bookshop
Average price: Inexpensive
Area: New Town
Address: 129-130 Princes Street
Edinburgh EH2 4AH
Phone: 0131 225 7008

#185
Houseproud of Morningside
Category: Hardware Store
Average price: Expensive
Area: Morningside
Address: 169 Morningside Road
Edinburgh EH10 4AX
Phone: 0131 452 9012

#186
Clarks
Category: Shoe Shop
Average price: Modest
Area: New Town
Address: 79 Princes Street
Edinburgh EH2 2ER
Phone: 0131 220 1261

#187
Build A Bear
Category: Toy Shop
Average price: Exclusive
Area: New Town
Address: 119 Princes St
Edinburgh EH2 4AA
Phone: 0131 226 5780

#188
Sports Direct
Category: Sports Wear, Shoe Shop
Average price: Inexpensive
Area: New Town
Address: 11/13 St James Ctr
Edinburgh EH1 3SS
Phone: 0870 333 9509

#189
The Ugly Duckling Shop
Category: Vintage
Average price: Modest
Area: Bruntsfield
Address: 3 Churchill Place
Edinburgh EH10 4BE
Phone: 0131 447 0867

#190
Swatch Group
Category: Watches, Flowers & Gifts
Average price: Expensive
Area: New Town
Address: 40-42 Princes Street
Edinburgh EH2 2BY
Phone: 0131 558 9214

#191
Walker Slater
Category: Men's Clothing,
Women's Clothing
Average price: Expensive
Area: Old Town
Address: 20 Victoria Street
Edinburgh EH1 2HG
Phone: 0131 220 2636

#192
Gap
Category: Men's Clothing, Women's
Clothing, Children's Clothing
Average price: Modest
Area: New Town
Address: 84a Princes St
Edinburgh EH2 2ER
Phone: 0131 220 2846

#193
French Connection
Category: Fashion
Average price: Expensive
Area: New Town
Address: 70 George Street
Edinburgh EH2 2LT
Phone: 0131 220 1276

#194
Avizandum Law Book Shop
Category: Bookshop
Average price: Expensive
Area: Old Town
Address: 56a Candlemaker Row
Edinburgh EH1 2QE
Phone: 0131 220 3373

#195
Kakao By K
Category: Women's Clothing
Average price: Expensive
Area: New Town
Address: 45 Thistle St
Edinburgh EH2 1DY
Phone: 0131 226 3584

#196
D L Cavanagh
Category: Antiques
Average price: Modest
Area: Old Town, Royal Mile
Address: 49 Cockburn Street
Edinburgh EH1 1BS
Phone: 0131 226 3391

#197
Rikkis Music Shop
Category: Musical Instruments
Average price: Modest
Area: Leith
Address: 102 Leith Walk
Edinburgh EH6 5DT
Phone: 0131 553 5084

#198
Enigma
Category: Fashion
Average price: Expensive
Area: New Town
Address: 138 Rose Street
Edinburgh EH2 3JD
Phone: 0131 624 7186

#199
New Look
Category: Women's Clothing
Average price: Inexpensive
Area: New Town
Address: 121/123 Princes Street
Edinburgh EH2 4AD
Phone: 0131 240 1460

#200
Edinburgh Farmers' Market
Category: Shopping
Average price: Modest
Area: Old Town
Address: Castle Terrace
Edinburgh EH1 2EN
Phone: 0131 652 5940

#201
Mountain Warehouse
Category: Outdoor Gear
Average price: Expensive
Area: New Town
Address: 126 Princes Street
Edinburgh EH2 4AD
Phone: 0131 226 3183

#202
Aga Shop
Category: Kitchen & Bath
Average price: Expensive
Area: New Town
Address: 51 Frederick Street
Edinburgh EH2 1LH
Phone: 0131 225 7293

#203
Pipe Shop
Category: Tobacconists
Average price: Exclusive
Area: Leith
Address: 92 Leith Walk
Edinburgh EH6 5HB
Phone: 0131 553 3561

#204
Supa Kuru
Category: Cards & Stationery
Average price: Expensive
Area: Old Town, Newington
Address: 33 Cockburn Street
Edinburgh EH1 1BP
Phone: 0131 622 7317

#205
Royal Mile Armouries
Category: Antiques
Average price: Modest
Area: Old Town, Royal Mile
Address: 555 Castlehill
Edinburgh EH1 2ND
Phone: 0131 226 4171

#206
Interflora
Category: Florist
Average price: Expensive
Area: Old Town, Newington
Address: St Mary's Street
Edinburgh EH8 8
Phone: 0131 447 4445

#207
J Barbour & Sons
Category: Outdoor Gear
Average price: Expensive
Area: New Town
Address: 21 Frederick Street
Edinburgh EH2 2NE
Phone: 0131 226 3160

#208
The Bike Station
Category: Bicycles
Average price: Modest
Area: Marchmont
Address: 250 Causewayside
Edinburgh EH9 1UU
Phone: 0131 668 1996

#209
Save The Children
Category: Charity Shop, Vintage
Average price: Inexpensive
Area: Old Town, Newington
Address: 34-36 South Bridge
Edinburgh EH1 1LL
Phone: 0131 556 3334

#210
Lindsay & Gilmour
Category: Pharmacy
Average price: Inexpensive
Area: Leith
Address: 19 Smith's Place
Edinburgh EH6 8NU
Phone: 0131 554 1551

#211
Mev Taylor's
Category: Musical Instruments
Average price: Inexpensive
Area: Newington
Address: 58 Clerk St
Edinburgh EH8 9JB
Phone: 0131 667 6520

#212
Ness
Category: Women's Clothing, Accessories
Average price: Modest
Area: Old Town, Newington, Royal Mile
Address: 367 High St
Edinburgh EH1 1
Phone: 0131 226 5227

#213
One World Shop
Category: Department Store
Average price: Inexpensive
Area: Old Town
Address: Princes Street
Edinburgh EH2 4BJ
Phone: 0131 229 4541

#214
Focus
Category: Sporting Goods,
Men's Clothing
Average price: Expensive
Area: Old Town, Royal Mile
Address: 270 Canongate
Edinburgh EH8 8AA
Phone: 0131 629 9196

#215
Solo Clothing
Category: Men's Clothing, Accessories
Average price: Expensive
Area: Old Town, Royal Mile
Address: Canongate
Edinburgh EH8 8AA
Phone: 0131 558 7682

#216
Specsavers
Category: Eyewear & Opticians
Average price: Inexpensive
Area: West End
Address: 14-16 Shandwick Place
Edinburgh EH2 4RN
Phone: 0131 240 8860

#217
Monkey Temple
Category: New Age Shop
Average price: Expensive
Area: Bruntsfield, The Meadows
Address: 16 Leven Street
Edinburgh EH3 9LJ
Phone: 0131 229 9532

#218
User 2 Computers
Category: Computer Repair, Computers
Average price: Modest
Area: Newington
Address: 4 South Clerk Street
Edinburgh EH8 9JE
Phone: 0131 662 9955

#219
Scribbler
Category: Cards & Stationery
Average price: Modest
Area: New Town
Address: 80A Princes Street
Edinburgh EH2 2ER
Phone: 0131 220 5793

#220
Marchmont Hardware
Category: Hardware Store
Average price: Modest
Area: Marchmont
Address: 8 Warrender Park Road
Edinburgh EH9 1JQ
Phone: 0131 667 6389

#221
Affordable Antiques
Category: Antiques
Average price: Modest
Area: Newington
Address: 69 Causewayside
Edinburgh EH9 1QG
Phone: 0131 478 3006

#222
Pippin
Category: Flowers & Gifts,
Jewellery, Home Decor
Average price: Modest
Area: Haymarket, West End
Address: 30 Haymarket Terrace
Edinburgh EH12 5JZ
Phone: 0131 347 8657

#223
The Little Bead Shop
Category: Arts & Crafts, Hobby Shop
Average price: Modest
Area: Bruntsfield, The Meadows
Address: 120 Bruntsfield Place
Edinburgh EH10 4ES
Phone: 0131 228 5058

#224
Banana Row
Category: Musical Instruments
Average price: Modest
Area: Cannonmills
Address: 47 Eyre Pl
Edinburgh EH3 5EY
Phone: 0131 557 2088

#225
Homebase
Category: Hardware Store,
Home Decor, Electronics
Average price: Modest
Area: Newington
Address: 102 St Leonards Street
Edinburgh EH8 9RD
Phone: 0131 668 3663

#226
Garlands
Category: Florist
Average price: Modest
Area: Leith
Address: 29 Elm Row
Edinburgh EH7 4AH
Phone: 0131 556 6111

#227
Cancer Research UK
Category: Charity Shop, Vintage
Average price: Inexpensive
Area: Stockbridge
Address: 30 Raeburn Place
Edinburgh EH4 1HN
Phone: 0131 343 6343

#228
Eero & Riley
Category: Cards & Stationery
Average price: Modest
Area: Leith
Address: 7 Easter Rd
Edinburgh EH7 5PH
Phone: 0131 661 0533

#229
Galerie Mirages
Category: Jewellery
Average price: Expensive
Area: Stockbridge
Address: 46a Raeburn Pl
Edinburgh EH4 1HL
Phone: 0131 315 2603

#230
Museum Of Childhood
Category: Museum, Art Gallery
Average price: Inexpensive
Area: Old Town, Newington, Royal Mile
Address: 42 High Street
Edinburgh EH1 1TG
Phone: 0131 529 4142

#231
Cookie
Category: Women's Clothing
Average price: Modest
Area: Old Town, Royal Mile
Address: 29 Cockburn St
Edinburgh EH1 1BP
Phone: 0131 622 7260

#232
A & A Traders
Category: Home & Garden
Average price: Modest
Area: Leith
Address: 56-60 Easter Road
Edinburgh EH7 5RQ
Phone: 0131 661 4157

#233
Stills
Category: Art Gallery
Average price: Modest
Area: Old Town, Royal Mile
Address: 23 Cockburn Street
Edinburgh EH1 1BP
Phone: 0131 622 6200

#234
Schuh
Category: Shoe Shop, Accessories
Average price: Expensive
Area: Old Town, Royal Mile
Address: 32 North Bridge
Edinburgh EH1 1QG
Phone: 0131 225 6552

#235
Superdrug Store
Category: Pharmacy,
Beauty & Cosmetics
Average price: Modest
Area: Newington
Address: 70 Nicolson Street
Edinburgh EH8 9DT
Phone: 0131 667 5070

#236
Cult Clothing
Category: Men's Clothing,
Women's Clothing, Accessories
Average price: Modest
Area: Old Town, Royal Mile
Address: 7-9 N Bridge
Edinburgh EH1 1SB
Phone: 0131 558 1495

#237
Accessorize
Category: Accessories
Average price: Expensive
Area: New Town
Address: 45 Princes St
Edinburgh EH2 2BY
Phone: 0131 556 2162

#238
Palenque
Category: Jewellery, Accessories
Average price: Expensive
Area: New Town
Address: 99 Rose Street
Edinburgh EH2 3DT
Phone: 0131 225 7194

#239
Ryman Stationary
Category: Cards & Stationery
Average price: Expensive
Area: Newington
Address: 7-11 Nicolson St
Edinburgh EH8 9BE
Phone: 0131 668 1223

#240
Bruntsfield News
Category: Newsagent
Average price: Inexpensive
Area: Bruntsfield
Address: 115 Bruntsfield Place
Edinburgh EH10 4EQ
Phone: 0131 229 3836

#241
Toys Galore
Category: Toy Shop
Average price: Expensive
Area: Morningside
Address: 193 Morningside Rd
Edinburgh EH10 4QP
Phone: 0131 447 1006

#242
Concrete Wardrobe
Category: Arts & Crafts
Average price: Expensive
Area: New Town
Address: 50A Broughton St
Edinburgh EH1 3SA
Phone: 0131 558 7130

#243
USC
Category: Fashion
Average price: Expensive
Area: New Town
Address: 97-98 Princes Street
Edinburgh EH2 2ER
Phone: 0131 220 2210

#244
Spirit of China
Category: Flowers & Gifts,
Jewellery, Antiques
Average price: Inexpensive
Area: Old Town, Newington
Address: 30 South Bridge
Edinburgh EH1 1LL
Phone: 0131 557 0990

#245
H&M
Category: Women's Clothing,
Men's Clothing, Accessories
Average price: Inexpensive
Area: New Town
Address: 85 Princes Street
Edinburgh EH2 2ER
Phone: 0131 226 0790

#246
Brora
Category: Women's Clothing,
Men's Clothing, Children's Clothing
Average price: Expensive
Area: New Town
Address: 48 Frederick St
Edinburgh EH2 1EX
Phone: 0131 220 6404

#247
Helen Bateman
Category: Shoe Shop, Accessories
Average price: Expensive
Area: West End
Address: 16 William Street
Edinburgh EH3 7NH
Phone: 0131 220 4495

#248
Hilary's Bazaar
Category: Flowers & Gifts,
Musical Instruments
Average price: Exclusive
Area: Old Town, Royal Mile
Address: 297 Canongate
Edinburgh EH8 8BD
Phone: 0131 556 0408

#249
Hi Fi Corner
Category: Electronics
Average price: Exclusive
Area: New Town
Address: 1 Haddington Place
Edinburgh EH7 4AE
Phone: 0131 556 7901

#250
Hector Russell Kilt maker
Category: Personal Shopping
Average price: Modest
Area: New Town
Address: 95-96 Princes Street
Edinburgh EH2 2ER
Phone: 0131 558 1254

#251
Accessorize
Category: Accessories
Average price: Expensive
Area: New Town
Address: 99a Princes Street
Edinburgh EH2 3AA
Phone: 0131 225 8056

#252
Oddbins
Category: Flowers & Gifts
Average price: Modest
Area: Old Town, Royal Mile
Address: 223 High Street
Edinburgh EH1 1PE
Phone: 0131 220 3516

#253
Whiplash Trash
Category: Adult, Accessories
Average price: Modest
Area: Old Town, Royal Mile
Address: 53 Cockburn St
Edinburgh EH1 1BS
Phone: 0131 226 1005

#254
Pound Savers
Category: Home & Garden, Pound Shop
Average price: Inexpensive
Area: Newington
Address: 37-41 Nicolson Street
Edinburgh EH8 9BE
Phone: 0131 668 2736

#255
Jane Davidson
Category: Women's Clothing
Average price: Exclusive
Area: New Town
Address: 52 Thistle Street
Edinburgh EH2 1EN
Phone: 0131 225 3280

#256
Whistles
Category: Women's Clothing, Accessories
Average price: Expensive
Area: New Town
Address: 97 George Street
Edinburgh EH2 3ES
Phone: 0131 226 4398

#257
Futon Company
Category: Home & Garden
Average price: Modest
Area: Old Town, West End
Address: 140 Lothian Road
Edinburgh EH3 9BG
Phone: 0131 228 4190

#258
Poundland
Category: Pound Shop
Average price: Inexpensive
Area: Newington
Address: Nicolson St
Edinburgh EH8 9DT
Phone: 0131 668 0982

#259
Khorwa
Category: Women's Clothing, Accessories
Average price: Modest
Area: Newington
Address: 52 Clerk Street
Edinburgh EH8 9JB
Phone: 0131 662 9218

#260
Dr. Martens
Category: Shoe Shop, Men's Clothing,
Women's Clothing
Average price: Modest
Area: New Town
Address: 76 Princes Street
Edinburgh EH2 2ER
Phone: 0131 220 1599

#261
Millets
Category: Outdoor Gear, Sports Wear
Average price: Exclusive
Area: New Town
Address: 12 Frederick Street
Edinburgh EH2 2HB
Phone: 0131 220 1551

#262
Hawick Cashmere
Category: Accessories, Men's Clothing,
Women's Clothing
Average price: Expensive
Area: Old Town, Grassmarket
Address: 81 Grassmarket
Edinburgh EH1 2HJ
Phone: 0131 225 8634

#263
Goodwins Jewellery
Category: Antiques
Average price: Expensive
Area: New Town
Address: 106-108 Rose Street
Edinburgh EH2 3JF
Phone: 0131 220 1230

#264
Bonkers
Category: Cards & Stationery
Average price: Modest
Area: New Town
Address: 54 Hanover Street
Edinburgh EH2 2DX
Phone: 0131 225 5538

#265
Ecco Shoes UK
Category: Shoe Shop, Outdoor Gear
Average price: Expensive
Area: New Town
Address: 107 Rose Street
Edinburgh EH2 3DT
Phone: 0131 225 3422

#266
Waterstones Book Sellers
Category: Bookshop
Average price: Modest
Area: New Town
Address: 13-14 Princes Street
Edinburgh EH2 2AN
Phone: 0131 556 3034

#267
Swarovski Store
Category: Accessories
Average price: Modest
Area: New Town
Address: 100a Princes Street
Edinburgh EH2 3AA
Phone: 0131 220 6565

#268
Key Player
Category: Musical Instruments
Average price: Modest
Area: New Town
Address: 14 Elm Row
Edinburgh EH7 4AA
Phone: 0131 556 3005

#269
Laura Ashley
Category: Fashion
Average price: Expensive
Area: New Town
Address: 51 George Street
Edinburgh EH2
Phone: 0131 225 1121

#270
High & Mighty
Category: Men's Clothing
Average price: Expensive
Area: New Town
Address: 4 Castle Street
Edinburgh EH2 3DW
Phone: 0131 226 6254

#271
QS
Category: Fashion
Average price: Inexpensive
Area: Newington
Address: 52 Nicolson Street
Edinburgh EH8 9DT
Phone: 0131 668 3002

#272

Edinburgh Arts
& Picture Framers
Category: Framing
Average price: Modest
Area: Newington
Address: 1-3 Nicolson Street
Edinburgh EH8 9BE
Phone: 0131 668 1255

#273
MAC
Category: Beauty & Cosmetics
Average price: Expensive
Area: New Town
Address: 30 - 34 St Andrew Square
Edinburgh EH2 2AD
Phone: 0870 192 5582

#274
Clarksons Edinburgh
Category: Jewellery
Average price: Expensive
Area: Old Town, Grassmarket
Address: 87 West Bow
Edinburgh EH1 2JP
Phone: 0131 225 8141

#275
Hoochie Coochie
Category: Women's Clothing,
Men's Clothing
Average price: Modest
Area: Tollcross, West End
Address: 48 Home Street
Edinburgh EH3 9NA
Phone: 0131 629 6559

#276
Psycho Moda
Category: Women's Clothing
Average price: Modest
Area: Old Town, Royal Mile
Address: 22 St Mary's Street
Edinburgh EH1 1SU
Phone: 0131 557 6777

#277
Cotswold Outdoor
Category: Outdoor Gear
Average price: Expensive
Area: West End
Address: 72 Rose Street
Edinburgh EH2 2NN
Phone: 0131 464 9991

#278
Rae Macintosh
Category: Musical Instruments
Average price: Modest
Area: West End
Address: 6 Queensferry St
Edinburgh EH2 4PA
Phone: 0131 225 1171

#279
Belinda Robertson
Category: Fashion
Average price: Exclusive
Area: New Town
Address: 13a Dundas Street
Edinburgh EH3 6QG
Phone: 0131 557 8118

#280
Q Store
Category: Adult
Average price: Modest
Area: New Town
Address: 5 Barony Street
Edinburgh EH3 6PD
Phone: 0131 477 4756

#281
The Institute
Category: Art Gallery
Average price: Inexpensive
Area: Marchmont
Address: 14 Roseneath Street
Edinburgh EH9 1JH
Phone: 0131 229 1338

#282
Kiss The Fish
Category: Flowers & Gifts, Arts & Crafts
Average price: Modest
Area: Stockbridge
Address: 9 Dean Park Street
Edinburgh EH4 1JN
Phone: 0131 332 8912

#283
Tappit Hen
Category: Flowers & Gifts, Jewellery
Average price: Expensive
Area: Old Town, Royal Mile
Address: 89 High Street
Edinburgh EH1 1SG
Phone: 0131 557 1852

#284
La Senza
Category: Lingerie
Average price: Modest
Area: New Town
Address: 117 Princes Street
Edinburgh EH2 3AA
Phone: 0131 226 1689

#285
Age UK
Category: Shopping
Average price: Inexpensive
Area: Stockbridge
Address: 13 Raeburn Place
Edinburgh EH4 1HU
Phone: 0131 332 6306

#286
**Hatches, Matches
and Dispatches**
Category: Cards & Stationery
Average price: Modest
Area: Bruntsfield
Address: 166 Bruntsfield Pl
Edinburgh EH10 4
Phone: 0131 228 4441

#287
Paton & Finlay
Category: Pharmacy
Average price: Modest
Area: Bruntsfield
Address: 177 Bruntsfield Place
Edinburgh EH10 4DG
Phone: 0131 229 2110

#288
St Columba's Hospice Shop
Category: Charity Shop
Average price: Inexpensive
Area: Leith
Address: 352 Leith Walk
Edinburgh EH6 8
Phone: 0131 555 1526

#289
Elgin Cashmere
Category: Fashion
Average price: Expensive
Area: Old Town, Newington, Royal Mile
Address: 28 High Street
Edinburgh EH1 1TB
Phone: 0131 556 7165

#290
Republic Retail
Category: Accessories, Men's Clothing,
Women's Clothing
Average price: Expensive
Area: New Town
Address: 63 St James Centre
Edinburgh EH1 3SS
Phone: 0131 558 2657

#291
Moleta Munro
Category: Furniture Shop
Average price: Exclusive
Area: Old Town, Royal Mile
Address: 4 Jeffrey Street
Edinburgh EH1 1DT
Phone: 0131 557 4800

#292
State of Mind
Category: Men's Clothing
Average price: Expensive
Area: Old Town, Newington, Royal Mile
Address: 20 St Marys St
Edinburgh EH1 1SU
Phone: 0131 556 0215

#293
Edinburgh University Pharmacy
Category: Pharmacy
Average price: Modest
Area: Newington
Address: Bristo Square
Edinburgh EH8 9AL
Phone: 0131 668 2182

#294
SOLE
Category: Shoe Shop
Average price: Expensive
Area: New Town
Address: 16 Multrees Walk
Edinburgh EH1 3DQ
Phone: 0131 556 6660

#295
Edinburgh Printmakers
Category: Art Gallery
Average price: Modest
Area: New Town
Address: 23 Union Street
Edinburgh EH1 3LR
Phone: 0131 557 2479

#296
All Saints
Category: Men's Clothing,
Women's Clothing, Shoe Shop
Average price: Expensive
Area: New Town
Address: 99 Princes St
Edinburgh EH2 3AA
Phone: 0131 220 9810

#297
Lindsay & Gilmour
Category: Pharmacy
Average price: Modest
Area: Leith
Address: 257a Leith Walk
Edinburgh EH6 8NY
Phone: 0131 554 6591

#298
DL's Book Exchange
Category: Bookshop
Average price: Inexpensive
Area: Leith
Address: 46 Great Junction St
Edinburgh EH6 5LB
Phone: 0131 553 5590

#299
Remnant Kings
Category: Haberdashery & Fabrics
Average price: Modest
Area: Leith
Address: 169 Bonnington Road
Edinburgh EH6 5BQ
Phone: 0131 554 7733

#300
Freeze Proshop
Category: Outdoor Gear
Average price: Modest
Area: Leith
Address: 165 Bonnington Rd
Edinburgh EH6 5BQ
Phone: 0131 260 9677

#301
Cuttea Sark
Category: Flowers & Gifts
Average price: Modest
Area: Old Town, Grassmarket
Address: 26 Victoria St
Edinburgh EH1 2JW
Phone: 0131 226 6245

#302
H Samuel
Category: Jewellery, Flowers & Gifts
Average price: Modest
Area: New Town
Address: ST James Centre
Edinburgh EH1 3SL
Phone: 0131 557 1192

#303
Wonderland Models
Category: Hobby Shop, Toy Shop
Average price: Modest
Area: Old Town, West End
Address: 97 & 101 Lothian Road
Edinburgh EH3 9AN
Phone: 0131 229 6428

#304
Arkangel
Category: Women's Clothing
Average price: Modest
Area: West End
Address: 4 William Street
Edinburgh EH3 7NH
Phone: 0131 226 4466

#305
Mama Said
Category: Tobacconists, Supermarket
Average price: Modest
Area: Old Town, Royal Mile
Address: 40 Cockburn St
Edinburgh EH1 1PB
Phone: 0131 226 4829

#306
Bethany Shop
Category: Charity Shop
Average price: Inexpensive
Area: Leith
Address: 17 Duke Street
Edinburgh EH6 8HG
Phone: 0131 625 5400

#307
SimplyFixIt
Category: Computer Repair, Computers
Average price: Modest
Area: Bruntsfield, The Meadows
Address: 78 Bruntsfield Place
Edinburgh EH10 4HG
Phone: 0131 549 8820

#308
Coda Music
Category: Music & DVDs
Average price: Modest
Area: Old Town, Royal Mile
Address: 12 Bank Street
Edinburgh EH1 2LN
Phone: 0131 622 7246

#309
Marks and Spencer Simply Food
Category: Supermarket
Average price: Expensive
Area: Morningside
Address: 212-216 Morningside Rd
Edinburgh EH10 4DD
Phone: 0131 447 7369

#310
Offbeat Clothing Co.
Category: Men's Clothing, Women's
Clothing, Accessories
Average price: Modest
Area: Old Town, Newington
Address: 93-95 S Bridge
Edinburgh EH1 1HN
Phone: 0131 225 7733

#311
Ragamuffin
Category: Women's Clothing, Accessories
Average price: Modest
Area: Old Town, Royal Mile
Address: 278 Canongate
Edinburgh EH8 8AA
Phone: 0131 557 6007

#312
Who's Who
Category: Accessories, Men's Clothing,
Women's Clothing
Average price: Inexpensive
Area: Old Town, Royal Mile
Address: 8 North Bridge
Edinburgh EH1 1QN
Phone: 0131 226 3334

#313
White Stuff
Category: Sports Wear, Swimwear
Average price: Expensive
Area: New Town
Address: 89 George Street
Edinburgh EH2 2PA
Phone: 0131 226 3238

#314
Scottish Experience
Category: Flowers & Gifts
Average price: Expensive
Area: Old Town, Royal Mile
Address: 324-326 Lawnmarket
Edinburgh EH1 2PH
Phone: 0131 225 9505

#315
Castle Photographic
Category: Photography Shop
Average price: Modest
Area: Old Town, Royal Mile
Address: 16 Bank Street
Edinburgh EH1 2LN
Phone: 0131 225 4312

#316
MaMaison
Category: Furniture Shop
Average price: Expensive
Area: Leith
Address: 373-375 Leith Walk
Edinburgh EH7 4
Phone: 0131 553 0692

#317
River Island Clothing
Category: Accessories, Men's Clothing,
Women's Clothing
Average price: Expensive
Area: New Town
Address: 111 Princes Street
Edinburgh EH2 3AA
Phone: 0844 826 9782

#318
Nevisport
Category: Outdoor Gear
Average price: Expensive
Area: New Town
Address: 19 Rose Street
Edinburgh EH2 2PR
Phone: 0131 225 9498

#319
James Pringle Weavers
Category: Women's Clothing,
Men's Clothing, Accessories
Average price: Modest
Area: Old Town, Newington, Royal Mile
Address: 371 High St
Edinburgh EH1 1PW
Phone: 0131 225 3212

#320
Corniche
Category: Women's Clothing
Average price: Expensive
Area: Old Town, Royal Mile
Address: 2 Jeffrey Street
Edinburgh EH1 1DT
Phone: 0131 556 3707

#321
Slanj Clothing
Category: Men's Clothing, Accessories
Average price: Modest
Area: Old Town, Royal Mile
Address: 14 St Marys St
Edinburgh EH1 1SU
Phone: 0131 557 1666

#322
Pandora
Category: Jewellery
Average price: Expensive
Area: New Town
Address: 18 Multrees Walk
Edinburgh EH1 3DQ
Phone: 0131 557 0390

#323
Farmfoods
Category: Frozen Foods
Average price: Inexpensive
Area: Newington
Address: 76 Nicolson St
Edinburgh EH8 9DT
Phone: 0845 456 7890

#324
Vision Express
Category: Eyewear & Opticians
Average price: Exclusive
Area: New Town
Address: 12-14 St James Ctr
Edinburgh EH1 3SR
Phone: 0131 556 5656

#325
Bank
Category: Women's Clothing,
Men's Clothing, Accessories
Average price: Modest
Area: New Town
Address: St James Centre
Edinburgh EH1 3SS
Phone: 0131 558 3776

#326
L K Bennett
Category: Shoe Shop
Average price: Exclusive
Area: New Town
Address: George Street
Edinburgh EH2 2HT
Phone: 0131 226 3370

#327
Fabulous Jewels
Category: Jewellery
Average price: Modest
Area: Bruntsfield
Address: 170 Bruntsfield Place
Edinburgh EH10 4ER
Phone: 0131 228 1893

#328
Thrift Shop
Category: Charity Shop
Average price: Modest
Area: Bruntsfield, The Meadows
Address: 6 Bruntsfield Place
Edinburgh EH10 4HN
Phone: 0131 229 4646

#329
Ann Summers
Category: Lingerie, Adult
Average price: Modest
Area: New Town
Address: 89 Princes St
Edinburgh EH2 2ER
Phone: 0131 225 5257

#330
Chic & Unique
Category: Jewellery, Vintage
Average price: Expensive
Area: Stockbridge
Address: 8 Deanhaugh St
Edinburgh EH4 1LY
Phone: 0131 332 9889

#331
Calvin Klein Underwear
Category: Men's Clothing,
Women's Clothing, Lingerie
Average price: Expensive
Area: New Town
Address: St Andrews Square
Edinburgh EH1 3DQ
Phone: 0131 557 6971

#332
Cash Converters UK
Category: Pawn Shop
Average price: Modest
Area: Newington
Address: 21 South Clerk Street
Edinburgh EH8 9JD
Phone: 0131 662 8200

#333
Le Chariot Express Shop
Category: Vintage, Charity Shop
Average price: Expensive
Area: Newington
Address: 47a South Clerk Street
Edinburgh EH8 9NZ
Phone: 0131 667 3456

#334
O2
Category: Mobile Phones
Average price: Expensive
Area: New Town
Address: 135 Princes St
Edinburgh EH2 4BL
Phone: 0131 225 5723

#335
Still Life
Category: Antiques
Average price: Modest
Area: Old Town
Address: 54 Candlemaker Row
Edinburgh EH1 2QE
Phone: 0131 225 8524

#336
Underground Nation
Category: Accessories, Men's Clothing,
Women's Clothing
Average price: Modest
Area: Old Town
Address: 46 Candlemaker Row
Edinburgh EH1 2QE
Phone: 0131 220 0006

#337
Watches Of Switzerland
Category: Accessories
Average price: Expensive
Area: New Town
Address: 76 Princes St
Edinburgh EH2 2DF
Phone: 0131 225 6867

#338
Cash Converters
Category: Pawn Shop
Average price: Modest
Area: Leith
Address: 368 Leith Walk
Edinburgh EH7 4PE
Phone: 0131 554 2296

#339
Peter Bell
Category: Bookshop
Average price: Modest
Area: Old Town, Grassmarket
Address: 68 West Port
Edinburgh EH1 2LD
Phone: 0131 229 0562

#340
Radley
Category: Fashion
Average price: Expensive
Area: New Town
Address: 3 Frederick St
Edinburgh EH2 2EY
Phone: 0131 226 1908

#341
Ottimo Lighting
Category: Home Decor
Average price: Expensive
Area: New Town
Address: 44 Queen St
Edinburgh EH2 3NL
Phone: 0131 226 4750

#342
Castle Fine Art
Category: Art Gallery
Average price: Exclusive
Area: New Town
Address: 20 Multrees Walk
Edinburgh EH1 3DQ
Phone: 0131 261 9181

#343
Ness
Category: Women's Clothing, Shoe Shop, Accessories
Average price: Modest
Area: Old Town, Royal Mile
Address: 336-340 Lawnmarket
Edinburgh EH1 2PH
Phone: 0131 225 8815

#344
Big Ideas
Category: Women's Clothing
Average price: Expensive
Area: Old Town, Grassmarket
Address: 96 West Bow
Edinburgh EH1 2HH
Phone: 0131 226 2532

#345
Little Ox
Category: Art Gallery
Average price: Modest
Area: Old Town
Address: 23 Candlemaker Row
Edinburgh EH1 2QG
Phone: 0131 629 0474

#346
Orvis Store
Category: Sporting Goods
Average price: Expensive
Area: New Town
Address: 19 Hope St
Edinburgh EH2 4EL
Phone: 0131 226 6227

#347
SimplyFixIT
Category: Computer Repair, Computers
Average price: Exclusive
Area: Old Town
Address: 1 Forrest Road
Edinburgh EH1 2QH
Phone: 0131 549 8820

#348
Frayed Hem
Category: Vintage
Average price: Modest
Area: Old Town, Royal Mile
Address: 45 Cockburn Street
Edinburgh EH1 1BS
Phone: 0131 225 9831

#349
The Fruitmarket
Gallery Bookshop
Category: Cards & Stationery, Bookshop
Average price: Modest
Area: Old Town, Royal Mile
Address: 45 Market Street
Edinburgh EH1 1DF
Phone: 0131 225 2383

#350
21st Century Kilts
Category: Women's Clothing,
Men's Clothing
Average price: Modest
Area: New Town
Address: 48 Thistle Street
Edinburgh EH2 1EN
Phone: 0131 220 9450

#351
21st Century Kilts
Category: Fashion
Average price: Expensive
Area: New Town
Address: 48 Thistle St
Edinburgh EH2 1EN
Phone: 07774 757222

#352
Edinburgh Coin Shop
Category: Hobby Shop
Average price: Inexpensive
Area: Newington
Address: 11 West Crosscauseway
Edinburgh EH8 9JW
Phone: 0131 668 2928

#353
Black & Lizars
Category: Eyewear & Opticians
Average price: Expensive
Area: Old Town, West End
Address: 96 Lothian Road
Edinburgh EH3 9BE
Phone: 0131 229 7738

#354
Frontiers
Category: Women's Clothing, Accessories
Average price: Modest
Area: West End
Address: 16 Stafford Street
Edinburgh EH3 7AU
Phone: 0131 476 3449

#355
Kinross Cashmere
Category: Accessories, Men's Clothing,
Women's Clothing
Average price: Expensive
Area: Old Town, Royal Mile
Address: 2 St Giles St
Edinburgh EH1 1PT
Phone: 0131 225 5178

#356
Union Gallery
Category: Art Gallery
Average price: Modest
Area: New Town
Address: 45 Broughton Street
Edinburgh EH1 3JU
Phone: 0131 556 7707

#357
Chalon
Category: Furniture Shop
Average price: Exclusive
Area: New Town
Address: 6 York Buildings
Edinburgh EH2 1HY
Phone: 0131 557 2909

#358
O2 Shop
Category: Mobile Phones
Average price: Modest
Area: New Town
Address: 33 St James Centre
Edinburgh EH1 3SJ
Phone: 0131 556 1877

#359
Unicorn Antiques
Category: Antiques
Average price: Expensive
Area: New Town
Address: 65 Dundas Street
Edinburgh EH3 6RS
Phone: 0131 556 7176

#360
SemiChem
Category: Pharmacy, Beauty & Cosmetics,
Pound Shop
Average price: Inexpensive
Area: Newington
Address: 112 Nicolson St
Edinburgh EH8 9EJ
Phone: 0131 667 3414

#361
Barnets Shoes
Category: Shoe Shop
Average price: Modest
Area: Old Town, Royal Mile
Address: 7 High Street
Edinburgh EH1 1SR
Phone: 0131 556 3577

#362
Mr James
Category: Men's Clothing
Average price: Modest
Area: West End
Address: 7 Drumsheugh Place
Edinburgh EH3 7PT
Phone: 0131 226 5582

#363
Brew Store
Category: Hobby Shop
Average price: Modest
Area: Newington
Address: 61 South Clerk Street
Edinburgh EH8 9PP
Phone: 0131 667 1296

#364
Annie Smith
Category: Jewellery
Average price: Exclusive
Area: Bruntsfield, The Meadows
Address: 106 Bruntsfield Place
Edinburgh EH10 4ES
Phone: 0131 228 4877

#365
National Gallery Art Shop
Category: Art Supplies, Bookshop, Cards &
Stationery
Average price: Modest
Area: New Town
Address: National Gallery of Scotland
Edinburgh EH2 2EL
Phone: 0131 624 6200

#366
Chie Chie
Category: Fashion
Average price: Modest
Area: Bruntsfield
Address: 144 Bruntsfield Pl
Edinburgh EH10 4ER
Phone: 0131 228 3577

#367
Beautifully Boudoir
Category: Lingerie
Average price: Modest
Area: Haymarket, West End
Address: 30 Haymarket Ter
Edinburgh EH12 5JZ
Phone: 0131 337 5552

#368
Tippi
Category: Antiques
Average price: Expensive
Area: Bruntsfield
Address: 144 Bruntsfield
Edinburgh EH10 4ER
Phone: 0131 229 4422

#369
Oxfam
Category: Charity Shop
Average price: Inexpensive
Area: Stockbridge
Address: 25 Raeburn Place
Edinburgh EH4 1HJ
Phone: 0131 332 7593

#370
Gullivers Toys and Gifts
Category: Toy Shop,
Baby Accessories & Furniture
Average price: Modest
Area: Bruntsfield
Address: 165b Bruntsfield Place
Edinburgh EH10 4DG
Phone: 0131 629 9424

#371
Paton & Finlay
Category: Pharmacy
Average price: Inexpensive
Area: Bruntsfield
Address: 177 Bruntsfield Pl
Edinburgh EH10 4DG
Phone: 0131 229 2110

#372
The Luckenbooth
Category: Flowers & Gifts
Average price: Expensive
Area: Old Town, Royal Mile
Address: 215 High Street
Edinburgh EH1 1PE
Phone: 0131 220 1840

#373
Spirit Hair & Beauty
Category: Hairdressers,
Beauty & Cosmetics, Nail Salons
Average price: Modest
Area: Marchmont
Address: 58 Ratcliffe Terrace
Edinburgh EH9 1ST
Phone: 0131 662 9553

#374
Ivor & Ineta's Hair 'n' Beauty
Category: Blow Dry/Out Services, Beauty &
Cosmetics, Barbers
Average price: Inexpensive
Area: Leith
Address: 355 Leith Walk
Edinburgh EH6 8SD
Phone: 07442 050911

#375
Cash Generator
Category: Pawn Shop
Average price: Modest
Area: Old Town, Newington
Address: 47-49 S Bridge
Edinburgh EH1 1LL
Phone: 0131 556 5455

#376
The Mulberry Bush
Category: Toy Shop
Average price: Modest
Area: Morningside
Address: 77 Morningside Road
Edinburgh EH10 4AY
Phone: 0131 447 5145

#377
Vacuum Exchange
Category: Electronics, Appliances
Average price: Inexpensive
Area: Leith
Address: 317 Leith Walk
Edinburgh EH6 8SA
Phone: 0131 554 5050

#378
Time & TIde
Category: Home Decor
Average price: Modest
Area: Morningside
Address: 225 Morningside Road
Edinburgh EH10 4QT
Phone: 0131 447 7640

#379
Joyce Forsyth
Category: Accessories,
Women's Clothing
Average price: Expensive
Area: Old Town
Address: 42 Candlemaker Row
Edinburgh EH1 2QE
Phone: 0131 220 4112

#380
Underground Solution Records
Category: Music & DVDs
Average price: Expensive
Area: Old Town, Royal Mile
Address: 9 Cockburn Street
Edinburgh EH1 1BP
Phone: 0131 226 2242

#381
Andrew Pringle
Category: Bookshop
Average price: Expensive
Area: Old Town, Grassmarket
Address: 62 West Port
Edinburgh EH1 2LD
Phone: 0131 228 8880

#382
WH Smith
Category: Bookshop, Newsagent
Average price: Modest
Area: Old Town
Address: Waverley Railway Station
Edinburgh EH1 1BB
Phone: 0131 557 1175

#383
Barnardos
Category: Charity Shop, Furniture Shop
Average price: Inexpensive
Area: Leith
Address: 144-148 Leith Walk
Edinburgh EH6 5DT
Phone: 0131 554 4099

#384
Christopher Ross
Category: Men's Clothing
Average price: Expensive
Area: New Town
Address: 39 Leith Street
Edinburgh EH1 3AT
Phone: 0131 557 2226

#385
Southside Pharmacy
Category: Pharmacy
Average price: Modest
Area: Newington
Address: 79 Nicolson St
Edinburgh EH8 9BZ
Phone: 0131 667 4032

#386
Antiques and Stuff
Category: Antiques
Average price: Modest
Area: Newington
Address: 102 Causewayside
Edinburgh EH9 1PU
Phone: 0131 667 2501

#387
**The Creepy Wee Shop
in the Graveyard**
Category: Cards & Stationery
Average price: Inexpensive
Area: Old Town
Address: 26B Candlemaker Row
Edinburgh EH1 2QG
Phone: 0131 225 9044

#388
Jack Wills
Category: Women's Clothing,
Men's Clothing
Average price: Expensive
Area: New Town
Address: 63-65 George St
Edinburgh EH2 2JL
Phone: 0131 252167

#389
Central Carpets
Category: Home & Garden
Average price: Inexpensive
Area: Leith
Address: 1 Mill Lane Great Junction Street,
Edinburgh EH6 5LD
Phone: 0131 553 6092

#390
Wright Of Comiston
Category: Florist
Average price: Modest
Area: Morningside
Address: 111 Comiston Road
Edinburgh EH10 6AQ
Phone: 0131 447 7648

#391
Ripping Records
Category: Music & DVDs, Music Venues,
Vinyl Records
Average price: Modest
Area: Old Town, Newington
Address: 91 South Bridge
Edinburgh EH1 1HN
Phone: 0131 226 7010

#392
Yekta
Category: Accessories
Average price: Inexpensive
Area: Old Town, Newington
Address: 97 South Bridge
Edinburgh EH1 1HN
Phone: 0131 225 9706

#393
Jeneil Jewellers
Category: Jewellery
Average price: Modest
Area: Leith
Address: A 48 Great Junction Street
Edinburgh EH6 5LB
Phone: 0131 476 9706

#394
River Island
Category: Accessories, Men's Clothing,
Women's Clothing
Average price: Modest
Area: New Town
Address: St James Ctr
Edinburgh EH1 3SS
Phone: 0131 557 0602

#395
C M Marr
Category: Framing
Average price: Modest
Area: Leith
Address: 7 Ferry Road
Edinburgh EH6 4AD
Phone: 0131 554 0500

#396
Barratt Shoes
Category: Shoe Shop
Average price: Inexpensive
Area: New Town
Address: Princes St
Edinburgh EH2 2ER
Phone: 0131 225 5066

#397
Wallaces
Category: Appliances
Average price: Inexpensive
Area: Haymarket, West End
Address: 87-93 Dalry Road
Edinburgh EH11 2AB
Phone: 0131 337 6362

#398
Apothecary
Category: New Age, Ethnic Shop
Average price: Modest
Area: Newington
Address: 47 Clerk St
Edinburgh EH8 9JQ
Phone: 0131 667 5536

#399
Sports Warehouse
Category: Sports Equipments
Average price: Modest
Area: Leith
Address: 24-26 Coburg Street
Edinburgh EH6 6HB
Phone: 0131 553 6003

#400
Oka Direct
Category: Furniture Shop
Average price: Exclusive
Area: Leith
Address: 94 Commercial Street
Edinburgh EH6 6LX
Phone: 0131 555 6463

#401
News Plus
Category: Newsagent
Average price: Inexpensive
Area: Bruntsfield
Address: 196 Bruntsfield Pl
Edinburgh EH10 4DF
Phone: 0131 229 3415

#402
BHS
Category: Department Store,
Home & Garden, Women's Clothing
Average price: Inexpensive
Area: New Town
Address: 64 Princes St
Edinburgh EH2 2DJ
Phone: 0131 226 2621

#403
Bacchus Antiques
Category: Antiques
Average price: Exclusive
Area: Old Town, Grassmarket
Address: 95 W Bow
Edinburgh EH1 2JP
Phone: 0131 225 6183

#404
Auld Christmas Shop
Category: Flowers & Gifts, Home Decor
Average price: Expensive
Area: Old Town, Royal Mile
Address: 515 Lawnmarket
Edinburgh EH1 2PE
Phone: 0131 225 3449

#405
Petals By The Shore
Category: Florist
Average price: Modest
Area: Leith
Address: 57 Bernard Street
Edinburgh EH6 6SL
Phone: 0131 554 2624

#406
Hamilton & Inches
Category: Jewellery
Average price: Exclusive
Area: New Town
Address: 87 George Street
Edinburgh EH2 3EY
Phone: 0131 225 4898

#407
Alchemia Jewellers
Category: Jewellery
Average price: Exclusive
Area: New Town
Address: 37 Thistle St
Edinburgh EH2 1DY
Phone: 0131 220 4795

#408
Anne Fontaine
Category: Fashion
Average price: Expensive
Area: New Town
Address: 4 Multrees Walk
Edinburgh EH1 3DQ
Phone: 0131 558 1284

#409
Princes Mall
Category: Shopping Centre
Average price: Modest
Area: Old Town
Address: Waverley Bridge
Edinburgh EH1 1BQ
Phone: 0131 557 3759

#410
WH Smith
Category: Office Equipment, Newsagent,
Bookshop
Average price: Modest
Area: New Town, West End
Address: 10b Queensferry St
Edinburgh EH2 4PG
Phone: 0131 225 9672

#411
Thrift Shop Two
Category: Electronics
Average price: Inexpensive
Area: Bruntsfield, The Meadows
Address: 26 Lochrin Buildings
Edinburgh EH3 9NB
Phone: 0131 229 6939

#412
Nomads Tent
Category: Antiques, Home Decor,
Art Gallery
Average price: Exclusive
Area: Newington
Address: 21 St Leonard's Ln
Edinburgh EH8 9SH
Phone: 0131 662 1612

#413
Lindsay & Gilmour
Category: Pharmacy
Average price: Modest
Area: New Town
Address: 11 Elm Row
Edinburgh EH7 4AA
Phone: 0131 556 4316

#414
Shiraz Newsagent
Category: Newsagent
Average price: Inexpensive
Area: Marchmont
Address: 21 Sciennes Rd
Edinburgh EH9 1NX
Phone: 0131 667 4811

#415
Argento
Category: Jewellery
Average price: Modest
Area: New Town
Address: 18a Frederick Street
Edinburgh EH2 2HB
Phone: 0131 226 1704

#416
Ye Olde Christmas Shoppe
Category: Flowers & Gifts, Hobby Shop
Average price: Expensive
Area: Old Town, Royal Mile
Address: 145 Canongate
Edinburgh EH8 8BN
Phone: 0131 557 9220

#417
Adeel Electrical Goods
Category: Appliances
Average price: Modest
Area: Leith
Address: 72 Elm Row
Edinburgh EH7 4AQ
Phone: 0131 556 9769

#418
Heritage Of Scotland
Category: Men's Clothing,
Women's Clothing, Souvenir Shop
Average price: Modest
Area: Old Town, Royal Mile
Address: 459-461 Lawnmarket
Edinburgh EH1 2NT
Phone: 0131 225 1140

#419
G-Star Raw Store
Multrees Walk
Category: Men's Clothing,
Women's Clothing
Average price: Expensive
Area: New Town
Address: Unit 8 Multrees Walk
Edinburgh EH1 3DQ
Phone: 0131 558 3975

#420
Chest Heart & Stroke Scotland
Category: Vintage
Average price: Inexpensive
Area: Newington
Address: 76 Newington Road
Edinburgh EH9 1QN
Phone: 0131 667 1901

#421
Levi Strauss
Category: Fashion
Average price: Expensive
Area: New Town
Address: 109-112 Princes St
Edinburgh EH2 3AA
Phone: 0131 220 0480

#422
Argos
Category: Toys, Home Furnishings,
Personal Care
Average price: Inexpensive
Area: Old Town, Royal Mile
Address: 11-15 N Bridge
Edinburgh EH1 1SB
Phone: 0131 558 1474

#423
Toys Galore
Category: Toy Shop
Average price: Modest
Area: Stockbridge
Address: 13 Comely Bank Road
Edinburgh EH4 1DR
Phone: 0131 343 1244

#424
PDSA
Category: Charity Shop
Average price: Modest
Area: Old Town, Royal Mile
Address: 115 High Street
Edinburgh EH1 1EH
Phone: 0131 556 1575

#425
Joseph H Bonnar
Category: Jewellery
Average price: Exclusive
Area: New Town
Address: 72 Thistle Street
Edinburgh EH2 1EN
Phone: 0131 226 2811

#426
Makin Allan Sons Pianos
Category: Musical Instruments
Average price: Exclusive
Area: Stockbridge
Address: 4-5 Summer Place
Edinburgh EH3 5NR
Phone: 0131 556 1287

#427
Vintage + Reclaimed
Category: Antiques
Average price: Expensive
Area: Newington
Address: 179 Causewayside
Edinburgh EH9 1PN
Phone: 0131 662 1300

#428
Superdrug
Category: Pharmacy,
Beauty & Cosmetics
Average price: Inexpensive
Area: West End
Address: 144 Lothian Road
Edinburgh EH3 9BG
Phone: 0131 229 8175

#429
Pride Of Scotland
Category: Tartan Products
Average price: Modest
Area: New Town
Address: 121-121a Princes Street
Edinburgh EH2 4AD
Phone: 0131 557 1414

#430
Slaters
Category: Men's Clothing,
Tailors & Alterations
Average price: Modest
Area: New Town
Address: 100 George Street
Edinburgh EH2 3DF
Phone: 0131 220 4343

#431
Poundstretcher
Category: Pound Shop
Average price: Inexpensive
Area: West End
Address: 42 Shandwick Place
Edinburgh EH2 4RT
Phone: 0131 225 1611

#432
Edinburgh Bicycle Cooperative
Category: Bicycles
Average price: Modest
Area: Bruntsfield, The Meadows
Address: 5-11 Alvanley Terrace
Edinburgh EH9 1DU
Phone: 0131 331 5010

#433
Historic Connections
Category: Arts & Crafts, Jewellery
Average price: Modest
Area: Old Town, Royal Mile
Address: 173 Canongate
Edinburgh EH8 8BN
Phone: 0131 556 5305

#434
The Kilt Hire Co.
Category: Men's Clothing
Average price: Modest
Area: Haymarket, West End
Address: 54-56 Haymarket Terrace
Edinburgh EH12 5LA
Phone: 0131 337 3333

#435
Kilberry Bagpipes
Category: Musical Instruments
Average price: Expensive
Area: Newington
Address: 93 Causewayside
Edinburgh EH9 1QG
Phone: 0131 668 3303

#436
The Scotland Shop
Category: Shopping
Average price: Modest
Area: Old Town, Newington, Royal Mile
Address: 18-20 High St
Edinburgh EH1 1SR
Phone: 0131 557 2030

#437
Edinburgh Castle Gift Shop
Category: Flowers & Gifts
Average price: Exclusive
Area: Old Town, Royal Mile
Address: Castle Hill
Edinburgh EH1 2NG
Phone: 0131 225 6685

#438
Mellstock Quire
Category: Cards & Stationery
Average price: Expensive
Area: Morningside
Address: 310 Morningside Road
Edinburgh EH10 4QH
Phone: 0131 452 8493

#439
Royal Mile Curios
Category: Antiques
Average price: Expensive
Area: Old Town, Royal Mile
Address: 363 High Street
Edinburgh EH1 1PW
Phone: 0131 226 4050

#440
Pringle Booksellers
Category: Antiques, Bookshop
Average price: Expensive
Area: Old Town, Grassmarket
Address: 62 W Port
Edinburgh EH1 2LD
Phone: 0131 228 8880

#441
Flowers by Arkadius
Category: Florist
Average price: Modest
Area: New Town
Address: 48 Princes Street
Edinburgh EH2 2YJ
Phone: 0131 226 5972

#442
Boots
Category: Pharmacy,
Beauty & Cosmetics
Average price: Modest
Area: Old Town, Royal Mile
Address: 40-44 North Bridge
Edinburgh EH1 1QN
Phone: 0131 220 1879

#443
Phone Box
Category: Mobile Phones
Average price: Modest
Area: Old Town, Newington
Address: 26 South Bridge
Edinburgh EH1 1LL
Phone: 0131 557 0459

#444
Spar
Category: Supermarket, Tobacconists
Average price: Modest
Area: Old Town, Newington
Address: 44-46 South Bridge
Edinburgh EH1 1LL
Phone: 0131 622 7678

#445
East
Category: Fashion
Average price: Expensive
Area: New Town
Address: 35 George Street
Edinburgh EH2 2EN
Phone: 0131 226 6944

#446
Mappin & Webb
Category: Jewellery
Average price: Exclusive
Area: New Town
Address: 88 George Street
Edinburgh EH2 3DF
Phone: 0131 225 5502

#447
Palenque
Category: Jewellery
Average price: Modest
Area: Old Town, Newington, Royal Mile
Address: 56 High Street
Edinburgh EH1 1TB
Phone: 0131 557 9553

#448
Thomas Pink
Category: Men's Clothing
Average price: Exclusive
Area: New Town
Address: 32a Castle Street
Edinburgh EH2 3HT
Phone: 0131 225 4264

#449
Print That T-Shirts
Category: Printing & Photocopying
Average price: Modest
Area: New Town
Address: 196 Rose Street
Edinburgh EH2 4AT
Phone: 0870 042 4350

#450
Latest News Newsagent
Category: Newsagent
Average price: Inexpensive
Area: Old Town
Address: 49 Lothian Road
Edinburgh EH1 2DJ
Phone: 0131 556 5818

#451
Mulberry Co
Category: Luggage, Leather Goods,
Accessories
Average price: Exclusive
Area: New Town
Address: 7 Multrees Walk
Edinburgh EH1 3DQ
Phone: 0131 557 5439

#452
Phase Eight
Category: Fashion
Average price: Expensive
Area: New Town
Address: St James Centre
Edinburgh EH1 3SP
Phone: 0131 556 9121

#453
Marie Curie Cancer Care
Category: Charity Shop
Average price: Inexpensive
Area: Newington
Address: 72 Nicolson Street
Edinburgh EH8 9DT
Phone: 0131 668 1673

#454
Main Point Books
Category: Bookshop
Average price: Inexpensive
Area: Old Town
Address: 77 Bread Street
Edinburgh EH3 9AH
Phone: 0131 228 4837

#455
Oasis Store
Category: Women's Clothing, Accessories
Average price: Modest
Area: New Town
Address: 14-16 Frederick St
Edinburgh EH2 2HB
Phone: 0131 225 4624

#456
Gamefish Angling Equipment
Category: Sporting Goods
Average price: Expensive
Area: New Town
Address: 6a Howe Street
Edinburgh EH3 6TD
Phone: 0131 220 6465

#457
Linzi Crawford
Category: Women's Clothing
Average price: Expensive
Area: New Town
Address: 27 Dublin Street
Edinburgh EH3 6NL
Phone: 0131 558 7558

#458
Edinburgh Newsagent
Category: Newsagent
Average price: Modest
Area: Haymarket
Address: 33 Roseburn Terrace
Edinburgh EH12 5NQ
Phone: 0131 337 9764

#459
The Clothing Bank
Category: Vintage
Average price: Inexpensive
Area: Newington
Address: 136 Nicolson Street
Edinburgh EH8 9EH
Phone: 07970 234234

#460
The Torrance Gallery
Category: Art Gallery, Museum
Average price: Inexpensive
Area: New Town
Address: 36 Dundas Street
Edinburgh EH3 6JN
Phone: 0131 556 6366

#461
The Ring Maker
Category: Jewellery
Average price: Expensive
Area: New Town
Address: 46 Dundas St
Edinburgh EH3 6JN
Phone: 0131 558 8800

#462
Louis Vuitton
Category: Leather Goods, Shoe Shop
Average price: Exclusive
Area: New Town
Address: 1-2 Multrees Walk
Edinburgh EH1 3QD
Phone: 0131 652 5900

#463
Capital Newsagent
Category: Newsagent
Average price: Inexpensive
Area: Newington
Address: 26 Clerk St
Edinburgh EH8 9HX
Phone: 0131 667 0266

#464
Dolly & Mop Beauty & Hair
Category: Hairdressers, Hair Removal,
Beauty & Cosmetics
Average price: Expensive
Area: Marchmont
Address: 25 Marchmont Crescent
Edinburgh EH9 1HQ
Phone: 0131 221 9360

#465
Royal Artizana
Category: Furniture Shop
Average price: Expensive
Area: Leith
Address: 115 Leith Walk
Edinburgh EH6 8NP
Phone: 0131 555 3999

#466
The Smart Stork
Category: Children's Clothing
Average price: Modest
Area: Marchmont
Address: 92 Marchmont Crescent
Edinburgh EH9 1HD
Phone: 0131 447 8000

#467
Glamour Hair & Beauty
Category: Hairdressers, Beauty &
Cosmetics, Beauticians & Day Spa
Average price: Inexpensive
Area: West End
Address: 125 Gilmore Place
Edinburgh EH3 9PP
Phone: 0131 466 4523

#468
Poundstretcher
Category: Pound Shop, Home & Garden
Average price: Inexpensive
Area: Old Town, Newington
Address: 100-106 South Bridge
Edinburgh EH1 1HN
Phone: 0131 225 8540

#469
Lucie Fenton Gallery
Category: Jewellery, Framing,
Art Gallery
Average price: Modest
Area: Stockbridge
Address: 20 Raeburn Place
Edinburgh EH4 1HN
Phone: 0131 332 3999

#470
Palace of Holyroodhouse Shop
Category: Art Gallery
Average price: Modest
Area: Old Town
Address: Holyrood Palace
Edinburgh EH8 8BA
Phone: 0131 556 5100

#471
Private Lines
Category: Adult
Average price: Modest
Area: Leith
Address: 60 Elm Row
Edinburgh EH7 4AQ
Phone: 0131 557 6842

#472
Caoba Gift Shop
Category: Flowers & Gifts
Average price: Modest
Area: Stockbridge
Address: 56 Raeburn Place
Edinburgh EH4 1HJ
Phone: 0131 343 2757

#473
Scotland T Shirt Company
Category: T-Shirts
Average price: Modest
Area: Old Town, Royal Mile
Address: 491 Lawnmarket
Edinburgh EH1 2NT
Phone: 0131 226 2514

#474
Fraser Hart
Category: Jewellery
Average price: Modest
Area: New Town
Address: 77 Princes Street
Edinburgh EH2 2DF
Phone: 0131 225 2233

#475
Maddie and Mark's Shoes
Category: Children's Clothing
Average price: Expensive
Area: Bruntsfield
Address: 205 Bruntsfield Pl
Edinburgh EH10 4DH
Phone: 0131 447 9779

#476
Get Shirty
Category: T-Shirts
Average price: Inexpensive
Area: New Town
Address: 134 Rose Street
Edinburgh EH2 3JD
Phone: 0131 220 4628

#477
Garage Shoes
Category: Shoe Shop
Average price: Inexpensive
Area: New Town
Address: 54-56 St James Centre
Edinburgh EH1 3SL
Phone: 0131 557 8952

#478
Fopp
Category: Books, Mags, Music & Video
Average price: Inexpensive
Area: Old Town, Royal Mile
Address: 55 Cockburn Street
Edinburgh EH1 1BS
Phone: 0131 220 0133

#479
Oasis Store
Category: Women's Clothing
Average price: Modest
Area: New Town
Address: 145 Princes Street
Edinburgh EH2 4BL
Phone: 0131 226 1523

#480
Hutchison Pharmacy
Category: Pharmacy
Average price: Modest
Area: Marchmont
Address: 2 Fountainhall Road
Edinburgh EH9 2NN
Phone: 0131 667 4462

#481
The Football Programme Shop
Category: Bookshop, Football
Average price: Modest
Area: Leith
Address: 5 Albion Rd
Edinburgh EH7 5QJ
Phone: 0131 652 1444

#482
Bathstore
Category: Kitchen & Bath
Average price: Modest
Area: New Town
Address: Queen Street
Edinburgh EH2 1HY
Phone: 0131 556 0333

#483
Fantastic Scotland
Category: Fashion
Average price: Modest
Area: Old Town, Royal Mile
Address: 156 Canongate
Edinburgh EH8 8DD
Phone: 0131 558 1114

#484
Outrageous Art
Category: Art Gallery
Average price: Expensive
Area: Bruntsfield, The Meadows
Address: 17-19 Barclay Place
Edinburgh EH10 4HW
Phone: 0131 477 2933

#485
Gamesmasters
Category: Videos & Video Game Rental
Average price: Inexpensive
Area: Leith
Address: 287 Leith Walk
Edinburgh EH6 8PD
Phone: 0131 555 5188

#486
Bobbies
Category: Bookshop
Average price: Inexpensive
Area: West End
Address: 220 Morrison Street
Edinburgh EH3 8EA
Phone: 0131 538 7069

#487
Those Were The Days Vintage
Category: Vintage
Average price: Modest
Area: Stockbridge, New Town
Address: 26 St Stephen Street
Edinburgh EH3 5AL
Phone: 0131 225 4400

#488
Powerhouse Fitness
Category: Sporting Goods
Average price: Expensive
Area: New Town
Address: 14 Antigua Street
Edinburgh EH1 3NH
Phone: 0131 558 3727

#489
Ingleby Gallery
Category: Art Gallery
Average price: Exclusive
Area: Old Town
Address: 6 Carlton Terrace
Edinburgh EH7 5DD
Phone: 0131 556 4441

#490
Leomax
Category: Mobile Phones,
Computer Repair
Average price: Modest
Area: Leith
Address: 75 Elm Row
Edinburgh EH7 4AQ
Phone: 0131 558 9090

#491
Fopp
Category: Bookshop, Comic Books
Average price: Inexpensive
Area: New Town
Address: 3-15 Rose Street
Edinburgh EH2 2PR
Phone: 0131 243 0870

#492
Azalay The Tropics Edinburgh
Category: Flowers & Gifts
Average price: Modest
Area: Morningside
Address: 392 Morningside Road
Edinburgh EH10 5HX
Phone: 0131 452 9444

#493
Liliana Dabic
Category: Fashion
Average price: Expensive
Area: Morningside
Address: 410 Morningside Road
Edinburgh EH10 5HY
Phone: 0131 466 7272

#494
Hawkin's Bazaar
Category: Toy Shop
Average price: Expensive
Area: New Town
Address: 16 St James Shopping Centre
Edinburgh EH1 3SR
Phone: 0131 556 4030

#495
Beautiful Things
Category: Arts & Crafts, Gift Shop
Average price: Expensive
Area: Morningside
Address: 414 Morningside Road
Edinburgh EH10 5HY
Phone: 0131 466 6333

#496
HMV
Category: Music & DVDs, Bookshop
Average price: Expensive
Area: New Town
Address: Unit 44-48
Edinburgh EH1 3SL
Phone: 0131 556 1236

#497
Superdrug
Category: Pharmacy,
Beauty & Cosmetics
Average price: Modest
Area: Morningside
Address: 216 Morningside Road
Edinburgh EH10 4QQ
Phone: 0131 447 9055

#498
Shoe Zone
Category: Shoe Shop
Average price: Modest
Area: Leith
Address: 36 Newkirkgate Centre
Edinburgh EH6 6AA
Phone: 0131 553 2767

#499
Evans Cycles
Category: Bicycles
Average price: Modest
Area: West End
Address: 88 Fountain Bridge
Edinburgh EH3 9
Phone: 0131 255 0500

#500
Shelter
Category: Charity Shop, Vintage
Average price: Inexpensive
Area: Haymarket, West End
Address: 27 Dalry Rd
Edinburgh EH11 2BQ
Phone: 0131 346 2468

TOP 500 RESTAURANTS

The Most Recommended by Locals & Trevelers

(From #1 to #500)

#1
The Edinburgh Larder
Cuisines: Deli, Coffee & Tea
Average price: Under £10
Area: Old Town, Newington
Address: 15 Blackfriars Street
Edinburgh EH1 1NB
Phone: 0131 556 6922

#2
Baked Potato Shop
Cuisines: Fast Food & Takeaways,
Vegetarian, Vegan
Average price: Under £10
Area: Old Town, Royal Mile
Address: 56 Cockburn Street
Edinburgh EH1 1PB
Phone: 0131 225 7572

#3
Hanedan
Cuisines: Turkish
Average price: £11-25
Area: Newington
Address: 41-42 West Preston Street
Edinburgh EH8 9PY
Phone: 0131 667 4242

#4
Oink
Cuisines: Sandwiches,
Fast Food & Takeaways
Average price: Under £10
Area: Old Town, Grassmarket
Address: 34 Victoria Street
Edinburgh EH1 2JW
Phone: 07771 968233

#5
Kismot
Cuisines: Indian
Average price: £11-25
Area: Newington
Address: 29 St Leonard's Street
Edinburgh EH8 9QN
Phone: 0131 667 0123

#6
Palmyra
Cuisines: Middle Eastern,
Fast Food & Takeaways
Average price: Under £10
Area: Newington
Address: 22 Nicolson Street
Edinburgh EH8 9DH
Phone: 0131 667 6655

#7
Mums
Cuisines: British, Breakfast & Brunch
Average price: £11-25
Area: Old Town
Address: 4a Forrest Road
Edinburgh EH1 2QN
Phone: 0131 260 9806

#8
Kim's Mini Meals
Cuisines: Korean
Average price: Under £10
Area: Newington
Address: 5 Buccleuch Street
Edinburgh EH8 9JN
Phone: 0131 629 7951

#9
Mark Greenaway
Cuisines: British
Average price: £26-45
Area: New Town
Address: 69 North Castle Street
Edinburgh EH2 3LJ
Phone: 0131 226 1155

#10
Wings Edinburgh
Cuisines: Chicken Wings
Average price: Under £10
Area: Old Town, Newington, Royal Mile
Address: 5/7 Old Fishmarket Close
Edinburgh EH1 1RW
Phone: 0131 629 1234

#11
Union of Genius
Cuisines: Soup, Coffee & Tea
Average price: Under £10
Area: Old Town
Address: 8 Forrest Road
Edinburgh EH1 2QN
Phone: 0131 226 4436

#12
La Favorita
Cuisines: Italian, Pizza
Average price: £11-25
Area: Leith
Address: 325 Leith Walk
Edinburgh EH6 8SA
Phone: 0131 554 2430

#13
The Holyrood 9A
Cuisines: Brewery, Burgers
Average price: £11-25
Area: Old Town
Address: 9a Holyrood Road
Edinburgh EH8 8AE
Phone: 0131 556 5044

#14
Café Marlayne
Cuisines: French
Average price: £11-25
Area: New Town
Address: 76 Thistle Street
Edinburgh EH2 1EN
Phone: 0131 226 2230

#15
The Dogs
Cuisines: British
Average price: £11-25
Area: New Town
Address: 110 Hanover Street
Edinburgh EH2 1DR
Phone: 0131 220 1208

#16
L'Escargot Blanc
Cuisines: French
Average price: £11-25
Area: New Town, West End
Address: 17 Queensferry St
Edinburgh EH2 4QP
Phone: 0131 226 1890

#17
Vittoria
Cuisines: Italian, Pizza
Average price: £11-25
Area: Old Town
Address: 19 George IV Bridge
Edinburgh EH1 1EN
Phone: 0131 225 1740

#18
Kanpai
Cuisines: Japanese
Average price: £11-25
Area: Old Town
Address: 8 Grindlay Street
Edinburgh EH3 9AS
Phone: 0131 228 1602

#19
BrewDog
Cuisines: Pub, Burgers, Pizza
Average price: £11-25
Area: Old Town, Newington
Address: 143 Cowgate
Edinburgh EH1 1JS
Phone: 0131 220 6517

#20
The Outsider
Cuisines: European, Mediterranean
Average price: £11-25
Area: Old Town, Grassmarket
Address: 15/16 George IV Bridge
Edinburgh EH1 1EE
Phone: 0131 226 3131

#21
Kebab Mahal
Cuisines: Indian, Fast Food & Takeaways
Average price: Under £10
Area: Newington
Address: 7 Nicolson Square
Edinburgh EH8 9BH
Phone: 0131 622 7228

#22
Phuket Pavillion
Cuisines: Thai
Average price: £11-25
Area: New Town
Address: 8 Union Street
Edinburgh EH1 3LU
Phone: 0131 556 4323

#23
Field
Cuisines: Scottish
Average price: £11-25
Area: Newington
Address: 41 West Nicolson Street
Edinburgh EH8 9DB
Phone: 0131 667 7010

#24
Ondine
Cuisines: Seafood
Average price: £26-45
Area: Old Town, Grassmarket
Address: 2 George IV Bridge
Edinburgh EH1 1AD
Phone: 0131 226 1888

#25
Brass Monkey
Cuisines: Pub, Sandwiches, Lounge
Average price: £11-25
Area: Newington
Address: 14 Drummond Street
Edinburgh EH8 9TU
Phone: 0131 556 1961

#26
Victor & Carina Contini Ristorante
Cuisines: Italian, Breakfast & Brunch
Average price: £11-25
Area: New Town
Address: 103 George Street
Edinburgh EH2 3ES
Phone: 0131 225 1550

#27
Mussel Inn Restaurant
Cuisines: Seafood
Average price: £11-25
Area: New Town
Address: 61 Rose Street
Edinburgh EH2 2NH
Phone: 0131 225 5979

#28
The Dome
Cuisines: British
Average price: £26-45
Area: New Town
Address: 14 George Street
Edinburgh EH2 2PF
Phone: 0131 624 8624

#29
The Mussel and Steak Bar
Cuisines: Seafood, Steakhouse
Average price: £11-25
Area: Old Town, Grassmarket
Address: 110 West Bow
Edinburgh EH1 2HH
Phone: 0131 225 5028

#30
Ecco Vino
Cuisines: Brasserie, Wine Bar, Italian
Average price: £11-25
Area: Old Town, Royal Mile
Address: 19 Cockburn Street
Edinburgh EH1 1BP
Phone: 0131 225 1441

#31
The Tailend
Cuisines: Fish & Chips
Average price: £11-25
Area: Leith
Address: 14-15 Albert Place
Edinburgh EH7 5HN
Phone: 0131 555 3577

#32
Spirit of Thai
Cuisines: Thai
Average price: £11-25
Area: Old Town
Address: 44 Grindlay Street
Edinburgh EH3 9AP
Phone: 0131 228 9333

#33
The Piemaker
Cuisines: Fast Food & Takeaways, Coffee
& Tea, Bakery
Average price: Under £10
Area: Old Town, Newington
Address: 38 South Bridge
Edinburgh EH1 1LL
Phone: 0131 558 1728

#34
Mother India's Cafe
Cuisines: Indian, Tapas
Average price: £11-25
Area: Old Town, Newington
Address: 3-5 Infirmary Street
Edinburgh EH1 1LT
Phone: 0131 524 9801

#35
Positano
Cuisines: Italian
Average price: £11-25
Area: Newington
Address: 85- 87 Newington Road
Edinburgh EH9 1QW
Phone: 0131 662 9977

#36
Martin Wishart
Cuisines: British, French
Average price: Above £46
Area: Leith
Address: 54 Shore
Edinburgh EH6 6
Phone: 0131 553 3557

#37
The Grain Store
Cuisines: French
Average price: £26-45
Area: Old Town, Grassmarket
Address: 30 Victoria Street
Edinburgh EH1 2JW
Phone: 0131 225 7635

#38
The Mosque Kitchen
Cuisines: Ethnic Food, Indian
Average price: Under £10
Area: Newington
Address: 31 Nicholson Square
Edinburgh EH8 9BX
Phone: 0131 667 4035

#39
Los Cardos
Cuisines: Mexican
Average price: Under £10
Area: Leith
Address: 281 Leith Walk
Edinburgh EH6 8PD
Phone: 0131 555 6619

#40
Toast
Cuisines: European, Breakfast & Brunch,
Brasserie
Average price: £11-25
Area: Marchmont
Address: 146 Marchmont Road
Edinburgh EH9 1AQ
Phone: 0131 446 9873

#41
Patisserie Madeleine
Cuisines: Coffee & Tea, French
Average price: £26-45
Area: Stockbridge
Address: 27b Raeburn Place
Edinburgh EH4 1HU
Phone: 0131 332 8455

#42
Fishers In The City
Cuisines: Seafood
Average price: £26-45
Area: New Town
Address: 58 Thistle Street
Edinburgh EH2 1EN
Phone: 0131 225 5109

#43
The Bon Vivant
Cuisines: European, Tapas
Average price: £11-25
Area: New Town
Address: 55 Thistle Street
Edinburgh EH2 1DY
Phone: 0131 225 3275

#44
The Kitchin
Cuisines: British, European
Average price: Above £46
Area: Leith
Address: 78 Commercial Street
Edinburgh EH6 6LX
Phone: 0131 555 1755

#45
The Witchery By The Castle
Cuisines: British
Average price: £26-45
Area: Old Town, Royal Mile
Address: 352 Castlehill
Edinburgh EH1 2NF
Phone: 0131 225 5613

#46
Urban Angel
Cuisines: Coffee & Tea
Average price: £11-25
Area: New Town
Address: 121 Hanover Street
Edinburgh EH2 1DJ
Phone: 0131 225 6215

#47
The Nile Valley Cafe
Cuisines: Coffee & Tea, African,
Sandwiches
Average price: Under £10
Area: Newington
Address: 6 Chapel Street
Edinburgh EH8 9AY
Phone: 0131 667 8200

#48
The Devil's Advocate
Cuisines: British, Gastropub
Average price: £11-25
Area: Old Town, Royal Mile
Address: 9 Advocate Close
Edinburgh EH1 1ND
Phone: 0131 225 4465

#49
Wedgwood the Restaurant
Cuisines: Brasserie
Average price: Above £46
Area: Old Town, Royal Mile
Address: 267 Canongate
Edinburgh EH8 8BQ
Phone: 0131 558 8737

#50
Timberyard
Cuisines: British
Average price: £26-45
Area: Old Town
Address: 10 Lady Lawson Street
Edinburgh EH3 9DS
Phone: 0131 221 1222

#51
Castle Terrace
Cuisines: British
Average price: Above £46
Area: Old Town
Address: 33-35 Castle Terrace
Edinburgh EH1 2EL
Phone: 0131 229 1222

#52
The Auld Hoose
Cuisines: Pub, British
Average price: £11-25
Area: Newington
Address: 23-25 St Leonard's Street
Edinburgh EH8 9QN
Phone: 0131 668 2934

#53
Ruan Thai Restaurant
Cuisines: Thai
Average price: £11-25
Area: New Town
Address: 48 Howe Street
Edinburgh EH3 6TH
Phone: 0131 226 3675

#54
Indaba Restaurant
Cuisines: Spanish, African, Tapas
Average price: £11-25
Area: Tollcross, West End
Address: 3 Lochrin Terrace
Edinburgh EH3 9QJ
Phone: 0131 221 1554

#55
Fishers
Cuisines: Seafood
Average price: £11-25
Area: Leith
Address: 1 Shore
Edinburgh EH6 6QW
Phone: 0131 554 5666

#56
WHISKI Bar & Restaurant
Cuisines: British
Average price: £11-25
Area: Old Town, Royal Mile
Address: 119 High Street
Edinburgh EH1 1SG
Phone: 0131 556 3095

#57
Peter's Yard
Cuisines: Scandinavian, Bakery
Average price: £11-25
Area: The Meadows
Address: 27 Simpson Loan
Edinburgh EH3 9GG
Phone: 0131 228 5876

#58
Villager
Cuisines: Bar, Burgers
Average price: £11-25
Area: Old Town
Address: 49 George IV Bridge
Edinburgh EH1 1EJ
Phone: 0131 226 2781

#59
Treacle
Cuisines: Bar, Gastropub
Average price: £11-25
Area: New Town
Address: 39 Broughton Street
Edinburgh EH1 3JU
Phone: 0131 557 0627

#60
Angels with Bagpipes
Cuisines: Bar, British
Average price: £26-45
Area: Old Town, Newington, Royal Mile
Address: 343 High St
Edinburgh EH1 1PW
Phone: 0131 220 1111

#61
Wildfire
Cuisines: Steakhouse, Seafood
Average price: £11-25
Area: New Town
Address: 192 Rose St
Edinburgh EH2 4AZ
Phone: 0131 225 3636

#62
Burger
Cuisines: Burgers, Fast Food & Takeaways
Average price: Under £10
Area: West End
Address: 94a Fountainbridge
Edinburgh EH3 9QA
Phone: 0131 228 5367

#63
Café Domenico
Cuisines: Italian
Average price: £11-25
Area: Leith
Address: 30 Sandport Street
Edinburgh EH6 6EP
Phone: 0131 467 7266

#64
Cloisters Bar
Cuisines: Pub, British
Average price: £11-25
Area: Tollcross, The Meadows
Address: 26 Brougham Street
Edinburgh EH3 9JH
Phone: 0131 221 9997

#65
Pierre Victoire
Cuisines: French
Average price: £11-25
Area: Cannonmills
Address: 18 Eyre Pl
Edinburgh EH3 5EP
Phone: 0131 556 0006

#66
Café Marlayne
Cuisines: Coffee & Tea, French
Average price: £11-25
Area: New Town
Address: 13 Antigua Street
Edinburgh EH1 3NH
Phone: 0131 558 8244

#67
The Bon Vivant's Companion
Cuisines: Deli
Average price: £26-45
Area: New Town
Address: 55 Thistle Street
Edinburgh EH2 1DY
Phone: 0131 225 6055

#68
Joseph Pearce
Cuisines: Gastropub, Scandinavian,
Breakfast & Brunch
Average price: £11-25
Area: New Town
Address: 23 Elm Row
Edinburgh EH7 4AA
Phone: 0131 556 4140

#69
El Quijote
Cuisines: Spanish, Tapas
Average price: £11-25
Area: Tollcross
Address: 13 A Brougham Street
Edinburgh EH3 9
Phone: 0131 478 2856

#70
The Cafe Royal
Cuisines: Seafood, Bar, British
Average price: £11-25
Area: New Town
Address: 19 W Register Street
Edinburgh EH2 2AA
Phone: 0131 556 1884

#71
Dubh Prais Restaurant
Cuisines: British
Average price: £26-45
Area: Old Town, Royal Mile
Address: 123b High St
Edinburgh EH1 1SG
Phone: 0131 557 5732

#72
The Engine Shed
Cuisines: Vegetarian
Average price: £11-25
Area: Newington
Address: 19 St Leonard's Lane
Edinburgh EH8 9SH
Phone: 0131 662 0040

#73
The Voodoo Room
Cuisines: British, Gastropub
Average price: £26-45
Area: New Town
Address: 19A West Register Street
Edinburgh EH2 2AA
Phone: 0131 556 7060

#74
Blackwood's Bar & Grill
Cuisines: Scottish, Bar
Average price: £26-45
Area: New Town
Address: 10 Gloucester Place
Edinburgh EH3 6EF
Phone: 0131 225 2720

#75
Guildford Arms
Cuisines: Pub, British
Average price: £11-25
Area: New Town
Address: 1-5 W Register Street
Edinburgh EH2 2AA
Phone: 0131 556 4312

#76
Karen's Unicorn
Cuisines: Chinese
Average price: £11-25
Area: Stockbridge, New Town
Address: 112 St Stephen St
Edinburgh EH3 5AD
Phone: 0131 220 6659

#77
Anima
Cuisines: Italian
Average price: £11-25
Area: Stockbridge
Address: 11 Henderson Row
Edinburgh EH3 5DH
Phone: 0131 558 2918

#78
Earthy Food Market
Cuisines: Deli, Sandwiches
Average price: £11-25
Area: Newington
Address: 33-41 Ratcliffe Terrace
Edinburgh EH9 1SX
Phone: 0131 667 2967

#79
Calistoga
Cuisines: American
Average price: £11-25
Area: New Town
Address: 70 Rose Street
Edinburgh EH2 3DX
Phone: 0131 225 1233

#80
Secret Arcade
Cuisines: Lounge, British
Average price: £11-25
Area: Old Town, Royal Mile
Address: 48 Cockburn Street
Edinburgh EH1 1PB
Phone: 0131 220 1297

#81
Shebeen
Cuisines: African, Barbeque, Bistro
Average price: £11-25
Area: West End
Address: 8 Morrison Street
Edinburgh EH3
Phone: 0131 629 0261

#82
Urban Angel
Cuisines: British, Coffee & Tea, Breakfast &
Brunch
Average price: £11-25
Area: New Town
Address: 1 Forth St
Edinburgh EH1 3JX
Phone: 0131 556 6323

#83
The Basement
Cuisines: Pub, British, Mexican
Average price: £26-45
Area: New Town
Address: 10a-12a Broughton Street
Edinburgh EH1 3RH
Phone: 0131 557 0097

#84
Brass Monkey Leith
Cuisines: Pub, British
Average price: £11-25
Area: Leith
Address: 362 Leith Walk
Edinburgh EH6 5BR
Phone: 0131 554 5286

#85
Divino Enoteca
Cuisines: Wine Bar, Italian
Average price: £26-45
Area: Old Town
Address: 5 Merchant St
Edinburgh EH1 2QD
Phone: 0131 225 1770

#86
Bell's Diner
Cuisines: American, Burgers, Steakhouse
Average price: £11-25
Area: Stockbridge, New Town
Address: 7 St Stephen Street
Edinburgh EH3 5AN
Phone: 0131 225 8116

#87
Pho Vietnam House
Cuisines: Vietnamese
Average price: £11-25
Area: West End
Address: 3 Grove Street
Edinburgh EH3 8AF
Phone: 0131 228 3383

#88
Henderson's
Cuisines: Vegetarian, Deli
Average price: £11-25
Area: New Town
Address: 94 Hanover Street
Edinburgh EH2 1DR
Phone: 0131 225 2131

#89
Roseleaf
Cuisines: Brasserie, Pub
Average price: £11-25
Area: Leith
Address: 23/24 Sandport Place
Edinburgh EH6 6EW
Phone: 0131 476 5268

#90
Red-Box Noodle Bar
Cuisines: Fast Food & Takeaways, Asian
Fusion, Japanese
Average price: Under £10
Area: Newington
Address: 51/53 West Nicolson Street
Edinburgh EH8 9DB
Phone: 0131 662 0828

#91
Under the Stairs
Cuisines: Lounge, Gastropub
Average price: £11-25
Area: Old Town
Address: 3A Merchant Street
Edinburgh EH1 2QD
Phone: 0131 466 8550

#92
Hewat's Restaurant
Cuisines: French, American, British
Average price: £26-45
Area: Newington
Address: 19 - 21b Causewayside
Edinburgh EH9 1QF
Phone: 0131 466 6660

#93
Galvin Brasserie de Luxe
Cuisines: Brasserie
Average price: £11-25
Area: Old Town, West End
Address: Princes Street
Edinburgh EH1 2AB
Phone: 0131 222 8988

#94
Café Andaluz
Cuisines: Tapas Bar, Spanish
Average price: £11-25
Area: New Town
Address: 77B George Street
Edinburgh EH2 3EE
Phone: 0131 220 9980

#95
Thai Orchid
Cuisines: Thai
Average price: £11-25
Area: Old Town, Grassmarket
Address: 5a Johnston Terrace
Edinburgh EH1 2PW
Phone: 0131 225 6633

#96
The Green Mantle
Cuisines: Lounge, Pub, European
Average price: Under £10
Area: Newington
Address: 44 W Crosscauseway
Edinburgh EH8 9JP
Phone: 0131 662 8741

#97
New York Steam Packet
Cuisines: American
Average price: £11-25
Area: New Town
Address: 31 Rose St Ln N
Edinburgh EH2 2NP
Phone: 0131 220 4825

#98
Teuchters Landing
Cuisines: Gastropub, Wine Bar
Average price: £11-25
Area: Leith
Address: 1a and 1c Dock Place
Edinburgh EH6 6LU
Phone: 0131 5547 4272

#99
No 12 Picardy Place
Cuisines: Lounge, European
Average price: £26-45
Area: New Town
Address: 12 Picardy Place
Edinburgh EH1 3JT
Phone: 0131 555 1289

#100
Word of Mouth
Cuisines: Coffee & Tea,
Breakfast & Brunch, Sandwiches
Average price: Under £10
Area: Leith
Address: 3A Albert Street
Edinburgh EH7 5HL
Phone: 0131 554 4344

#101
Wannaburger
Cuisines: Burgers
Average price: Under £10
Area: West End
Address: 7/8 Queensferry Street
Edinburgh EH2 4PA
Phone: 0131 220 0036

#102
The Vintage
Cuisines: British, Gastropub
Average price: £11-25
Area: Leith
Address: 60 Henderson Street
Edinburgh EH6
Phone: 0131 563 5293

#103
Social Bite
Cuisines: Coffee & Tea, Sandwiches
Average price: Under £10
Area: New Town
Address: 131 Rose Street
Edinburgh EH2 3DT
Phone: 0131 202 6866

#104
Tex Mex 2
Cuisines: Mexican, Tex-Mex
Average price: £11-25
Area: New Town
Address: 64 Thistle Street
Edinburgh EH2 1EN
Phone: 0131 260 9699

#105
Spoon
Cuisines: Coffee & Tea, Brasserie
Average price: £11-25
Area: Newington
Address: 6a Nicolson Street
Edinburgh EH8 9DH
Phone: 0131 623 1752

#106
The Honours
Cuisines: Brasserie
Average price: Above £46
Area: New Town
Address: 58A N Castle Street
Edinburgh EH2 3LU
Phone: 0131 225 2515

#107
Howies Scottish Restaurant
Cuisines: Scottish
Average price: £11-25
Area: Old Town
Address: 10 - 14 Victoria Street
Edinburgh EH1 2HG
Phone: 0131 225 1721

#108
Delicious Italian
Cuisines: Fast Food & Takeaways
Average price: Under £10
Area: Marchmont
Address: 27a Marchmont Road
Edinburgh EH9 1HY
Phone: 0131 228 3800

#109
I.J Mellis Cheesemongers
Cuisines: Cheese Shop, Deli
Average price: £26-45
Area: Old Town, Grassmarket
Address: 30A Victoria Street
Edinburgh EH1 2JW
Phone: 0131 226 6215

#110
Kampung Ali Malaysian Delight
Cuisines: Malaysian
Average price: £11-25
Area: West End
Address: 97-101 Fountainbridge
Edinburgh EH3 9QG
Phone: 0131 228 5069

#111
Tigerlily
Cuisines: British, Wine Bar
Average price: £26-45
Area: New Town
Address: 125 George St
Edinburgh EH3 5AG
Phone: 0131 225 5005

#112
Three Birds
Cuisines: British, Scottish
Average price: £26-45
Area: Bruntsfield
Address: 3 Viewforth
Edinburgh EH10 4JD
Phone: 0131 229 3252

#113
The Shore
Cuisines: Seafood
Average price: £26-45
Area: Leith
Address: 3 Shore
Edinburgh EH6 6QW
Phone: 0131 553 5080

#114
Kyloe Restaurant & Grill
Cuisines: Steakhouse
Average price: £26-45
Area: West End
Address: 1 - 3 Rutland Street
Edinburgh EH1 2AE
Phone: 0131 229 3402

#115
Bodega
Cuisines: Mexican
Average price: £11-25
Area: Leith
Address: 62 Elm Row
Edinburgh EH7 4AQ
Phone: 0131 556 7930

#116
Mediterranean Gate
Cuisines: Sandwiches, Mediterranean, Fast
Food & Takeaways
Average price: Under £10
Area: Old Town
Address: 48 George Iv Bridge
Edinburgh EH1 1EJ
Phone: 0131 220 3696

#117
The Clock
Cuisines: Coffee & Tea, Burgers,
Sandwiches
Average price: Under £10
Area: Haymarket, West End
Address: 125 Dalry Road
Edinburgh EH11 2
Phone: 0131 538 7035

#118
Olive Branch Bistro
Cuisines: Mediterranean, Brasserie
Average price: £11-25
Area: New Town
Address: 91 Broughton Street
Edinburgh EH1 3RX
Phone: 0131 557 8589

#119
Tonic
Cuisines: British, Gastropub
Average price: £26-45
Area: New Town
Address: 34a North Castle Street
Edinburgh EH2 3BN
Phone: 0131 225 6431

#120
Sweet Melindas
Cuisines: Seafood
Average price: £26-45
Area: Marchmont
Address: 11 Roseneath Street
Edinburgh EH9 1JH
Phone: 0131 229 7953

#121
Iglu
Cuisines: British, Gastropub
Average price: £11-25
Area: New Town
Address: 2 Jamaica St
Edinburgh EH3 6HH
Phone: 0131 476 5333

#122
Time 4 Thai
Cuisines: Thai
Average price: £11-25
Area: New Town
Address: 45 N Castle Street
Edinburgh EH2 3BG
Phone: 0131 225 8822

#123
Tanjore
Cuisines: Indian
Average price: £11-25
Area: Newington
Address: 6-8 Clerk Street
Edinburgh EH8 9HX
Phone: 0131 478 6518

#124
Nobles Cafe Bar & Venue
Cuisines: British, Gastropub
Average price: £11-25
Area: Leith
Address: 44a Constitution Street
Edinburgh EH6 6RS
Phone: 0131 629 7215

#125
The King's Wark
Cuisines: Pub, Gastropub,
Breakfast & Brunch, British
Average price: £11-25
Area: Leith
Address: 36 The Shore
Edinburgh EH6 6QU
Phone: 0131 554 9260

#126
City Restaurant
Cuisines: British, Fast Food & Takeaways,
Fish & Chips
Average price: Under £10
Area: Newington
Address: 33-35 Nicolson Street
Edinburgh EH8 9BE
Phone: 0131 667 2819

#127
Royal Mcgregor
Cuisines: British, Gastropub,
Breakfast & Brunch
Average price: £11-25
Area: Old Town, Royal Mile
Address: 154 High Street
Edinburgh EH1 1QS
Phone: 0131 225 7064

#128
Benes Fish Chip Shop
Cuisines: Fish & Chips
Average price: Under £10
Area: Old Town, Royal Mile
Address: 162 Canongate
Edinburgh EH8 8DD
Phone: 0131 557 1092

#129
Stack Dim Sum Bar
Cuisines: Dim Sum
Average price: £11-25
Area: Leith
Address: 42 Dalmeny Street
Edinburgh EH6 8RG
Phone: 0131 553 7330

#130
Illegal Jack's
Cuisines: Tex-Mex
Average price: £11-25
Area: Old Town
Address: 113-117 Lothian Road
Edinburgh EH3 9AN
Phone: 0131 622 7499

#131
The Apartment
Cuisines: American
Average price: £11-25
Area: Bruntsfield, The Meadows
Address: 7-13 Barclay Place
Edinburgh EH10 4HW
Phone: 0131 228 6456

#132
Gusto
Cuisines: Italian
Average price: £11-25
Area: New Town
Address: 135 George Street
Edinburgh EH2 4JH
Phone: 0131 225 2555

#133
Sushiya
Cuisines: Japanese, Sushi Bar
Average price: £11-25
Area: Haymarket, West End
Address: 19 Dalry Road
Edinburgh EH11 2BQ
Phone: 0131 313 3222

#134
Kampong Ah Lee
Cuisines: Malaysian, Chinese
Average price: £11-25
Area: Newington
Address: 28 Clerk Street
Edinburgh EH8 9HX
Phone: 0131 662 9050

#135
The City Cafe
Cuisines: Bar, American
Average price: £11-25
Area: Old Town, Newington
Address: 19 Blair Street
Edinburgh EH1 1QR
Phone: 0131 220 0125

#136
Katie's Diner
Cuisines: American
Average price: £11-25
Area: Bruntsfield, The Meadows
Address: 12 Barclay Terrace
Edinburgh EH10 4HP
Phone: 0131 229 1394

#137
Noor Indian Takeaway
Cuisines: Indian, Fast Food & Takeaways
Average price: £11-25
Area: Newington
Address: 56 South Clerk Street
Edinburgh EH8 9PS
Phone: 0131 667 0404

#138
Lancers Brasserie
Cuisines: Indian, Pakistani,
Fast Food & Takeaways
Average price: £26-45
Area: Stockbridge
Address: 5 Hamilton Place
Edinburgh EH3 5BA
Phone: 0131 332 3444

#139
Los Argentinos
Cuisines: Argentine, Steakhouse
Average price: £11-25
Area: Newington
Address: 28 - 30 W Preston Street
Edinburgh EH8 9PZ
Phone: 0131 668 3111

#140
Bread & Olives
Cuisines: Deli
Average price: £11-25
Area: New Town, West End
Address: 17a Queensferry Street
Edinburgh EH2 4QW
Phone: 0131 226 3005

#141
Papilio
Cuisines: Italian
Average price: £11-25
Area: Bruntsfield
Address: 158 Bruntsfield Place
Edinburgh EH10 4ER
Phone: 0131 229 3325

#142
Tempus
Cuisines: Wine Bar, French, Scottish
Average price: £11-25
Area: New Town
Address: 25 George Street
Edinburgh EH2 2PB
Phone: 0131 240 7197

#143
Iris
Cuisines: American
Average price: £11-25
Area: New Town
Address: 47A Thistle Street
Edinburgh EH2 1DY
Phone: 0131 220 2111

#144
Bonsai Bar Bistro
Cuisines: Japanese, Sushi Bar
Average price: £11-25
Area: Newington
Address: 46 W Richmond Street
Edinburgh EH8 9DZ
Phone: 0131 668 3847

#145
Fair Trade Coffee Shop
Cuisines: Coffee & Tea,
Breakfast & Brunch
Average price: £11-25
Area: Leith
Address: 30-31 Albert Place
Edinburgh EH7 5HN
Phone: 0131 476 2698

#146
Love India
Cuisines: Indian, Pakistani
Average price: £11-25
Area: Old Town
Address: 50 E Fountainbridge
Edinburgh EH3 9BH
Phone: 0131 228 6666

#147
Global
Cuisines: Deli, Sandwiches
Average price: Under £10
Area: Old Town, Grassmarket
Address: 13 George Iv Bridge
Edinburgh EH1 1EE
Phone: 0131 220 3690

#148
Silver Bowl
Cuisines: Fast Food & Takeaways,
Chinese, Thai
Average price: £11-25
Area: Leith
Address: 311 Leith Walk
Edinburgh EH6 8SA
Phone: 0131 554 5709

#149
The Bailie
Cuisines: British, Gastropub
Average price: £11-25
Area: New Town
Address: 2 St Stephen Street
Edinburgh EH3 5AL
Phone: 0131 225 4673

#150
Browns
Cuisines: Breakfast & Brunch, Gastropub
Average price: £11-25
Area: New Town
Address: 131-133 George Street
Edinburgh EH2 4JS
Phone: 0131 225 4442

#151
Mercat Bar
Cuisines: British, Gastropub
Average price: £11-25
Area: West End
Address: 28 W Maitland Street
Edinburgh EH12 5DS
Phone: 0131 225 8716

#152
Amber Restaurant
Cuisines: Scottish
Average price: £11-25
Area: Old Town, Royal Mile
Address: 354 Castlehill
Edinburgh EH1 2NE
Phone: 0131 477 8477

#153
Loudons Cafe & Bakery
Cuisines: Breakfast & Brunch,
Bakery, Cafe
Average price: £11-25
Area: West End
Address: 94B Fountainbridge
Edinburgh EH3 9QA
Phone: 0131 228 9774

#154
Purslane
Cuisines: British
Average price: £26-45
Area: Stockbridge, New Town
Address: 33A St Stephen's Street
Edinburgh EH3 5AH
Phone: 0131 226 3500

#155
Greyfriars Bobby's Bar
Cuisines: Pub, British
Average price: £11-25
Area: Old Town
Address: 30-34 Candlemaker Row
Edinburgh EH1 2QE
Phone: 0131 225 8328

#156
Vittoria Restaurant
Cuisines: Italian
Average price: £11-25
Area: Leith
Address: 113 Brunswick Street
Edinburgh EH7 5HR
Phone: 0131 556 6171

#157
The Abbotsford
Cuisines: Pub, European
Average price: £11-25
Area: New Town
Address: 3-5 Rose Street
Edinburgh EH2 2PR
Phone: 0131 225 5276

#158
Victor & Carina Contini The Scottish Cafe and Restaurant
Cuisines: Breakfast & Brunch, European, Tea Room
Average price: £11-25
Area: Old Town
Address: National Gallery Complex
Edinburgh EH2 2EL
Phone: 0131 226 6524

#159
Gurkha Cafe & Restaurant
Cuisines: Indian, Himalayan/Nepalese
Average price: £11-25
Area: Old Town, Royal Mile
Address: 25/27 Cockburn Street
Edinburgh EH1 1BP
Phone: 0131 225 2832

#160
A Room in the West End
Cuisines: Scottish
Average price: £26-45
Area: West End
Address: 26 William Street
Edinburgh EH3 7NH
Phone: 0131 226 1036

#161
The Elephant House
Cuisines: Coffee & Tea, Sandwiches, Brasserie
Average price: £11-25
Area: Old Town
Address: 21 George IV Bridge
Edinburgh EH1 1EN
Phone: 0131 220 5355

#162
Le Marche Francais
Cuisines: French
Average price: £11-25
Area: West End
Address: 9a W Maitland Street
Edinburgh EH12 5DS
Phone: 0131 221 1894

#163
Imans
Cuisines: Indian
Average price: £11-25
Area: Tollcross, West End
Address: 4-8 Lochrin Buildings
Edinburgh EH3 9NB
Phone: 0131 221 1115

#164
Taste of Italy
Cuisines: Coffee & Tea, Italian
Average price: Under £10
Area: New Town
Address: 9 Baxter's Place
Edinburgh EH1 3AF
Phone: 0131 557 9998

#165
The Southern
Cuisines: British, Gastropub
Average price: £11-25
Area: Newington
Address: 22-26 South Clerk Street
Edinburgh EH8 9PR
Phone: 0131 662 8926

#166
Blue Parrot Cantina
Cuisines: Tex-Mex, Mexican
Average price: £11-25
Area: Stockbridge, New Town
Address: 49 ST. Stephen Street
Edinburgh EH3 5AH
Phone: 0131 225 2941

#167
The Orchard
Cuisines: Bar, British
Average price: £11-25
Area: Stockbridge
Address: 1-2 Howard Place
Edinburgh EH3 5JZ
Phone: 0131 550 0850

#168
Petit Paris
Cuisines: French
Average price: £26-45
Area: Old Town, Grassmarket
Address: 38-40 Grassmarket
Edinburgh EH1 2JU
Phone: 0131 226 2442

#169
Tuk Tuk Indian Street Food
Cuisines: Indian
Average price: £11-25
Area: Tollcross
Address: 1 Leven Street
Edinburgh EH3 9LH
Phone: 0131 228 3322

#170
Clarinda's Tea Room
Cuisines: Coffee & Tea, British
Average price: Under £10
Area: Old Town, Royal Mile
Address: 69 Canongate
Edinburgh EH8 8BS
Phone: 0131 557 1888

#171
10-to-10 In Delhi
Cuisines: Indian, Desserts,
Coffee & Tea
Average price: Under £10
Area: Newington
Address: 67 Nicolson Street
Edinburgh EH8 9BZ
Phone: 07536 757770

#172
Kama Sutra
Cuisines: Indian
Average price: Above £46
Area: Old Town, West End
Address: Lothian Road
Edinburgh EH3 9AN
Phone: 0131 229 7747

#173
La Piazza
Cuisines: Italian
Average price: £11-25
Area: West End
Address: 97-99 Shandwick Place
Edinburgh EH2 4SD
Phone: 0131 221 1150

#174
Biddy Mulligans
Cuisines: Irish, Pub
Average price: £11-25
Area: Old Town, Grassmarket
Address: 94-96 Grassmarket
Edinburgh EH1 2JR
Phone: 0131 220 1246

#175
Smoke Stack
Cuisines: American, Barbeque,
Steakhouse, British
Average price: £11-25
Area: New Town
Address: 53-55 Broughton Street
Edinburgh EH1 3RJ
Phone: 0131 556 6032

#176
Empires
Cuisines: Turkish, Ethnic Food
Average price: £11-25
Area: Old Town, Newington, Royal Mile
Address: 24 St Marys Street
Edinburgh EH1 1SU
Phone: 0131 466 0100

#177
Olly Bongo's
Cuisines: Coffee & Tea, Bagels,
Sandwiches
Average price: Under £10
Area: Old Town
Address: 4 Teviot Pl
Edinburgh EH1 2QZ
Phone: 0131 225 2849

#178
Made In France
Cuisines: Deli
Average price: Under £10
Area: Tollcross, West End
Address: 5 Lochrin Place
Edinburgh EH3 9QX
Phone: 0131 221 1184

#179
Always Sunday
Cuisines: Cafe
Average price: £11-25
Area: Old Town, Newington, Royal Mile
Address: 170 High Street
Edinburgh EH1 1QS
Phone: 0131 622 0667

#180
Mamma's
Cuisines: Pizza, Italian
Average price: £11-25
Area: Old Town, Grassmarket
Address: 30 The Grassmarket
Edinburgh EH1 2JU
Phone: 0131 225 6464

#181
Malones Irish Bar
Cuisines: Pub, Irish
Average price: £11-25
Area: Old Town
Address: 14 Forrest Road
Edinburgh EH1 2QN
Phone: 0131 226 5954

#182
The Spice Pavilion
Cuisines: Indian
Average price: £11-25
Area: New Town
Address: 3A1 Dundas Street
Edinburgh EH3 6QG
Phone: 0131 467 5506

#183
Café Renroc
Cuisines: Breakfast & Brunch, Sandwiches
Average price: £11-25
Area: Leith
Address: 91 Montgomery Street
Edinburgh EH7 5HZ
Phone: 0131 629 3727

#184
Sygn
Cuisines: Bar, Breakfast & Brunch
Average price: £11-25
Area: New Town
Address: 15 Charlotte Lane
Edinburgh EH2 4QZ
Phone: 0131 225 6060

#185
Pizza Paradise
Cuisines: Fast Food & Takeaways, Pizza,
Fish & Chips
Average price: Under £10
Area: Old Town
Address: 34 George IV Bridge
Edinburgh EH1 1EN
Phone: 0131 226 6706

#186
Al Dente
Cuisines: Italian
Average price: £11-25
Area: Leith
Address: 139 Easter Road
Edinburgh EH7 5QA
Phone: 0131 652 1932

#187
The Cellar Door
Cuisines: British
Average price: £26-45
Area: Old Town
Address: 44-46 George IV Bridge
Edinburgh EH1 1EJ
Phone: 0131 226 4155

#188
The Albanach
Cuisines: British, Gastropub
Average price: £11-25
Area: Old Town, Royal Mile
Address: 197 High Street
Edinburgh EH1 1PE
Phone: 0131 220 5277

#189
Lebowskis
Cuisines: Bar, Gastropub, Burgers
Average price: £11-25
Area: West End
Address: 18 Morrison St
Edinburgh EH3 8BJ
Phone: 0131 466 1779

#190
Kasbah Take Away
Cuisines: Fast Food & Takeaways
Average price: Under £10
Area: Marchmont
Address: 24 Marchmont Road
Edinburgh EH9 1HZ
Phone: 0131 229 2001

#191
Shapla Takeaway
Cuisines: Indian, Fast Food & Takeaways
Average price: £11-25
Area: Leith
Address: 87 Easter Rd
Edinburgh EH7 5PW
Phone: 0131 652 0405

#192
The Huxley
Cuisines: Bar, Gastropub
Average price: £11-25
Area: West End
Address: 1 Rutland Street
Edinburgh EH1 2AE
Phone: 0131 229 3402

#193
Tapa
Cuisines: Spanish, Tapas Bar,
Mediterranean
Average price: £11-25
Area: Leith
Address: 19 Shore Place
Edinburgh EH6 6SW
Phone: 0131 476 6776

#194
L'escargot Bleu
Cuisines: French
Average price: £26-45
Area: New Town
Address: 56 Broughton Street
Edinburgh EH1 3SA
Phone: 0131 557 1600

#195
Gaia
Cuisines: Italian, Deli
Average price: £11-25
Area: Leith
Address: 32 Crighton Place
Edinburgh EH7 4NY
Phone: 0131 553 7333

#196
52 Canoes Tiki Den
Cuisines: Bar, British
Average price: £11-25
Area: New Town, West End
Address: 13-14 Melville Place
Edinburgh EH3 8PR
Phone: 0131 226 4732

#197
Bobby's Sandwich Bar
Cuisines: Sandwiches, Coffee & Tea
Average price: Under £10
Area: Old Town
Address: 4 Greyfriars Place
Edinburgh EH1 2QQ
Phone: 0131 220 1133

#198
Rapido
Cuisines: Fish & Chips
Average price: £11-25
Area: New Town
Address: 77 - 79 Broughton Street
Edinburgh EH1 3RJ
Phone: 0131 556 2041

#199
Monteiths Restaurant
Cuisines: Wine Bar, European
Average price: £26-45
Area: Old Town, Royal Mile
Address: 61 High Street
Edinburgh EH1 1SR
Phone: 0131 557 0330

#200
La Tasca
Cuisines: Spanish, Basque
Average price: £26-45
Area: New Town
Address: 9 South Charlotte Street
Edinburgh EH2 4AS
Phone: 0131 220 0011

#201
Hellers Kitchen
Cuisines: American
Average price: £11-25
Area: Newington
Address: 15 Salisbury Place
Edinburgh EH9 1SL
Phone: 0131 667 4654

#202
**Michael Neave Kitchen
and Whisky Bar**
Cuisines: British, Bar
Average price: £26-45
Area: Old Town, Newington
Address: 21 Old Fishmarket Close
Edinburgh EH1 1RW
Phone: 0131 226 4747

#203
Clamshell
Cuisines: Fast Food & Takeaways
Average price: Under £10
Area: Old Town, Newington, Royal Mile
Address: 148 High Street
Edinburgh EH1 1QS
Phone: 0131 225 4338

#204
Made In Italy
Cuisines: Italian, Coffee & Tea
Average price: Under £10
Area: Old Town, Grassmarket
Address: 42 Grassmarket
Edinburgh EH1 2JU
Phone: 0131 622 7328

#205
Yak & Yeti
Cuisines: Asian Fusion
Average price: £11-25
Area: Newington
Address: 13 Newington Road
Edinburgh EH9 1QR
Phone: 0131 667 9897

#206
Victor Hugo
Cuisines: Deli, Coffee & Tea
Average price: £11-25
Area: Marchmont
Address: 26-27 Melville Terrace
Edinburgh EH9 1LP
Phone: 0131 667 1827

#207
The Ship on the Shore
Cuisines: Seafood
Average price: £26-45
Area: Leith
Address: 24-26 The Shore
Edinburgh EH6 6QN
Phone: 0131 555 0409

#208
Earthy Canonmills
Cuisines: Bakery, Cafe, Deli
Average price: £11-25
Area: Stockbridge
Address: 1-6 Canonmills Bridge
Edinburgh EH3 5HA
Phone: 0131 556 9699

#209
Kweilin Restaurant
Cuisines: Chinese
Average price: £26-45
Area: New Town
Address: 19-21 Dundas Street
Edinburgh EH3 6QG
Phone: 0131 557 1875

#210
Omar Khayyam
Cuisines: Indian, Fast Food & Takeaways
Average price: £11-25
Area: West End
Address: 1 Grosvenor Street
Edinburgh EH12 5ED
Phone: 0131 225 2481

#211
The Street
Cuisines: Gastropub
Average price: Under £10
Area: New Town
Address: 2b Picardy Place
Edinburgh EH1 3JT
Phone: 0131 556 4272

#212
Café Grande
Cuisines: Coffee & Tea, Brasserie
Average price: £11-25
Area: Bruntsfield
Address: 184 Bruntsfield Place
Edinburgh EH10 4DF
Phone: 0131 228 1188

#213
Ti Amo
Cuisines: Italian
Average price: Under £10
Area: Newington
Address: 16 Niolson Street
Edinburgh EH8 9DH
Phone: 0131 556 5678

#214
Turkish Kitchen
Cuisines: Turkish
Average price: Under £10
Area: New Town
Address: 120-122 Rose Street
Edinburgh EH2 3
Phone: 0131 226 2122

#215
Cacio Pepe
Cuisines: Italian
Average price: Under £10
Area: New Town
Address: 87 Hanover St
Edinburgh EH2 1EE
Phone: 0131 220 6733

#216
Pivo Caffe
Cuisines: Cafe
Average price: £11-25
Area: Old Town
Address: 1 Calton Road
Edinburgh EH8 8DL
Phone: 0131 557 2925

#217
Wagamama
Cuisines: Asian Fusion
Average price: £11-25
Area: Old Town
Address: 1 Castle Terrace
Edinburgh EH1 2DP
Phone: 0131 229 5506

#218
Ghillie Dhu
Cuisines: Wine Bar, British, Pub
Average price: £26-45
Area: West End
Address: 2-6 Rutland Place
Edinburgh EH1 2AD
Phone: 0131 222 9930

#219
Passorn
Cuisines: Thai
Average price: £11-25
Area: Tollcross, The Meadows
Address: 23-23a Brougham Pl
Edinburgh EH3 9JU
Phone: 0131 229 1537

#220
Sabor Criollo
Cuisines: Latin American
Average price: £26-45
Area: Stockbridge
Address: 36 Deanhaugh Street
Edinburgh EH4 1LY
Phone: 0131 332 3322

#221
The Roamin' Nose
Cuisines: Coffee & Tea, Bistro
Average price: £11-25
Area: Cannonmills
Address: 14 Eyre Place
Edinburgh EH3 5EP
Phone: 0131 629 3135

#222
Karen's Unicorn
Cuisines: Chinese
Average price: £26-45
Area: New Town
Address: 8b Abercromby Place
Edinburgh EH3 6LB
Phone: 0131 556 6333

#223
The West Room
Cuisines: Gastropub,
Breakfast & Brunch
Average price: £11-25
Area: West End
Address: 3 Melville Place
Edinburgh EH3 7PR
Phone: 0131 629 9868

#224
The Beehive Inn
Cuisines: Pub, Gastropub
Average price: £11-25
Area: Old Town, Grassmarket
Address: 18-20 Grassmarket
Edinburgh EH1 2JU
Phone: 0131 225 7171

#225
Negociants
Cuisines: Pub, Gastropub
Average price: £11-25
Area: Old Town, Newington
Address: 45-47 Lothian Street
Edinburgh EH11 1HB
Phone: 0131 225 6313

#226
Silver Bowl
Cuisines: Chinese
Average price: £11-25
Area: Leith
Address: 12 Albert Place
Edinburgh EH7 5HN
Phone: 0131 554 9830

#227
The Stockbridge Restaurant
Cuisines: British
Average price: £26-45
Area: Stockbridge, New Town
Address: 54 St Stephen Street
Edinburgh EH3 5AL
Phone: 0131 226 6766

#228
Bar Italia
Cuisines: Italian
Average price: £11-25
Area: West End
Address: 100-104 Lothian Road
Edinburgh EH3 9BE
Phone: 0131 228 6379

#229
First Coast
Cuisines: British
Average price: £11-25
Area: Haymarket, West End
Address: 97-101 Dalry Road
Edinburgh EH11 2AB
Phone: 0131 313 4404

#230
The Globe Deli
Cuisines: Cafe
Average price: £11-25
Area: Leith
Address: 23 Bernard Street
Edinburgh EH6 6PW
Phone: 0131 625 5552

#231
Buffalo Grill
Cuisines: American
Average price: £11-25
Area: Newington
Address: 12 Chapel Street
Edinburgh EH8 9AY
Phone: 0131 667 7427

#232
Hot Hot Chinese
Cuisines: Chinese
Average price: £11-25
Area: Old Town, West End
Address: 60 Home Street
Edinburgh EH3 9NA
Phone: 0131 656 0707

#233
TGI Fridays
Cuisines: American
Average price: £11-25
Area: New Town
Address: 22-26 Castle Street
Edinburgh EH2 3HT
Phone: 0131 226 6543

#234
The Living Room
Cuisines: American, British
Average price: £26-45
Area: New Town
Address: 113-115 George Street
Edinburgh EH2 4JN
Phone: 0131 226 0880

#235
Henderson's Bistro
Cuisines: Vegetarian
Average price: £11-25
Area: New Town
Address: 25 Thistle Street
Edinburgh EH2 1DX
Phone: 0131 225 2605

#236
Café Truva
Cuisines: Coffee & Tea, Turkish
Average price: £11-25
Area: Leith
Address: 77 Shore
Edinburgh EH6 6RG
Phone: 0131 554 5502

#237
Flip!
Cuisines: Sandwiches
Average price: £11-25
Area: Newington
Address: 54 Clerk Street
Edinburgh EH8 9JB
Phone: 0131 667 2727

#238
Montpeliers
Cuisines: Wine Bar, Brasserie
Average price: £11-25
Area: Bruntsfield
Address: 159-161 Bruntsfield Pl
Edinburgh EH10 4DG
Phone: 0131 229 3115

#239
Blonde Restaurants
Cuisines: British, European
Average price: £11-25
Area: Newington
Address: 75 St Leonards St
Edinburgh EH8 9QR
Phone: 0131 668 2917

#240
Zucca Restaurant
Cuisines: Italian
Average price: £11-25
Area: Old Town
Address: 15 Grindlay St
Edinburgh EH3 9AX
Phone: 0131 221 9323

#241
B'est
Cuisines: Mediterranean, French, Bistro
Average price: £11-25
Area: Newington
Address: 16 Drummond Street
Edinburgh EH8 9TX
Phone: 0131 556 4448

#242
Bonsai
Cuisines: Japanese, Sushi Bar
Average price: £11-25
Area: New Town
Address: 14 Broughton Street
Edinburgh EH1 3RH
Phone: 0131 557 5093

#243
Cafe Musa
Cuisines: Coffee & Tea,
Sandwiches, Tea Room
Average price: Under £10
Area: Old Town, Royal Mile
Address: 16 N Bank Street
Edinburgh EH1 2LP
Phone: 0131 226 7809

#244
La Favorita Morningside
Cuisines: Pizza, Italian
Average price: £11-25
Area: Morningside
Address: 350 Morningside Road
Edinburgh EH10 4QL
Phone: 0131 447 4000

#245
Indigo Yard
Cuisines: British, Gastropub
Average price: £11-25
Area: New Town
Address: 7 Charlotte Lane
Edinburgh EH2 4QZ
Phone: 0131 220 5603

#246
Dean Gallery Café
Cuisines: Cafe
Average price: £11-25
Area: West End
Address: 73 Belford Road
Edinburgh EH4 3DS
Phone: 0131 624 6200

#247
La P'tite Folie
Cuisines: French
Average price: £11-25
Area: New Town
Address: 61 Frederick St
Edinburgh EH2 1
Phone: 0131 225 7983

#248
The Filling Station
Cuisines: American, Fast Food &
Takeaways
Average price: £11-25
Area: Old Town, Royal Mile
Address: 235 High Street
Edinburgh EH1 1PE
Phone: 0131 226 2488

#249
Bombay Bicycle Club
Cuisines: Indian
Average price: £11-25
Area: The Meadows
Address: 6-6a Brougham Place
Edinburgh EH3 9HW
Phone: 0131 229 3839

#250
Namaste Kathmandu
Cuisines: Himalayan/Nepalese, Indian
Average price: £11-25
Area: Old Town
Address: 17-19 Forrest Road
Edinburgh EH1 2Q
Phone: 0131 220 2273

#251
Papa John's
Cuisines: Pizza, Fast Food & Takeaways
Average price: £26-45
Area: Newington
Address: 12 South Clerk Street
Edinburgh EH8 9PR
Phone: 0131 668 1122

#252
La Lanterna Ristorante
Cuisines: Italian
Average price: £11-25
Area: New Town
Address: 83 Hanover Street
Edinburgh EH2 1EE
Phone: 0131 226 3090

#253
Water of Leith Bistro
Cuisines: French
Average price: £11-25
Area: Leith
Address: 52 Coburg Street
Edinburgh EH6 6HJ
Phone: 0131 555 2613

#254
The Salisbury Arms
Cuisines: Pub, British
Average price: £26-45
Area: Newington
Address: 58 Dalkeith Road
Edinburgh EH16 5AD
Phone: 0131 667 4518

#255
New Lee On
Cuisines: Chinese
Average price: £11-25
Area: Bruntsfield, The Meadows
Address: 4-5 Bruntsfield Place
Edinburgh EH10 4HN
Phone: 0131 229 7732

#256
Mithas
Cuisines: Indian, Cocktail Bar
Average price: Above £46
Area: Leith
Address: 7 Dock Place
Edinburgh EH6 6LU
Phone: 0131 554 0008

#257
9 Cellars
Cuisines: Indian
Average price: £11-25
Area: New Town
Address: 1-3 York Place
Edinburgh EH2 1
Phone: 0131 557 9899

#258
Roxburghe Hotel
Cuisines: European
Average price: Above £46
Area: New Town
Address: 38 Charlotte Square
Edinburgh EH2 4HQ
Phone: 0131 240 5500

#259
No 1 Sushi Bar
Cuisines: Japanese, Sushi Bar
Average price: £11-25
Area: Tollcross
Address: 37 Home Street
Edinburgh EH3 9JP
Phone: 0131 229 6880

#260
The Advocate
Cuisines: Pub, Gastropub
Average price: Under £10
Area: Old Town, Newington
Address: 7 Hunter Square
Edinburgh EH1 1QW
Phone: 0131 226 2749

#261
Two Thin Laddies
Cuisines: Coffee & Tea,
Sandwiches, Bistro
Average price: £11-25
Area: Old Town, Tollcross
Address: 103 High Riggs
Edinburgh EH3 9RP
Phone: 0131 229 0653

#262
The Atelier Restaurant
Cuisines: European, British, Scottish
Average price: £11-25
Area: West End
Address: 159-161 Morrison Street
Edinburgh EH3 8AG
Phone: 0131 629 1344

#263
Bonningtons Eaterie
Cuisines: Coffee & Tea, Soup, Sandwiches
Average price: Under £10
Area: Newington
Address: 75 Clerk Street
Edinburgh EH8 9JG
Phone: 0131 668 1055

#264
My Big Fat Greek Kitchen
Cuisines: Greek
Average price: £11-25
Area: Tollcross
Address: 6 Brougham Street
Edinburgh EH3 9JH
Phone: 0131 228 1030

#265
The Edinburgh Larder Bistro
Cuisines: British, Scottish, Bistro
Average price: £11-25
Area: West End
Address: 1A Alva Street
Edinburgh EH2 4PH
Phone: 0131 225 4599

#266
Thai Lemongrass
Cuisines: Thai
Average price: £11-25
Area: Bruntsfield, The Meadows
Address: 40-41 Bruntsfield Pl
Edinburgh EH10 4HJ
Phone: 0131 229 2225

#267
The Cholas
Cuisines: Indian
Average price: £11-25
Area: Newington
Address: 63 Clerk Street
Edinburgh EH8 9JQ
Phone: 0131 667 8550

#268
La Garrigue
Cuisines: French
Average price: £11-25
Area: Cannonmills
Address: 14 Eyre Place
Edinburgh EH3 5EP
Phone: 0131 558 1608

#269
Room at 34
Cuisines: Lounge, British
Average price: £11-25
Area: Newington
Address: 32 Potterrow
Edinburgh EH8 9BT
Phone: 0131 662 9960

#270
Buffalo Grill Stockbridge
Cuisines: American, Steakhouse
Average price: £11-25
Area: Stockbridge
Address: 1 Raeburn Place
Edinburgh EH4 1HU
Phone: 0131 332 3864

#271
The Atrium
Cuisines: Specialty Food
Average price: £26-45
Area: Old Town
Address: 10 Cambridge Street
Edinburgh EH1 2ED
Phone: 0131 228 8882

#272
The Magnum
Cuisines: Pub, British
Average price: £26-45
Area: New Town
Address: 1 Albany Street
Edinburgh EH1 3PY
Phone: 0131 557 4366

#273
Baguette King
Cuisines: Sandwiches
Average price: Under £10
Area: Newington
Address: 59 Nicolson Street
Edinburgh EH8 9BZ
Phone: 0131 662 0805

#274
Tikka Mahal
Cuisines: Indian
Average price: Under £10
Area: Newington
Address: 53 Clerk Street
Edinburgh EH8 9JQ
Phone: 0131 662 9994

#275
Plumed Horse Restaurant
Cuisines: British
Average price: Above £46
Area: Leith
Address: 50-54 Henderson Street
Edinburgh EH6 6DE
Phone: 0131 554 5556

#276
The Lioness of Leith
Cuisines: Lounge, British, Cocktail Bar
Average price: £11-25
Area: Leith
Address: 21-25 Duke Street
Edinburgh EH6 8HH
Phone: 0131 629 0580

#277
Let Me Eat
Cuisines: Fast Food & Takeaways
Average price: Under £10
Area: Old Town
Address: 63 Holyrood Road
Edinburgh EH8 8
Phone: 07521 454052

#278
Zen Kitchen
Cuisines: Asian Fusion,
Fast Food & Takeaways
Average price: £26-45
Area: Stockbridge
Address: 138 Dundas Street
Edinburgh EH3 6
Phone: 0131 556 9988

#279
The New Bell
Cuisines: Italian, Seafood
Average price: £26-45
Area: Newington
Address: 233-235 Causewayside
Edinburgh EH9 1PH
Phone: 0131 668 2868

#280
Garibaldi's
Cuisines: Mexican
Average price: £11-25
Area: New Town
Address: 97a Hanover Street
Edinburgh EH2 1DJ
Phone: 0131 220 3007

#281
Rafael's Restaurant
Cuisines: Spanish
Average price: £26-45
Area: Stockbridge
Address: 2 Deanhaugh Street
Edinburgh EH4 1LY
Phone: 0131 332 1469

#282
Sambuca Restaurant
Cuisines: Italian
Average price: £11-25
Area: Newington
Address: 103-105 Causewayside
Edinburgh EH9 1QG
Phone: 0131 667 3307

#283
Zizzi Restaurants
Cuisines: Italian
Average price: £11-25
Area: West End
Address: Fountainbridge
Edinburgh EH3 9RU
Phone: 0131 225 9908

#284
Steak Edinburgh
Cuisines: Steakhouse
Average price: £26-45
Area: New Town
Address: 14 Picardy Place
Edinburgh EH1 3JT
Phone: 0131 556 1289

#285
The Other Place
Cuisines: Pub, Scottish, Brasserie
Average price: £11-25
Area: Cannonmills
Address: 2-4 Broughton Road
Edinburgh EH7 4EB
Phone: 0131 556 1024

#286
Glass and Thompson
Cuisines: Coffee & Tea,
Delicatessen, Deli
Average price: £26-45
Area: New Town
Address: 2 Dundass Street
Edinburgh EH3 6QG
Phone: 0131 557 0909

#287
David Bann
Cuisines: Vegetarian, Vegan
Average price: £26-45
Area: Old Town, Newington
Address: 56-58 St Marys Street
Edinburgh EH1 1SX
Phone: 0131 556 5888

#288
Doctors
Cuisines: Gastropub, Pub
Average price: Under £10
Area: Old Town
Address: 32 Forrest Rd
Edinburgh EH1 2QN
Phone: 0131 225 1819

#289
The Khukuri
Cuisines: Himalayan/Nepalese, Indian
Average price: £26-45
Area: West End
Address: 8 West Maitland Street
Edinburgh EH12 5DS
Phone: 0131 228 2085

#290
Herbie West End
Cuisines: Deli, Coffee & Tea, Sandwiches
Average price: £11-25
Area: West End
Address: 7 William Street
Edinburgh EH3 7NG
Phone: 0131 226 6366

#291
Rivage
Cuisines: Indian
Average price: £11-25
Area: Leith
Address: 126 - 130 Easter Road
Edinburgh EH7 5RJ
Phone: 0131 661 6888

#292
56 North
Cuisines: British, Wine Bar
Average price: £11-25
Area: Newington
Address: 2 West Crosscauseway
Edinburgh EH8 9JW
Phone: 0131 662 8860

#293
Khartoum Cafe
Cuisines: African, Fast Food & Takeaways
Average price: Under £10
Area: Bruntsfield
Address: 6 Gillespie Place
Edinburgh EH10 4HS
Phone: 0131 228 9797

#294
Ruan Thai
Cuisines: Thai
Average price: £11-25
Area: Old Town, Royal Mile
Address: 29 Cockburn St
Edinburgh EH1 1BP
Phone: 0131 225 7007

#295
Annabelle's Restaurant
Cuisines: Coffee & Tea, British
Average price: £11-25
Area: Marchmont
Address: 27 Sciennes Road
Edinburgh EH9 1NX
Phone: 0131 667 0700

#296
Blackfriars
Cuisines: Bar, British
Average price: Under £10
Area: Old Town, Newington
Address: 57-61 Blackfriars Street
Edinburgh EH1 1NB
Phone: 0131 558 8684

#297
Khublai Khan
Cuisines: Mongolian, Buffet
Average price: £26-45
Area: Leith
Address: 43 Assembly St
Edinburgh EH6 7BQ
Phone: 0131 555 0005

#298
Wok & Wine
Cuisines: Chinese
Average price: £11-25
Area: New Town
Address: 57a Frederick Street
Edinburgh EH2 1LH
Phone: 0131 225 2382

#299
Caffe Centro
Cuisines: Coffee & Tea, Italian
Average price: £11-25
Area: New Town
Address: 38 George Street
Edinburgh EH2 2LE
Phone: 0131 225 3419

#300
Wolfits
Cuisines: Sandwiches
Average price: Under £10
Area: New Town
Address: 200 Rose St
Edinburgh EH2 4AZ
Phone: 0131 225 5096

#301
Bristo Bar & Kitchen
Cuisines: British, Scottish
Average price: £11-25
Area: Old Town, Newington
Address: 41 Lothian Street
Edinburgh EH1 1HB
Phone: 0131 225 4186

#302
Hadrian's Brasserie
Cuisines: British
Average price: £26-45
Area: Old Town, Royal Mile
Address: N Bridge
Edinburgh EH1 1TR
Phone: 0131 557 5000

#303
Zest
Cuisines: Indian, Pakistani
Average price: £11-25
Area: New Town
Address: 15 North ST Andrew Street
Edinburgh EH2 1HJ
Phone: 0131 556 5028

#304
Le Di-Vin
Cuisines: Wine Bar, French
Average price: £26-45
Area: New Town
Address: 9 Randolph Pl
Edinburgh EH3 7TE
Phone: 0131 538 1815

#305
Yum Yum HK Diner
Cuisines: Chinese
Average price: £11-25
Area: Newington
Address: 13 W Richmond St
Edinburgh EH8 9EF
Phone: 0131 667 8263

#306
Ryan's Bar
Cuisines: Pub, Cafe, Wine Bar
Average price: £11-25
Area: New Town
Address: 2 - 4 Hope St
Edinburgh EH2 4DB
Phone: 0131 226 6669

#307
Ryrie's Bar
Cuisines: Pub, British
Average price: Under £10
Area: Haymarket, West End
Address: 1 Haymarket Terrace
Edinburgh EH12 5EY
Phone: 0131 337 0550

#308
Grand Cru
Cuisines: Bar, Gastropub
Average price: £11-25
Area: New Town
Address: 79 Hanover St
Edinburgh EH2 1EE
Phone: 0131 226 6427

#309
Bijou
Cuisines: French
Average price: £11-25
Area: Leith
Address: 2 Restalrig Road
Edinburgh EH6 8BN
Phone: 0131 538 0664

#310
Bar Kohl
Cuisines: Burgers, Cocktail Bar
Average price: £11-25
Area: Old Town
Address: 54 George IV Bridge
Edinburgh EH1 1EJ
Phone: 0131 225 6936

#311
Nonna's Kitchen
Cuisines: Pizza, Italian
Average price: £26-45
Area: Bruntsfield
Address: 45 Morningside Road
Edinburgh EH10 4AZ
Phone: 0131 466 6767

#312
The Howard
Cuisines: British
Average price: Above £46
Area: New Town
Address: 34 Great King Street
Edinburgh EH3 6QH
Phone: 0131 557 3500

#313
The Lot
Cuisines: Local Flavour
Average price: Under £10
Area: Old Town, Grassmarket
Address: 4-6 Grassmarket
Edinburgh EH1 2JU
Phone: 0131 225 9924

#314
Massimo Restaurant
Cuisines: Italian
Average price: £11-25
Area: New Town
Address: 10/11 Antigua Street
Edinburgh EH1 3NH
Phone: 0131 556 8383

#315
Yeni Meze Bar
Cuisines: Turkish, Mediterranean
Average price: Under £10
Area: New Town
Address: 73 Hanover Street
Edinburgh EH2 1EE
Phone: 0131 225 5755

#316
North Bridge Brasserie
Cuisines: Brasserie, Coffee & Tea
Average price: £26-45
Area: Old Town, Royal Mile
Address: 20 North Bridge
Edinburgh EH1 1TR
Phone: 0131 622 2900

#317
Greggs
Cuisines: Bakery, Fast Food & Takeaways
Average price: Under £10
Area: Newington
Address: 74 Nicolson Street
Edinburgh EH8 9DT
Phone: 0131 667 4156

#318
The Tattie Shop
Cuisines: British, Fast Food & Takeaways
Average price: £11-25
Area: Bruntsfield
Address: 3 Viewforth Garden
Edinburgh EH10 4ET
Phone: 0131 228 5282

#319
Topkapi
Cuisines: Middle Eastern
Average price: £26-45
Area: West End
Address: 109 Fountainbridge
Edinburgh EH3 9QG
Phone: 0131 229 2747

#320
Cosmo
Cuisines: Buffet
Average price: Under £10
Area: New Town
Address: Greenside Place
Edinburgh EH1 3AA
Phone: 0131 557 0808

#321
Olly Bongo's
Cuisines: Coffee & Tea,
Sandwiches, Bagels
Average price: Under £10
Area: West End
Address: 97-101 Morrison St
Edinburgh EH3 8BX
Phone: 0131 228 8335

#322
Ignite Restaurant
Cuisines: Indian, Pakistani
Average price: £11-25
Area: West End
Address: 272-274 Morrison Street
Edinburgh EH3 8DT
Phone: 0131 228 5666

#323
Saigon Saigon
Cuisines: Chinese
Average price: £11-25
Area: New Town
Address: 14 S St Andrew St
Edinburgh EH2 2AZ
Phone: 0131 557 3737

#324
Bistro Moderne
Cuisines: French
Average price: £26-45
Area: Stockbridge, New Town
Address: 15 NW Circus Place
Edinburgh EH3 6SX
Phone: 0131 225 4431

#325
Caffe e Cucina
Cuisines: Coffee & Tea, Italian
Average price: £11-25
Area: Morningside
Address: 372 Morningside Road
Edinburgh EH10 5HS
Phone: 0131 447 0345

#326
Biblos
Cuisines: Pub, Gastropub
Average price: £11-25
Area: Old Town, Newington
Address: 1a Chambers Street
Edinburgh EH1 1HR
Phone: 0131 226 7177

#327
Chiquito
Cuisines: Mexican
Average price: £11-25
Area: New Town
Address: 29 Frederick St
Edinburgh EH2 2ND
Phone: 0131 225 4579

#328
Bisque Bar and Brasserie
Cuisines: British
Average price: £26-45
Area: Bruntsfield, The Meadows
Address: 69 Bruntsfield Place
Edinburgh EH10 4HH
Phone: 0131 622 8163

#329
Marmaris Kebab House
Cuisines: Fast Food & Takeaways
Average price: Under £10
Area: Newington
Address: 35 Clerk St
Edinburgh EH8 9JH
Phone: 0131 622 7555

#330
Haq's
Cuisines: Indian, Fast Food & Takeaways
Average price: Under £10
Area: Leith
Address: 4 Albert Place
Edinburgh EH7 5HN
Phone: 0131 554 3430

#331
International Starters
Cuisines: British
Average price: Under £10
Area: Leith
Address: 82 Commercial Street
Edinburgh EH6 6LX
Phone: 0131 555 2546

#332
The Rosehip
Cuisines: British
Average price: Under £10
Area: New Town
Address: 43 Rose Street
Edinburgh EH2 2NH
Phone: 0131 225 8028

#333
Bar Frizzante
Cuisines: Italian
Average price: £11-25
Area: Old Town
Address: 95 Lothian Road
Edinburgh EH3 9AW
Phone: 0131 229 7788

#334
Good Seed Bistro
Cuisines: Vegetarian, Mediterranean
Average price: £11-25
Area: Haymarket, West End
Address: 100-102 Dalry Rd
Edinburgh EH11 2DW
Phone: 0131 337 3803

#335
Cafe Nom De Plume
Cuisines: Cafe
Average price: Under £10
Area: New Town
Address: 60 Broughton St
Edinburgh EH1 3SA
Phone: 0131 478 1372

#336
Sandwich Express
Cuisines: Coffee & Tea, Sandwiches
Average price: Under £10
Area: Leith
Address: 9A Albert Pl
Edinburgh EH7 5HN
Phone: 0131 554 5005

#337
Pork Butcher George Bowman
Cuisines: Butchers, Fast Food &
Takeaways
Average price: £26-45
Area: Leith
Address: 44 Great Jcn Street
Edinburgh EH6 5LB
Phone: 0131 554 4046

#338
**The Newington Traditional
Fish Bar**
Cuisines: Fish & Chips
Average price: Under £10
Area: Newington
Address: 23 South Clerk Street
Edinburgh EH8 9JD
Phone: 0131 667 0203

#339
Foodies at Holyrood
Cuisines: Deli, Sandwiches
Average price: Under £10
Area: Old Town
Address: 67 Holyrood Rd
Edinburgh EH8 8AU
Phone: 0131 557 6836

#340
Gennaro Ristorante
Cuisines: Italian
Average price: £11-25
Area: Old Town, Grassmarket
Address: 64 Grassmarket
Edinburgh EH1 2JR
Phone: 0131 226 3706

#341
Vigo Delicatessen
Cuisines: Deli
Average price: £11-25
Area: Haymarket
Address: 2a Roseburn Terrace
Edinburgh EH12 6AW
Phone: 0131 467 5589

#342
Lazeez Tandoori
Cuisines: Fast Food & Takeaways
Average price: £11-25
Area: Haymarket
Address: 191 Dalry Road
Edinburgh EH11 2EB
Phone: 0131 337 7977

#343
The Deli
Cuisines: Deli
Average price: Under £10
Area: Morningside
Address: 324 Morningside Road
Edinburgh EH10 4QJ
Phone: 0131 447 0004

#344
Maxi's Cafe
Cuisines: Breakfast & Brunch
Average price: £11-25
Area: Stockbridge
Address: 33 Raeburn Pl
Edinburgh EH4 1HX
Phone: 0131 343 3007

#345
Finnegan's Wake
Cuisines: Irish, Pub
Average price: £11-25
Area: Old Town, Grassmarket
Address: 9B Victoria Street
Edinburgh EH1 2HE
Phone: 0131 225 9348

#346
Rocket Café
Cuisines: Coffee & Tea,
Breakfast & Brunch, Cafe
Average price: Under £10
Area: Bruntsfield
Address: 41 Morningside Rd
Edinburgh EH10 4DR
Phone: 0131 447 0377

#347
YummyTori
Cuisines: Japanese
Average price: £26-45
Area: Old Town, West End
Address: 90-92 Lothian Road
Edinburgh EH3 9BE
Phone: 0131 229 2206

#348
Nanyang Malaysian Restaurant
Cuisines: Asian Fusion, Dim Sum,
Malaysian
Average price: £26-45
Area: The Meadows
Address: Unit 1 3-5 Lister Square
Edinburgh EH3 9GL
Phone: 0131 629 1797

#349
Yocoko Noodle Bar
Cuisines: Japanese
Average price: Under £10
Area: Old Town, Newington
Address: 44-46 South Bridge
Edinburgh EH1 1LL
Phone: 0131 558 3889

#350
Pig In A Poke
Cuisines: Fast Food & Takeaways
Average price: Under £10
Area: New Town
Address: Rose Street
Edinburgh EH2 3DT
Phone: 0131 226 1616

#351
Zico's Brazilian Grill Bar
Cuisines: Brazilian, Latin American
Average price: £11-25
Area: West End
Address: 97 Morrison Street
Edinburgh EH3
Phone: 0131 478 1222

#352
Blackcherry Cafe
Cuisines: European
Average price: Under £10
Area: Old Town, Grassmarket
Address: 29 Grassmarket
Edinburgh EH1 2HS
Phone: 0131 225 8387

#353
New Saffrani
Cuisines: Indian, Pakistani
Average price: £11-25
Area: Old Town, Newington
Address: 11 South College Street
Edinburgh EH8 9AA
Phone: 0131 667 1597

#354
Good 2 Go
Cuisines: Deli
Average price: Under £10
Area: Newington
Address: 39 West Nicolson Street
Edinburgh EH8 9DB
Phone: 0131 667 2720

#355
Bees
Cuisines: Bar, Cafe
Average price: Under £10
Area: Old Town
Address: 21 Candlemaker Row
Edinburgh EH1 2QG
Phone: 0131 225 9996

#356
The Gold Sea
Cuisines: Fish & Chips
Average price: £11-25
Area: Leith
Address: 243 Ferry Road
Edinburgh EH6 4NN
Phone: 0131 554 2195

#357
Gourmet Burger Kitchen
Cuisines: American, Burgers, Gastropub
Average price: £11-25
Area: New Town
Address: 137 George Street
Edinburgh EH2 4JY
Phone: 0131 260 9896

#358
WHISKI Room
Cuisines: British
Average price: £11-25
Area: Old Town, Royal Mile
Address: 4 - 7 North Bank Street
Edinburgh EH1 2LP
Phone: 0131 225 7224

#359
The Everest
Cuisines: Indian
Average price: £11-25
Area: Tollcross, West End
Address: 52 Home Street
Edinburgh EH3 9
Phone: 0131 229 1348

#360
Mandarin House
Cuisines: Chinese
Average price: Under £10
Area: Haymarket
Address: 10 Roseburn Ter
Edinburgh EH12 5
Phone: 0131 337 5165

#361
Maialino
Cuisines: Delicatessen, Italian
Average price: £11-25
Area: West End
Address: 34 William Street
Edinburgh EH3 7LJ
Phone: 0131 477 7778

#362
Ivory Lounge
Cuisines: Pub, British
Average price: Under £10
Area: New Town
Address: 126-128 George Street
Edinburgh EH2 4JN
Phone: 0131 220 6180

#363
Ong Gie
Cuisines: Korean
Average price: £11-25
Area: Tollcross, The Meadows
Address: 22 Brougham Place
Edinburgh EH3 9JU
Phone: 0131 229 0869

#364
Greens Deli
Cuisines: Deli
Average price: £26-45
Area: Newington
Address: 34 Buccleuch Street
Edinburgh EH8 9LP
Phone: 07773 034608

#365
Bengal Spice
Cuisines: Indian
Average price: £11-25
Area: Leith
Address: 8 Montagu Terrace
Edinburgh EH3 5QX
Phone: 0131 467 0651

#366
Bluerapa Thai
Cuisines: Thai
Average price: Under £10
Area: West End
Address: 6 Torphichen Place
Edinburgh EH3 8DU
Phone: 0131 629 0447

#367
Butterflies Cafe
Cuisines: British
Average price: £11-25
Area: Marchmont
Address: 1A Kilgraston Road
Edinburgh EH9 2DW
Phone: 0131 447 4359

#368
Pomegranate Restaurant
Cuisines: Middle Eastern
Average price: £11-25
Area: New Town
Address: 1 Antigua Street
Edinburgh EH1 3NH
Phone: 0131 556 8337

#369
Elm Rose Cafe and Diner
Cuisines: Cafe
Average price: Under £10
Area: Leith
Address: Elm Row
Edinburgh EH7 4
Phone: 0131 557 8888

#370
Restaurant At The Bonham
Cuisines: French
Average price: £11-25
Area: West End
Address: 35 Drumsheugh Garden
Edinburgh EH3 7RN
Phone: 0131 623 9319

#371
San Marco Restaurant
Cuisines: Italian
Average price: £11-25
Area: Stockbridge
Address: 9-11 Marys Place
Edinburgh EH4 1JH
Phone: 0131 332 1569

#372
Forth Floor Restaurant
Cuisines: Bar, British
Average price: £26-45
Area: New Town
Address: 30-34 St Andrew Square
Edinburgh EH2 2AD
Phone: 0131 524 8350

#373
Cafe Cassis
Cuisines: Mediterranean, French
Average price: £11-25
Area: Newington
Address: 43-45 Salisbury Road
Edinburgh EH16 5AA
Phone: 0131 667 8991

#374
Cafe No 9
Cuisines: Breakfast & Brunch
Average price: Under £10
Area: Leith
Address: 9 Croall Place
Edinburgh EH7 4LT
Phone: 0131 629 6289

#375
Bodrum Express
Cuisines: Fast Food & Takeaways
Average price: £11-25
Area: Cannonmills
Address: 52-54 Rodney Street
Edinburgh EH7 4DX
Phone: 0131 556 8397

#376
The Stockbridge Tap
Cuisines: British, Pub, Gastropub
Average price: £11-25
Area: Stockbridge
Address: 2-4 Raeburn Pl
Edinburgh EH4 1HN
Phone: 0131 343 3000

#377
Olive Tree
Cuisines: Mediterranean
Average price: £11-25
Area: Newington
Address: 27 Marshall Street
Edinburgh EH8 9BJ
Phone: 0131 667 9997

#378
Ciao Roma
Cuisines: Italian
Average price: £11-25
Area: Old Town, Newington
Address: 64 South Bridge
Edinburgh EH1 1LS
Phone: 0131 557 3777

#379
Café Turquaz
Cuisines: Turkish, Juice Bar
Average price: £11-25
Area: Newington
Address: 119 Nicolson Street
Edinburgh EH8 9ER
Phone: 0131 667 6664

#380
Pret A Manger
Cuisines: Coffee & Tea, Soup, Sandwiches
Average price: Under £10
Area: New Town
Address: 51 Hanover St
Edinburgh EH2 2
Phone: 020 7932 5338

#381
Sandwich Culture
Cuisines: Deli, Coffee & Tea, Sandwiches
Average price: £11-25
Area: Haymarket, West End
Address: 24 Haymarket Terrace
Edinburgh EH12 5JZ
Phone: 0131 337 1814

#382
Deep Sea Carry-Out
Cuisines: Fish & Chips
Average price: £11-25
Area: New Town
Address: 2 Antigua Street
Edinburgh EH1 3NH
Phone: 0131 557 0276

#383
Slug & Lettuce
Cuisines: Pub, Gastropub
Average price: £11-25
Area: New Town
Address: Unit 8 Omni Ctr
Edinburgh EH1 3BN
Phone: 0131 524 7700

#384
Vintners Room
Cuisines: Mediterranean
Average price: Above £46
Area: Leith
Address: 87 Giles St
Edinburgh EH6 6BZ
Phone: 0131 554 6767

#385
Chilli Connection
Cuisines: Indian, Fast Food & Takeaways
Average price: Under £10
Area: Newington
Address: 47 S Clerk St
Edinburgh EH8 9NZ
Phone: 0131 668 1171

#386
Fredericks Coffee House
Cuisines: Breakfast & Brunch, Cafe, Deli
Average price: Under £10
Area: New Town
Address: 30 Frederick Street
Edinburgh EH2 2
Phone: 0131 260 9997

#387
One Square
Cuisines: Wine Bar, British
Average price: £26-45
Area: West End
Address: 1 Festival Square
Edinburgh EH3 9SR
Phone: 0131 221 6422

#388
Circus
Cuisines: Breakfast & Brunch
Average price: £11-25
Area: Old Town, Royal Mile
Address: 8 St Mary's Street
Edinburgh EH1 1SU
Phone: 0131 556 6963

#389
Cross & Corner
Cuisines: Gastropub, Pub
Average price: £11-25
Area: Cannonmills
Address: 1 Canonmills Edinburgh
Edinburgh EH3 5HA
Phone: 0131 558 7080

#390
Waiting Room
Cuisines: Pub, Gastropub
Average price: £11-25
Area: Morningside
Address: 7 Belhaven Terrace
Edinburgh EH10 5HZ
Phone: 0131 452 9707

#391
Eatalia's
Cuisines: Italian, Fast Food & Takeaways
Average price: Under £10
Area: Leith
Address: 1 Brunswick Place
Edinburgh EH7 5HP
Phone: 0131 557 8484

#392
Pizza Express
Cuisines: Pizza, Italian
Average price: Above £46
Area: Morningside
Address: 1 Nile Grove
Edinburgh EH10 4RE
Phone: 0131 447 6055

#393
New Happy Palace
Cuisines: Fast Food & Takeaways
Average price: £26-45
Area: Leith
Address: 145-147 Granton Road
Edinburgh EH5 3NL
Phone: 0131 552 6151

#394
Sportsters
Cuisines: Sports Bar, American
Average price: Under £10
Area: Old Town, Royal Mile
Address: 1A Market St
Edinburgh EH1 1DE
Phone: 0131 226 9560

#395
Tiles
Cuisines: Pub, Lounge, British
Average price: £11-25
Area: New Town
Address: 1 St Andrew's Square
Edinburgh EH2 2BD
Phone: 0131 558 1507

#396
The Crafters Barn
Cuisines: Tapas, Brasserie, Pizza
Average price: £26-45
Area: Old Town, Royal Mile
Address: 9 North Bank Street
Edinburgh EH1 2LP
Phone: 0131 226 1178

#397
Elfalafel
Cuisines: Falafel
Average price: £11-25
Area: Old Town
Address: 15 Bristo Pl
Edinburgh EH1 1EZ
Phone: 0131 477 2455

#398
Athena Greek Restaurant
Cuisines: Greek, Mediterranean
Average price: £11-25
Area: New Town
Address: 89 Hanover Street
Edinburgh EH2 1EE
Phone: 0131 226 3451

#399
Bar Soba
Cuisines: Bar, Asian Fusion
Average price: £11-25
Area: New Town
Address: 104 Hanover Street
Edinburgh EH2 1DR
Phone: 0131 225 6220

#400
Koyama
Cuisines: Sushi Bar
Average price: £11-25
Area: Old Town
Address: 20 Forrest Road
Edinburgh EH1 2QN
Phone: 0131 225 6555

#401
Café Milk
Cuisines: Coffee & Tea,
Breakfast & Brunch, Sandwiches
Average price: Under £10
Area: West End
Address: 232 Morrison St
Edinburgh EH3 8EA
Phone: 0131 629 6022

#402
Franco's Chip Shop
Cuisines: Fish & Chips,
Fast Food & Takeaways
Average price: Under £10
Area: Stockbridge
Address: 5-7 Comely Bank Road
Edinburgh EH4 1DR
Phone: 0131 332 3557

#403
Pallucci
Cuisines: Italian
Average price: £11-25
Area: Old Town
Address: 100 Percent Authentic Italian
Edinburgh EH1 2QN
Phone: 0131 220 5553

#404
St Vincent
Cuisines: Pub, Gastropub
Average price: £11-25
Area: Stockbridge, New Town
Address: 11 St Vincent Street
Edinburgh EH3 6SW
Phone: 0131 226 6861

#405
Real Rajput Indian Cuisine
Cuisines: Indian
Average price: £26-45
Area: Old Town, Royal Mile
Address: 209-213 High Street
Edinburgh EH1 1PZ
Phone: 0131 220 2335

#406
Thyme
Cuisines: Sandwiches, Deli
Average price: £11-25
Area: Old Town, Tollcross, West End
Address: 44 Earl Grey Street
Edinburgh EH3 9BN
Phone: 07946 819982

#407
Fresco
Cuisines: Fast Food & Takeaways
Average price: Under £10
Area: Old Town, Royal Mile
Address: 223 Canongate
Edinburgh EH8 8BJ
Phone: 0131 556 9641

#408
Henderson's
Cuisines: Vegetarian
Average price: Under £10
Area: Old Town
Address: Princes St
Edinburgh EH2 4BJ
Phone: 0131 229 0212

#409
Tian Tian
Cuisines: Chinese
Average price: £11-25
Area: Bruntsfield, The Meadows
Address: 8 Gillespie Place
Edinburgh EH10 4HS
Phone: 0131 622 0482

#410
Ravenous
Cuisines: Cafe
Average price: Under £10
Area: New Town
Address: 42 Dundas Street
Edinburgh EH3 6JN
Phone: 0131 558 1168

#411
Bella Italia
Cuisines: Italian
Average price: £26-45
Area: New Town
Address: 9/11 Hanover Street
Edinburgh EH2 2DL
Phone: 0131 225 4808

#412
Sala Cafe Bar
Cuisines: Coffee & Tea, Gay Bar
Average price: £11-25
Area: New Town
Address: 58a Broughton Street
Edinburgh EH1 3SA
Phone: 0131 556 5758

#413
Lune Town Cantonese Restaurant
Cuisines: Chinese
Average price: £11-25
Area: West End
Address: 38 William Street
Edinburgh EH3 7LJ
Phone: 0131 220 1688

#414
Hanam's
Cuisines: Middle Eastern
Average price: £11-25
Area: Old Town
Address: 3 Johnston Terrace
Edinburgh EH1 2PW
Phone: 0131 225 1329

#415
Bruntsfield Bistro
Cuisines: British, Breakfast & Brunch
Average price: £26-45
Area: Bruntsfield, The Meadows
Address: 69 Bruntsfield Pl
Edinburgh EH10 4HH
Phone: 0131 229 1393

#416
Ravenous
Cuisines: Coffee & Tea, Sandwiches
Average price: £11-25
Area: Stockbridge
Address: 12 Raeburn Place
Edinburgh EH4
Phone: 0131 558 1168

#417
Pataka Restaurant
Cuisines: Indian, Pakistani
Average price: £11-25
Area: Newington
Address: 190 Causewayside
Edinburgh EH9 1PN
Phone: 0131 668 1167

#418
Cafe Artista
Cuisines: Italian, Seafood, Pizza
Average price: £11-25
Area: Marchmont
Address: 94-96 Marchmont Crescent
Edinburgh EH9 1HD
Phone: 0131 447 6477

#419
Central Takeaway and Pizzeria
Cuisines: Fish & Chips, Fast Food &
Takeaways
Average price: Under £10
Area: Old Town
Address: 15-16 Teviot Place
Edinburgh EH1 2QZ
Phone: 0131 226 6898

#420
La Rusticana
Cuisines: Italian
Average price: £11-25
Area: New Town
Address: 90 Hanover Street
Edinburgh EH2 1EL
Phone: 0131 225 2227

#421
Beirut
Cuisines: Middle Eastern
Average price: £26-45
Area: Newington
Address: 24 Nicholson Square
Edinburgh EH8 9BX
Phone: 0131 667 9919

#422
Morningside Glory
Cuisines: Pub, Gastropub
Average price: £11-25
Area: Morningside
Address: 1 Comiston Road
Edinburgh EH10 6AA
Phone: 0131 447 1205

#423
Happiness
Cuisines: Chinese
Average price: £11-25
Area: Newington
Address: 34 W Preston Street
Edinburgh EH8 9PY
Phone: 0131 662 1133

#424
The Filling Station
Cuisines: American, Burgers
Average price: £26-45
Area: West End
Address: 66 Rose St
Edinburgh EH2 2NN
Phone: 0131 226 2802

#425
Circle Cafe
Cuisines: Cafe, Breakfast & Brunch
Average price: £11-25
Area: Stockbridge, Cannonmills
Address: 1 Brandon Terrace
Edinburgh EH3 5AE
Phone: 0131 624 4666

#426
The Verandah Restaurant
Cuisines: Indian, Bangladeshi
Average price: £26-45
Area: Haymarket, West End
Address: 17 Dalry Road
Edinburgh EH11 2BQ
Phone: 0131 337 5828

#427
No1 Grange Road
Cuisines: British, Gastropub
Average price: Under £10
Area: Newington
Address: 1 Grange Road Edinburgh
Edinburgh EH9 1UH
Phone: 0131 667 2335

#428
The Curry Leaf
Cuisines: Indian
Average price: £26-45
Area: Bruntsfield
Address: 139 Bruntsfield Place
Edinburgh EH10 4EB
Phone: 0131 229 9194

#429
The Courtyard Bar & Brasserie
Cuisines: British, Pub
Average price: £11-25
Area: Leith
Address: 2 Bonnington Road Lane
Edinburgh EH6 5BJ
Phone: 0131 554 1314

#430
Miso & Sushi
Cuisines: Japanese, Chinese
Average price: £11-25
Area: Haymarket
Address: 46 Haymarket Terrace
Edinburgh EH12 5LA
Phone: 0131 337 7466

#431
Salvatore's
Cuisines: Fish & Chips
Average price: Under £10
Area: Marchmont
Address: 16 Roseneath Street
Edinburgh EH9 1JH
Phone: 0131 229 4087

#432
The Dome Garden Café
Cuisines: Sandwiches, Coffee & Tea
Average price: £11-25
Area: New Town
Address: 14 George St
Edinburgh EH2 2
Phone: 0131 624 8624

#433
Dario's
Cuisines: Italian
Average price: Under £10
Area: Old Town
Address: 85-87 Lothian Road
Edinburgh EH3 9AW
Phone: 0131 229 9625

#434
Coffee Corner
Cuisines: Pizza, Coffee & Tea
Average price: Under £10
Area: Old Town
Address: 68 ST. Marys Street
Edinburgh EH1 1SX
Phone: 07974 528241

#435
The Bon Vivant Stockbridge
Cuisines: Gastropub, Lounge
Average price: £11-25
Area: Stockbridge
Address: Dean Street
Edinburgh EH4 1LW
Phone: 0131 315 3311

#436
Quattrozero
Cuisines: Italian
Average price: Under £10
Area: New Town
Address: 40/41 Queensferry Street
Edinburgh EH2 4RA
Phone: 0131 220 5622

#437
Stac Polly
Cuisines: British
Average price: £26-45
Area: New Town
Address: 29-33 Dublin Street
Edinburgh EH3 6NL
Phone: 0131 556 2231

#438
Dersim Kebab House
Cuisines: Turkish
Average price: £11-25
Area: Haymarket
Address: 166 Dalry Road
Edinburgh EH11 2EG
Phone: 0131 346 8396

#439
The Forest
Cuisines: Local Flavour, Cafe
Average price: Under £10
Area: Tollcross
Address: 141 Lauriston Place
Edinburgh EH3 9JN
Phone: 0131 229 4922

#440
Yo! Sushi
Harvey Nichols Edinburgh
Cuisines: Sushi Bar
Average price: £11-25
Area: New Town
Address: St Andrew Sq
Edinburgh EH2 2AD
Phone: 0131 341 1771

#441
Falko Konditormeister
Cuisines: Bakery, German
Average price: £11-25
Area: Bruntsfield
Address: 185 Bruntsfield Place
Edinburgh EH10 4DG
Phone: 0131 656 0763

#442
G Y Chinese Take Away
Cuisines: Chinese, Fast Food & Takeaways
Average price: Under £10
Area: Marchmont
Address: 27 Roseneath Place
Edinburgh EH9 1JD
Phone: 0131 229 9922

#443
Bona Deli
Cuisines: Deli, Ethnic Food
Average price: £11-25
Area: Newington
Address: 86 S Clerk Street
Edinburgh EH8 9PT
Phone: 0131 662 0962

#444
Miros Cantina Mexicana
Cuisines: Mexican
Average price: £11-25
Area: New Town
Address: 184 Rose Street
Edinburgh EH2 4BA
Phone: 0131 225 4376

#445
Globetrotter Fish & Chips
Cuisines: Fish & Chips
Average price: Under £10
Area: Bruntsfield
Address: 169 Bruntsfield Place
Edinburgh EH10 4DG
Phone: 0131 229 3522

#446
KFC
Cuisines: Fast Food & Takeaways, Chicken Wings
Average price: Above £46
Area: Leith
Address: 134-137 Leith Walk
Edinburgh EH6 8NP
Phone: 0131 554 6647

#447
Viva Mexico
Cuisines: Mexican, Tex-Mex
Average price: £11-25
Area: Old Town, Royal Mile
Address: 41 Cockburn Street
Edinburgh EH1 1BS
Phone: 0131 226 5145

#448
Stac Polly Restaurant Edinburgh
Cuisines: European
Average price: £26-45
Area: Old Town
Address: 8-10 Grindlay Street
Edinburgh EH3 9AS
Phone: 0131 229 5405

#449
Filament Coffee
Cuisines: Coffee & Tea, Wine Bar
Average price: Under £10
Area: Old Town, Grassmarket
Address: 5 India Buildings
Edinburgh EH1 2EX
Phone: 07914 189590

#450
Castle Rock Chip Shop
Cuisines: Fish & Chips
Average price: Under £10
Area: Old Town, Grassmarket
Address: 87 Grassmarket
Edinburgh EH1 2HJ
Phone: 0131 220 1110

#451
Ping On Chinese Restaurant
Cuisines: Chinese
Average price: £11-25
Area: Stockbridge
Address: 26-32 Deanhaugh Street
Edinburgh EH4 1LY
Phone: 0131 332 3621

#452
Café Truva Art College
Cuisines: Turkish
Average price: £11-25
Area: Old Town
Address: 46 Lady Lawson Street
Edinburgh EH3
Phone: 0131 629 5057

#453
Marcella Italian Bakery
Cuisines: Bakery, Italian, Coffee & Tea
Average price: Under £10
Area: Tollcross, The Meadows
Address: 20a Brougham Place
Edinburgh EH3 9JU
Phone: 0131 622 5781

#454
The Globe
Cuisines: Fast Food & Takeaways, Coffee & Tea, Sandwiches
Average price: Under £10
Area: New Town
Address: 42 Broughton Street
Edinburgh EH1 3SA
Phone: 0131 558 3837

#455
La Sal
Cuisines: Spanish
Average price: £11-25
Area: Newington
Address: 6-8 Howden Street
Edinburgh EH8 9HL
Phone: 0131 667 3600

#456
Jones & Son Bespoke BBQs
Cuisines: Barbeque
Average price: Under £10
Area: New Town
Address: Cathedral Ln
Edinburgh EH1 3JD
Phone: 07825 908597

#457
Simple Feast
Cuisines: Cafe
Average price: Under £10
Area: New Town
Address: 32 Howe Street
Edinburgh EH3 6TH
Phone: 0131 629 0663

#458
Concord Fish Bar
Cuisines: Fish & Chips
Average price: £11-25
Area: Tollcross
Address: 49 Home Street
Edinburgh EH3 9JP
Phone: 0131 228 1182

#459
Tempting Tattie
Cuisines: Fast Food & Takeaways, Coffee
& Tea, Do-It-Yourself Food
Average price: Under £10
Area: Old Town, Royal Mile
Address: 18 Jeffrey Street
Edinburgh EH1 1DT
Phone: 0131 556 7960

#460
Leven's
Cuisines: Thai, Asian Fusion
Average price: £11-25
Area: Bruntsfield, The Meadows
Address: 30-32 Leven Street
Edinburgh EH3 9LJ
Phone: 0131 229 8988

#461
Mc Kirdy's Steakhouse
Cuisines: British
Average price: £26-45
Area: West End
Address: 151-155 Morrison Street
Edinburgh EH3 8AG
Phone: 0131 229 6660

#462
La Bruschetta
Cuisines: Italian
Average price: £26-45
Area: Haymarket, West End
Address: 13 Clifton Terrace
Edinburgh EH12 5DR
Phone: 0131 467 7464

#463
Chop Chop
Cuisines: Chinese
Average price: £11-25
Area: West End
Address: 248 Morrison Street
Edinburgh EH3 8DT
Phone: 0131 221 1155

#464
Eastern Spices
Cuisines: Food Delivery Services, Indian
Average price: £11-25
Area: Stockbridge
Address: 6 Howard Street
Edinburgh EH3 5JP
Phone: 0131 558 3609

#465
The Wild Restaurant
Cuisines: French, European, Italian
Average price: Under £10
Area: Newington
Address: 21 Newington Road
Edinburgh EH9 1QR
Phone: 0131 667 1210

#466
Bollywood The Coffee Box
Cuisines: Street Vendor, Indian
Average price: Under £10
Area: Bruntsfield
Address: 99A Bruntsfield Place
Edinburgh EH10 4HG
Phone: 07814 603938

#467
Naked
Cuisines: Soul Food, Gluten-Free, Fast
Food & Takeaways
Average price: £26-45
Area: West End
Address: 35 Palmerston Place
Edinburgh EH12 5AU
Phone: 0131 516 2988

#468
Stac Polly Bistro
Cuisines: Brasserie
Average price: £26-45
Area: Old Town
Address: 38 St Mary's Street
Edinburgh EH1 1SX
Phone: 0131 557 5754

#469
Il'Castello Restaurant
Cuisines: Italian
Average price: £11-25
Area: Old Town
Address: 36 Castle Terrace
Edinburgh EH1 2EL
Phone: 0131 229 2730

#470
East India Takeaway
Cuisines: Fast Food & Takeaways, Cafe
Average price: £11-25
Area: Leith
Address: 103 Brunswick Street
Edinburgh EH7 5HR
Phone: 0131 558 8488

#471
Piano Cafe
Cuisines: Cafe
Average price: Under £10
Area: Stockbridge
Address: 5 Howard Street
Edinburgh EH3 5JP
Phone: 0131 629 0618

#472
Starbucks
Cuisines: Coffee & Tea, Desserts,
Sandwiches
Average price: Under £10
Area: Old Town
Address: 123 Lothian Rd
Edinburgh EH3 9AN
Phone: 0131 229 4899

#473
Marchmont Takeaway
Cuisines: Fast Food & Takeaways
Average price: Under £10
Area: Marchmont
Address: 98 Marchmont Road
Edinburgh EH9 1HR
Phone: 0131 447 8439

#474
Karen Wong Chinese Restaurant
Cuisines: Chinese, Fast Food & Takeaways
Average price: Under £10
Area: Newington
Address: 107 Saint Leonard's Street
Edinburgh EH8 9QY
Phone: 0131 662 0777

#475
Goodwill Chinese Carryout
Cuisines: Fast Food & Takeaways
Average price: Under £10
Area: Newington
Address: 6 Newington Road
Edinburgh EH9 1QS
Phone: 0131 667 6688

#476
Deli Italia
Cuisines: Deli
Average price: £11-25
Area: Newington
Address: 75 Nicolson Street
Edinburgh EH8 9BZ
Phone: 0131 668 2900

#477
In Touch
Cuisines: Indian
Average price: £26-45
Area: Leith
Address: 8 Inverleith Garden
Edinburgh EH3 5PU
Phone: 0131 551 6892

#478
**Gurkha Brigade Nepalese
Restaurant**
Cuisines: Himalayan/Nepalese
Average price: Under £10
Area: New Town
Address: 9a Antigua Street
Edinburgh EH1 3NH
Phone: 0131 557 8855

#479
Dovecot Cafe by Stag Espresso
Cuisines: Coffee & Tea, Soup
Average price: Under £10
Area: Old Town, Newington
Address: 10 Infirmary St
Edinburgh EH1 1LT
Phone: 07590 728974

#480
Auld Jocks Pie Shoppe
Cuisines: British, Bakery
Average price: Under £10
Area: Old Town, Grassmarket
Address: 24 George IV Bridge
Edinburgh EH1 1EN
Phone: 0131 226 4449

#481
Patisserie Valerie
Cuisines: Bakery, Cafe
Average price: Under £10
Area: Old Town, Royal Mile
Address: 25 North Bridge
Edinburgh EH1
Phone: 0131 557 1533

#482
Tony's Fish Bar
Cuisines: Fish & Chips,
Fast Food & Takeaways
Average price: Under £10
Area: Newington
Address: 7 Ratcliffe Terrace
Edinburgh EH9 1SX
Phone: 0131 667 0310

#483
Sonar Gao
Cuisines: Fast Food & Takeaways
Average price: £11-25
Area: Leith
Address: 191 Great Junction Street
Edinburgh EH6 5LQ
Phone: 0131 555 2424

#484
Mamma Roma Restaurante
Cuisines: Italian
Average price: £26-45
Area: New Town
Address: 4 Antigua Street
Edinburgh EH1 3NH
Phone: 0131 558 1628

#485
Deacons House Cafe
Cuisines: Coffee & Tea, Scottish
Average price: £11-25
Area: Old Town, Royal Mile
Address: 3 Brodie's Close
Edinburgh EH1 2PS
Phone: 0131 226 1894

#486
Marie Délices
Cuisines: Patisserie/Cake Shop, Cafe
Average price: £11-25
Area: Morningside
Address: 125 Comiston Road
Edinburgh EH10 6AQ
Phone: 0131 447 1909

#487
Valvona & Crolla
Cuisines: Deli, Italian
Average price: £26-45
Area: New Town
Address: 19 Elm Row
Edinburgh EH7 4AA
Phone: 0131 556 6066

#488
Hanks Sandwich Bar
Cuisines: Sandwiches
Average price: £11-25
Area: West End
Address: 162 Fountainbridge
Edinburgh EH3
Phone: 0131 228 4050

#489
Riverlife
Cuisines: Caribbean, French
Average price: £11-25
Area: Haymarket, West End
Address: 84 Dalry Road
Edinburgh EH11 2AX
Phone: 07724 822386

#490
Roseburn Cafe
Cuisines: Coffee & Tea,
Breakfast & Brunch
Average price: Under £10
Area: Haymarket
Address: 8 Roseburn Terrace
Edinburgh EH12 6AW
Phone: 0131 313 0331

#491
Beanscene
Cuisines: Cafe
Average price: £11-25
Area: Leith
Address: 76 Commercial Street
Edinburgh EH6 6LX
Phone: 0131 555 7033

#492
Caffe Nero
Cuisines: Cafe
Average price: Under £10
Area: Old Town, Newington
Address: 1 Parliment Square
Edinburgh EH1 1RF
Phone: 0131 220 0383

#493
Subway
Cuisines: Fast Food & Takeaways
Average price: £11-25
Area: Old Town, Royal Mile
Address: 160 High Street
Edinburgh EH1 1QS
Phone: 0131 260 9719

#494
Khushi's
Cuisines: Indian
Average price: £11-25
Area: New Town
Address: 10 Antigua Street
Edinburgh EH1 3NH
Phone: 0131 558 1947

#495
La P'Tite Folie
Cuisines: French
Average price: £11-25
Area: New Town
Address: 9 Randolph Pl
Edinburgh EH3 7TE
Phone: 0131 225 8678

#496
Henri's French Food and Wines
Cuisines: Deli, Cheese Shop, French
Average price: £26-45
Area: Morningside
Address: 376 Morningside Road
Edinburgh EH10 5HX
Phone: 0131 447 8877

#497
Maison Bleue
Cuisines: French
Average price: £26-45
Area: Old Town, Grassmarket
Address: 36-38 Victoria Street
Edinburgh EH1 2JW
Phone: 0131 226 1900

#498
Derya Kebabs
Cuisines: Turkish
Average price: Under £10
Area: Haymarket, West End
Address: 72 Dalry Road
Edinburgh EH11 2AY
Phone: 0131 313 3433

#499
Bar Napoli
Cuisines: Italian
Average price: £11-25
Area: New Town
Address: 75 Hanover Street
Edinburgh EH2 1EE
Phone: 0131 225 2600

#500
The Dining Room
Cuisines: French, British, Vegetarian
Average price: £11-25
Area: New Town
Address: 28 Queen Street
Edinburgh EH2 1JX
Phone: 0131 220 2044

TOP 500 ATTRACTIONS

The Most Recommended by Locals & Trevelers
(From #1 to #500)

#1
Edinburgh Castle
Category: Museum, Landmark, Historical Building
Area: Old Town, Royal Mile
Address: Castle Hill
Edinburgh EH1 2HG
Phone: 0131 225 9846

#2
Royal Botanic Garden Edinburgh
Category: Park, Botanical Garden
Address: Arboretum Place / Inverleith Row,
Edinburgh EH3 5LR

#3
Silver Reels
Category: Amusement Park
Area: Newington
Address: 48 Nicolson Street
Edinburgh EH8 9DT
Phone: 0131 667 4888

#4
The Scotch Malt Whisky Society
Category: Social Club
Area: Leith
Address: 87 Giles Street
Edinburgh EH6 6BZ
Phone: 0131 554 3451

#5
Edinburgh Leisure
Category: Leisure Centre
Area: Newington
Address: 54 Nicolson Street
Edinburgh EH8 9DT
Phone: 0131 650 1001

#6
Gorgie City Farm
Category: Zoo
Address: 51 Gorgie Road
Edinburgh EH11 2LA

#7
Retro Recycles
Category: Recycling Centre,
Mountain Biking
Area: Old Town, Royal Mile
Address: Cockburn St
Edinburgh EH1
Phone: 07772 940373

#8
Scottish National Gallery
Category: Art Gallery
Area: Old Town
Address: The Mound
Edinburgh EH2 2EL
Phone: 0131 624 6200

#9
Culture & Leisure
Category: Leisure Centre
Address: 23-25 Waterloo Place
Edinburgh EH1 3BH

#10
Inverleith Park
Category: Park
Address: Arboretum Pl
Edinburgh EH3 5NY

#11
Gold Rush Amusements
Category: Amusement Park
Area: Tollcross, West End
Address: 14a Home Street
Edinburgh EH3 9LY
Phone: 0131 229 4888

#12
Royal Botanic Garden Edinburgh
Category: Park, Botanical Garden
Address: Arboretum Place / Inverleith Row,
Edinburgh EH3 5LR

#13
Fitness First
Category: Gym
Area: New Town
Address: 30a Abercromby Place
Edinburgh EH3 6QE
Phone: 0121 328 0762

#14
Camera Obscura
Category: Local Flavour, Museum
Area: Old Town, Royal Mile
Address: 549 Castlehill
Edinburgh EH1 2ND
Phone: 0131 226 3709

#15
**Han Wong Tae Kwon
Do Academy**
Category: Sports Club
Area: Tollcross, West End
Address: 9 Thornybauk
Edinburgh EH3 9QH
Phone: 0131 229 2722

#16
Holyrood Park
Category: Park
Address: Holyrood Park Road
Edinburgh EH16 5BT

#17
AM Fitness
Category: Personal Trainers
Area: Newington
Address: 46 Pleasance
Edinburgh EH8 9TJ
Phone: 07734 284004

#18
Filmhouse
Category: Cinema
Area: Old Town, West End
Address: 88 Lothian Road
Edinburgh EH3 9BZ
Phone: 0131 229 5932

#19
Royale Amusements
Category: Amusement Park
Area: West End
Address: 18 Shandwick Place
Edinburgh EH2 4RN
Phone: 0131 225 1331

#20
The Dominion
Category: Cinema
Address: 18 Newbattle Terrace
Edinburgh EH10 4RT

#21
Slot Casino
Category: Sports & Leisure
Area: Old Town, Newington
Address: South Bridge
Edinburgh EH8

#22
Edinburgh Playhouse
Category: Theatre, Music Venues
Area: New Town
Address: 18-22 Greenside Place
Edinburgh EH1 3AA
Phone: 0131 524 3333

#23
Trout Anglers Club
Category: Sports Club
Area: New Town
Address: 29 Dundas Street
Edinburgh EH3 6QQ
Phone: 0131 556 6656

#24
George Square Garden
Category: Park
Area: The Meadows
Address: George Square Lane
Edinburgh EH8 9

#25
Edinburgh Bowling Club
Category: Sports Club
Area: Newington
Address: 4 Meadow Lane
Edinburgh EH8 9NR
Phone: 0131 667 5665

#26
**Edinburgh International
Book Festival**
Category: Bookshop, Festival
Area: New Town
Address: A 5 Charlotte Sq
Edinburgh EH2 4DR
Phone: 0131 718 5666

#27
Factory Gym
Category: Gym
Address: Calton Rd
Edinburgh EH1 3

#28
The Voodoo Rooms
Category: Lounge, Music Venues
Area: New Town
Address: 19A West Register Street
Edinburgh EH2 2AA
Phone: 0131 556 7060

#29
Marco's Leisure
Category: Leisure Centre
Area: West End
Address: 55 Grove Street
Edinburgh EH3 8AB
Phone: 0131 228 2141

#30
Cabaret Voltaire
Category: Club, Music Venues
Area: Old Town, Newington
Address: 36-38 Blair Street
Edinburgh EH1 1QR
Phone: 0131 247 4704

#31
Ceroc Scotland
Category: Club, Dance Studio
Area: Stockbridge, New Town
Address: St Stephens Street
Edinburgh EH3 5AB
Phone: 07528 694901

#32
Museum Of Childhood
Category: Museum, Art Gallery
Area: Old Town, Newington, Royal Mile
Address: 42 High Street
Edinburgh EH1 1TG
Phone: 0131 529 4142

#33
Pilates Work Education
Category: Gym
Address: Leith Street
Edinburgh EH1 3AU

#34
Festival Theatre Edinburgh
Category: Music Venues
Area: Newington
Address: 13-29 Nicolson Street
Edinburgh EH8 9FT
Phone: 0131 529 6000

#35
**Edinburgh West End
Bowling Club**
Category: Sports Club
Area: Bruntsfield
Address: Hailes Street
Edinburgh EH3 9NF
Phone: 0131 229 8308

#36
Leith Circle Gallery
Category: Art Gallery
Area: Leith
Address: 115 Leith Walk
Edinburgh EH6 8NP
Phone: 07564 138768

#37
Systema Scotland
Category: Sports & Leisure
Area: Stockbridge, New Town
Address: 37 Saint Stephen Street
Edinburgh EH3 5AH
Phone: 07801 888344

#38
Ripping Records
Category: Music Venues
Area: Old Town, Newington
Address: 91 South Bridge
Edinburgh EH1 1HN
Phone: 0131 226 7010

#39
Ayatana Yoga
Category: Yoga
Area: West End
Address: 25 Palmerston Place
Edinburgh EH12 5AP
Phone: 07966 502085

#40
St Andrew Square Garden
Category: Park, Landmark,
Historical Building
Area: New Town
Address: St Andrew Square
Edinburgh EH2

#41
Lutton Place Bowling Club
Category: Sports Club
Area: Newington
Address: 18 Lutton Place
Edinburgh EH8 9PE
Phone: 0131 668 2707

#42
Kings Theatre
Category: Theatre
Area: The Meadows
Address: 2 Leven St
Edinburgh EH3 9
Phone: 0131 221 0606

#43
**Dean Lawn Tennis
& Squash Club**
Category: Sports Club
Area: Stockbridge
Address: 24 Lennox Street
Edinburgh EH4 1QA
Phone: 0131 315 2836

#44
HMV Picture House
Category: Club, Music Venues
Area: Old Town
Address: 31 Lothian Road
Edinburgh EH1 2DJ
Phone: 0131 221 2280

#45
Yoga Shop
Category: Yoga
Area: Cannonmills
Address: 25 Rodney Street
Edinburgh EH7 4EL
Phone: 0131 558 3593

#46
Tynecastle Stadium
Category: Stadium, Football
Address: Gorgie Rd
Edinburgh EH11 2NL

#47
**Johnny's Entertainment
& Amusement**
Category: Amusement Park
Area: Haymarket, West End
Address: 26 Dalry Road
Edinburgh EH11 2BA
Phone: 0131 346 8475

#48
Cameo
Category: Cinema
Area: Tollcross, West End
Address: 38 Home Street
Edinburgh EH3 9LZ
Phone: 0871 902 5723

#49
Edinburgh Golf Centre
Category: Golf
Area: Haymarket, West End
Address: 58 Dalry Road
Edinburgh EH11 2AY
Phone: 0131 337 5888

#50
Nobles Cafe Bar & Venue
Category: Music Venues
Area: Leith
Address: 44a Constitution Street
Edinburgh EH6 6RS
Phone: 0131 629 7215

#51
Golfing-Lady
Category: Sports Club
Area: Haymarket, West End
Address: 18 Haymarket Terrace
Edinburgh EH12 5JZ
Phone: 0131 313 4446

#52
Vegas in the Garden
Category: Club, Park
Area: New Town
Address: Princes Street
Edinburgh EH2 3AA
Phone: 0131 529 4068

#53
Forth Canoe Club
Category: Sports Club
Address: 24 Hartington Place
Edinburgh EH10 4LE

#54
Peckhams
Category: Winery
Area: Newington
Address: 49 South Clerk Street
Edinburgh EH10 4DG
Phone: 0131 668 3939

#55
The Edinburgh Academy
Category: Sports Club
Area: Stockbridge, New Town
Address: 9 Kinnear Road
Edinburgh EH3 5PQ
Phone: 0131 552 4197

#56
Henry's Cellar Bar
Category: Music Venues
Area: West End
Address: 8-16 Morrison Street
Edinburgh EH3 8BJ
Phone: 0131 629 4101

#57
Whitehouse & Grange Bowling Club
Category: Sports Club
Area: Marchmont
Address: 18a Hope Terrace
Edinburgh EH9 2AR
Phone: 0131 447 9606

#58
Queen S Hall Edinburgh
Category: Music Venues
Area: Newington
Address: 85-89 Clerk Street
Edinburgh EH8
Phone: 0131 668 3456

#59
City Of Edinburgh Swimming
Category: Sports Club
Address: 21 Dalkeith Road
Edinburgh EH16 5BB

#60
Holyrood Park
Category: Park
Address: Queens Drive
Edinburgh EH8

#61
Ceroc Scotland
Category: Club, Dance Studio
Area: Leith
Address: 1 Shrub Place Lane
Edinburgh EH7 4PB
Phone: 07528 694901

#62
The Edinburgh International Film Festival
Category: Festival, Local Flavour
Area: Old Town, West End
Address: 88 Lothian Rd
Edinburgh EH3 9BZ
Phone: 0131 228 4051

#63
Parkide Bowling Club
Category: Sports Club
Address: Holyrood Park Road
Edinburgh EH16 5BG

#64
Out of the Blue
Category: Music Venues
Area: Leith
Address: 36 Dalmeny St
Edinburgh EH6 8RG
Phone: 0131 555 7100

#65
Edinburgh Sports Club
Category: Sports Club
Address: 7 Belford Place
Edinburgh EH4 3DH

#66
Scotsman's Lounge
Category: Pub, Music Venues
Area: Old Town
Address: 73 Cockburn Street
Edinburgh EH1 1BU
Phone: 0131 225 7726

#67
Fit-Foundations
Category: Fitness, Instruction
Address: Murdoch Terrace
Edinburgh EH11 1BB

#68
Dean Bowling Club
Category: Bowling Alley
Area: Stockbridge
Address: Comely Bank Terrace
Edinburgh EH4 1AS
Phone: 0131 332 0015

#69
C K T Leisure
Category: Gym
Address: 10 Beaverhall Road
Edinburgh EH7 4JE

#70
Malones Irish Bar
Category: Music Venues
Area: Old Town
Address: 14 Forrest Road
Edinburgh EH1 2QN
Phone: 0131 226 5954

#71
Pleasance Courtyard
Category: Theatre
Area: Newington
Address: 60 Pleasance
Edinburgh EH8 9TJ

#72
Liquid Room
Category: Club, Music Venues
Area: Old Town, Grassmarket
Address: 9c Victoria Street
Edinburgh EH1 2HE
Phone: 0131 225 2564

#73
The Banshee Labyrinth
Category: Pub, Cinema
Area: Old Town, Newington
Address: 29-35 Niddry Street
Edinburgh EH1 1LG
Phone: 0131 558 8209

#74
Surgeons' Hall Museum
Category: Museum
Area: Newington
Address: Nicolson Street
Edinburgh EH8 9DW
Phone: 0131 527 1600

#75
Electric Circus
Category: Karaoke, Music Venues, Club
Area: Old Town, Royal Mile
Address: 36-39 Market Street
Edinburgh EH1 1DF
Phone: 0131 226 4224

#76
The Jazz Bar
Category: Pub, Jazz & Blues
Area: Old Town, Newington
Address: 1A Chambers Street
Edinburgh EH1 1HR
Phone: 0131 220 4298

#77
Murrayfield Ice Rink
Category: Ice Rinks
Address: 13 Riversdale Cres
Edinburgh EH12 5XN

#78
Studio 24
Category: Club, Music Venues
Area: Old Town
Address: 24-26 Calton Road
Edinburgh EH8 8
Phone: 0131 558 3758

#79
Leith Links
Category: Park, Bowling Alley, Football
Area: Leith
Address: Links Pl
Edinburgh EH6 7

#80
Royal Edinburgh Military Tattoo
Category: Festival
Area: Old Town, Royal Mile
Address: Castle Hill
Edinburgh EH1 2HG
Phone: 0131 225 1188

#81
Harrison Park
Category: Park
Address: West Bryson Road
Edinburgh EH11 1EH

#82
Edinburgh College Of Art
Category: College, Art Gallery
Area: Old Town
Address: 74 Lauriston Pl
Edinburgh EH3 9DF
Phone: 0131 221 6000

#83
The People's Story Museum
Category: Museum
Area: Old Town, Royal Mile
Address: 163 Canongate
Edinburgh EH8 8BN
Phone: 0131 529 4057

#84
Beltane Fire Festival
Category: Festival
Address: Calton Hill
Edinburgh EH1

#85
The Meadows
Category: Park
Area: Marchmont
Address: 5 Millerfield Place
Edinburgh EH9
Phone: 0131 667 5316

#86
Our Dynamic Earth
Category: Museum
Address: 112-116 Holyrood Road
Edinburgh EH8 8AS

#87
Alba Flamenca
Category: Theatre, Dance Studio
Area: Newington
Address: 74 East Crosscauseway
Edinburgh EH8 9HQ
Phone: 0131 667 3600

#88
Scottish Storytelling Centre
Category: Museum
Area: Old Town, Newington, Royal Mile
Address: 43-45 High Street
Edinburgh EH1 1SR
Phone: 0131 556 9579

#89
Tenpin Bowling
Category: Bowling Alley
Address: Fountain Park
Edinburgh EH11 1AW

#90
The Queens Hall
Category: Music Venues
Area: Newington
Address: 85-89 Clerk Street
Edinburgh EH8 9JG
Phone: 0131 668 2019

#91
The Bongo Club
Category: Club, Music Venues
Area: Old Town
Address: 66 Cowgate
Edinburgh EH1 1JX
Phone: 0131 558 8844

#92
Meadows Tennis
Category: Tennis
Area: Newington, The Meadows
Address: Melville Drive
Edinburgh EH8 9NL
Phone: 07766 774529

#93
The Writers' Museum
Category: Museum, Art Gallery
Area: Old Town, Royal Mile
Address: Lady Stairs House Lady Stair's
Close, Edinburgh EH1 2PA
Phone: 0131 529 4901

#94
**Craiglockhart Tennis
& Sports Centre**
Category: Leisure Centre
Address: 177 Colinton Road
Edinburgh EH14 1BZ

#95
Georgian House
Category: Museum
Area: New Town
Address: 7 Charlotte Square
Edinburgh EH2 4DR
Phone: 0131 225 2160

#96
Leith Waterworld
Category: Leisure Centre
Area: Leith
Address: 377 Easter Rd
Edinburgh EH6 8HU
Phone: 0131 555 6000

#97
**Teviot Library Bar
& Underground**
Category: Music Venues
Address: 13 Bristo Square
Edinburgh EH8 9AJ

#98
Duddingston Loch
Category: Park
Address: Queens Drive
Edinburgh EH15 3PY

#99
Museum Of Edinburgh
Category: Museum
Area: Old Town, Royal Mile
Address: 142-146 Canongate
Edinburgh EH8 8DD
Phone: 0131 529 4143

#100
Assembly Roxy
Category: Music Venues, Theatre
Area: Newington
Address: 2 Roxburgh Place
Edinburgh EH8 9SU
Phone: 0871 750 0077

#101
The Scotch Whisky Experience
Category: Museum
Area: Old Town, Newington
Address: 354 Castlehill
Edinburgh EH1 1PD
Phone: 0131 220 0441

#102
C Venues
Category: Theatre
Area: Old Town, Newington
Address: Chambers St
Edinburgh EH1 1HR
Phone: 0870 701 5105

#103
Clown Around
Category: Kids Activities
Area: Leith
Address: 109 Restalrig Road
Edinburgh EH6 7NY
Phone: 0131 553 7676

#104
Medina
Category: Music Venues
Area: Old Town, Newington
Address: 45-47 Lothian Street
Edinburgh EH1 1HB
Phone: 0131 220 4287

#105
Marchmont Gallery
Category: Art Gallery
Area: Marchmont
Address: 56 Warrender Park Road
Edinburgh EH9 1EX
Phone: 0131 228 8228

#106
Jam House
Category: British, Jazz & Blues
Area: New Town
Address: 5 Queen Street
Edinburgh EH2 1JE
Phone: 0131 226 4380

#107
Speakers Corner
Category: Sports & Leisure
Area: New Town
Address: Princes Street
Edinburgh EH2 2DF

#108
Tynecastle Stadium
Category: Stadium, Football
Address: Gorgie Rd
Edinburgh EH11 2NL

#109
National Portrait Gallery Cafe
Category: Art Gallery, Cafe
Area: New Town
Address: 20A 20a Dundas Street
Edinburgh EH3 6HZ
Phone: 0131 557 4569

#110
Hunter square
Category: Park
Area: Old Town, Newington, Royal Mile
Address: High Street
Edinburgh EH1 1QW

#111
Fountain Park Leisure Complex
Category: Cinema, Shopping Centre
Address: 130 Dundee St
Edinburgh EH11 1AF

#112
The Spiegel Garden
Category: Festival, Theatre, Pub
Area: Newington, The Meadows
Address: George Sq
Edinburgh EH8 9

#113
Edinburgh International Festival
Category: Festival, Theatre
Area: Old Town, Royal Mile
Address: 348-350 Castlehill
Edinburgh EH1 2NE
Phone: 0131 473 2000

#114
BBC at the Edinburgh Festival
Category: Festival, Local Flavour
Area: Newington
Address: 26-30 Potterrow
Edinburgh EH8 9BT

#115
Udderbelly
Category: Theatre
Area: Newington
Address: Bristo Sq
Edinburgh EH8 9AL

#116
Dunbar's Close Garden
Category: Botanical Garden, Park
Area: Old Town, Royal Mile
Address: Dunbar's Close
Edinburgh EH8 8BN

#117
Pleasance Theatre
Category: Theatre, Cinema,
Music Venues
Area: Newington
Address: 60 Pleasance
Edinburgh EH8 9TJ
Phone: 0131 556 1513

#118
**The Crags Community
Sports Centre**
Category: Leisure Centre
Area: Newington
Address: 10 Bowmont Place
Edinburgh EH8 9RY
Phone: 0131 667 3334

#119
**Edinburgh Police
Centre Museum**
Category: Museum
Area: Old Town, Royal Mile
Address: Royal Mile
Edinburgh EH1 1QS

#120
Hidden Door Festival
Category: Festival
Area: Old Town, Royal Mile
Address: Market Street
Edinburgh EH1 1DF

#121
The Big Red Door
Category: Theatre
Area: Old Town
Address: 10 Lady Lawson St
Edinburgh EH3 9DS
Phone: 0131 228 4567

#122
West Port Book Festival
Category: Festival
Area: Old Town, Grassmarket
Address: West Port
Edinburgh EH1 2JE

#123
Vue Cinema
Category: Cinema
Area: New Town
Address: Omni
Edinburgh EH1 3AT
Phone: 0871 224 0240

#124
No Fit State Fringe Tent
Category: Festival
Area: West End
Address: 207/9 Fountainbridge
Edinburgh EH3 9RU

#125
Heart of Midlothian F.C.
Category: Sports & Leisure
Area: Haymarket, West End
Address: Haymarket
Edinburgh EH11 2BG

#126
Sneaky Pete's
Category: Club, Music Venues
Area: Old Town
Address: 73 Cowgate
Edinburgh EH1 1JW
Phone: 0131 225 1757

#127
The Omni Centre
Category: Arcade, Pub, Cinema
Address: 28 Greenside Row
Edinburgh EH1 3AJ

#128
Finnegan's Wake
Category: Irish, Pub, Music Venues
Area: Old Town, Grassmarket
Address: 9B Victoria Street
Edinburgh EH1 2HE
Phone: 0131 225 9348

#129
Whisky Stramash
Category: Festival
Area: Newington
Address: Sturgeon's Hall
Edinburgh EH1

#130
**Mean Fiddler Picture House
Purchase Ledger**
Category: Music Venues
Area: Old Town
Address: 31 Lothian Road
Edinburgh EH1 2DJ
Phone: 0131 221 2282

#131
Excel Sports Academy
Category: Kids Activities
Address: Garscube Terrace
Edinburgh EH12 6BG

#132
Framers
Category: Art Gallery
Area: Bruntsfield, The Meadows
Address: 81 Bruntsfield Place
Edinburgh EH10 4HG

#133
Wasps
Category: Art Gallery
Area: Stockbridge
Address: 48A Hamilton Place
Edinburgh EH3 5AY
Phone: 0131 226 7126

#134
Banana Row
Category: Musical Instruments
Area: Cannonmills
Address: 47 Eyre Pl
Edinburgh EH3 5EY
Phone: 0131 557 2088

#135
Pilrig Park
Category: Park
Area: Leith
Address: Pilrig Street Edinburgh
Phone: 0131 529 5050

#136
Odeon Cinema
Category: Cinema
Area: West End
Address: 118 Lothian Rd
Edinburgh EH3 9BG
Phone: 0871 224 4007

#137
Church Hill Theatre
Category: Theatre
Area: Bruntsfield
Address: 33a Morningside Road
Edinburgh EH10 4DR
Phone: 0131 447 7597

#138
Tumble Tots
Category: Kids Activities
Address: Murrayfield Parish Church
Ormidale Terrace
Edinburgh EH12 6EQ

#139
Edinburgh Mela
Category: Festival
Area: Leith
Address: Leith Links
Edinburgh EH6 7
Phone: 0131 332 2888

#140
Potterow - Pleasance Dome
Category: Theatre
Area: Newington
Address: 1 Bristo Square
Edinburgh EH8 9AL
Phone: 0131 556 6550

#141
Assembly Hall
Category: Theatre, Music Venues
Area: Old Town, Royal Mile
Address: Mound Place
Edinburgh EH1 2LU

#142
Dr Neils Garden
Category: Park
Address: Old Church Lane
Edinburgh EH15 3PX

#143
Bedlam Theatre
Category: Theatre
Area: Old Town
Address: 2 Forrest Road
Edinburgh EH1 1EZ
Phone: 0131 225 9873

#144
Piershill Square East
Category: Park
Address: Piershill Sq E
Edinburgh EH8 7

#145
West End Craft and Design Fair
Category: Festival
Area: Old Town
Address: Princes Street
Edinburgh EH2 4BJ

#146
A Taste of Spain 2010
Category: Festival, Ethnic Food
Area: Old Town
Address: The Mound
Edinburgh EH2 2

#147
Provenance Wines
Category: Winery
Area: Tollcross, West End
Address: 39 Home Street
Edinburgh EH3 9JP
Phone: 0131 229 0841

#148
Oddbins
Category: Winery
Area: New Town, West End
Address: 5 Queensferry St
Edinburgh EH2 4PA
Phone: 0131 226 7589

#149
Alba Flamenca
Category: Theatre, Dance Studio
Area: Newington
Address: 74 East Crosscauseway
Edinburgh EH8 9HQ
Phone: 0131 667 3600

#150
Slot Casino
Category: Amusement Park
Area: Newington
Address: 21 Clerk Street
Edinburgh EH8 9JH
Phone: 0131 667 8585

#151
The Institute
Category: Art Gallery
Area: Marchmont
Address: 14 Roseneath Street
Edinburgh EH9 1JH
Phone: 0131 229 1338

#152
Gateway Theatre
Category: Theatre
Area: Leith
Address: Elm Row
Edinburgh EH7 4AH
Phone: 0131 317 3900

#153
Beanscene
Category: Music Venues
Area: West End
Address: 2 Grosvenor St
Edinburgh EH12 5EG
Phone: 0131 346 8043

#154
Roseburn Park
Category: Park
Address: Roseburn Park
Edinburgh EH12 5XN

#155
Edinburgh Printmakers
Category: Art Gallery
Area: New Town
Address: 23 Union Street
Edinburgh EH1 3LR
Phone: 0131 557 2479

#156
Walkabout
Category: Theatre, Pub
Area: Old Town, Royal Mile
Address: Unit 6 Omni Leisure Development
Edinburgh EH1 3AA
Phone: 0131 524 9300

#157
Murrayfield Stadium
Category: Stadium
Address: Murrayfield
Edinburgh EH12 5PJ

#158
Circus Casino
Category: Casino
Address: 124 Dundee Street
Edinburgh EH11 1AF

#159
Victoria Park
Category: Park, Playground
Area: Leith
Address: Craighall Rd
Edinburgh EH6 4

#160
Pleasance Cinema
Category: Cinema
Area: Newington
Address: 60 Pleasance
Edinburgh EH8 9TJ

#161
El Bar
Category: Theatre, Dance School
Area: Newington
Address: 6-8 Howden Street
Edinburgh EH8 9HQ
Phone: 0131 667 3600

#162
Ainslie Park Leisure Centre
Category: Stadium
Address: 92 Pilton Drive
Edinburgh EH5 2HF

#163
Festival of Politics
Category: Festival
Area: Old Town, Royal Mile
Address: Scottish Parliament
Edinburgh EH99 1SP
Phone: 0131 348 5000

#164
Clown Around
Category: Kids Activities
Area: Leith
Address: 109 Restalrig Road
Edinburgh EH6 7NY
Phone: 0131 553 7676

#165
Museum On the Mound
Category: Museum
Area: Old Town, Royal Mile
Address: The Mound
Edinburgh EH1 1YZ
Phone: 0131 243 5464

#166
St Margarets Lake
Category: Lake
Address: Holyrood Park
Edinburgh EH16

#167
George Square Theatre
Category: Theatre
Area: Newington, The Meadows
Address: 30 George Square
Edinburgh EH8 9LJ
Phone: 0131 651 1292

#168
Castle Fine Art
Category: Art Gallery
Area: New Town
Address: 20 Multrees Walk
Edinburgh EH1 3DQ
Phone: 0131 261 9181

#169
**Royal Scots Dragoon
Guards Museum**
Category: Museum, Art Gallery
Area: Old Town
Address: Castlehill
Edinburgh EH1 2YT
Phone: 0131 220 4387

#170
Hogmanay Street Party
Category: Festival
Area: New Town
Address: Princes Street Edinburgh

#171
Little Ox
Category: Art Gallery
Area: Old Town
Address: 23 Candlemaker Row
Edinburgh EH1 2QG
Phone: 0131 629 0474

#172
Arthurs Seat
Category: Hiking, Landmark,
Historical Building
Address: Arthur's Seat
Edinburgh EH8 8EQ

#173
New Club
Category: Social Club
Area: New Town
Address: 86 Princes Street
Edinburgh EH2 2BB
Phone: 0131 226 4881

#174
Meggatland Playing Fields
Category: Leisure Centre
Address: 60 Colinton Rd
Edinburgh EH14 1AH

#175
**Boroughmuir Rugby
Football Club**
Category: Sports Club
Address: 60j Colinton Road
Edinburgh EH14 1AS

#176
Dovecot Studio
Category: Art Gallery
Area: Old Town, Newington
Address: 10 Infirmary St
Edinburgh EH1 1LT
Phone: 0131 550 3660

#177
John Knox House
Category: Art Gallery
Area: Old Town, Royal Mile
Address: 43-45 High Street
Edinburgh EH1 1SR
Phone: 0131 556 9579

#178
Royal Scottish Academy Of Art
Category: Art Gallery
Area: Old Town
Address: The Mound
Edinburgh EH2
Phone: 0131 225 6671

#179
Piershill Square West
Category: Park
Address: Piershill Sq W
Edinburgh EH8 7

#180
Union Gallery
Category: Art Gallery
Area: New Town
Address: 45 Broughton Street
Edinburgh EH1 3JU
Phone: 0131 556 7707

#181
Anatomical Museum
Category: Museum
Address: Teviot Place
Edinburgh EH1

#182
Megabowl
Category: Bowling Alley
Address: Unit D Fountain Park
Edinburgh EH11 1AW

#183
Cairn O'Mohr
Category: Winery
Area: Old Town
Address: Castle Ter
Edinburgh EH1 2

#184
Axolotl Gallery
Category: Art Gallery
Area: New Town
Address: 35 Dundas Street
Edinburgh EH3 6QQ
Phone: 0131 557 1460

#185
Nicolson Square
Category: Park
Area: Newington
Address: Nicolson Sq
Edinburgh EH8 9BX

#186
Garage
Category: Art Gallery
Area: New Town
Address: 51A Northumberland St
Edinburgh EH3 6JQ
Phone: 07917 668044

#187
Kagyu Samye Dzong Edinburgh
Category: Buddhist Temple
Area: West End
Address: 4 Walker Street
Edinburgh EH3 7LA
Phone: 0131 225 8359

#188
Doubtfire Gallery
Category: Art Gallery
Area: New Town
Address: 1-3 SE Circus Place
Edinburgh EH3 6TJ

#189
Abbey Hill Park
Category: Park
Area: Old Town
Address: Regent Road
Edinburgh EH8 8EA

#190
Premier Bingo
Category: Social Club
Area: Newington
Address: 50 Nicolson Street
Edinburgh EH8 9DT
Phone: 0131 662 1448

#191
Dunbar's Close Garden
Category: Botanical Garden, Park
Area: Old Town, Royal Mile
Address: Dunbar's Close
Edinburgh EH8 8BN

#192
Murieston Park
Category: Park
Area: Haymarket
Address: Murieston Park
Edinburgh EH11 2LH

#193
Theatre Workshop Edinburgh
Category: Theatre, Music Venues
Area: Stockbridge
Address: 34 Hamilton Place
Edinburgh EH3 5AX
Phone: 0131 226 4366

#194
The Grove Gallery
Category: Art Gallery
Area: West End
Address: 17 Grove Street
Edinburgh EH3 8AF
Phone: 0131 229 7117

#195
Laughing Horse
Category: Theatre
Area: Newington
Address: 36 W Nicholson St
Edinburgh EH8 9DD
Phone: 0131 667 7533

#196
Alba Ballooning
Category: Hot Air Balloons
Area: Marchmont
Address: 12 Gladstone Terrace
Edinburgh EH9 1LT

#197
Inch Park
Category: Park
Address: 225 Gilmerton Rd
Edinburgh EH16 5UF

#198
Glassite Meeting House
Category: Theatre
Area: New Town
Address: 33 barony st
Edinburgh EH1 3SA

#199
There Will Be No Miracles Here
Category: Art Gallery
Area: West End
Address: 73 Belford Rd
Edinburgh EH4 3DS
Phone: 0131 624 6200

#200
London Road Garden
Category: Park
Address: Royal Ter
Edinburgh EH7 5

#201
European Christmas Market
Category: Christmas Market
Area: Old Town
Address: The Mound
Edinburgh EH2 2EL

#202
Churchill Theatre
Category: Theatre
Area: Bruntsfield
Address: 33a Morningside Road
Edinburgh EH10 4DR
Phone: 0131 447 7597

#203
West End Fair
Category: Festival
Area: Leith
Address: Lothian Rd
Edinburgh EH7 5HZ
Phone: 0131 661 6600

#204
Morningside Gallery
Category: Art Gallery
Address: 94 Morningside Rd
Edinburgh EH10 4BY

#205
Arthur's Seat
Category: Park, Landmark,
Historical Building
Address: Holyrood Road
Edinburgh EH8 8EQ

#206
The Ale House
Category: Pub, Music Venues
Area: Newington
Address: 18-22 Clerk Street
Edinburgh EH8 9HX
Phone: 0131 629 0275

#207
**Edinburgh Jazz
and Blues Festival**
Category: Festival, Jazz & Blues
Area: Leith
Address: 89 Giles St
Edinburgh EH6 6BZ
Phone: 0131 473 2000

#208
Blackford Pond
Category: Botanical Garden
Area: Marchmont
Address: Cluny Garden
Edinburgh EH9 3HR

#209
Royal Lyceum Theatre
Category: Theatre, Music Venues
Area: Old Town
Address: 30b Grindlay Street
Edinburgh EH3 9
Phone: 0131 248 4848

#210
Usher Hall
Category: Music Venues, Landmark,
Historical Building
Area: Old Town, West End
Address: Lothian Road
Edinburgh EH1 2EA
Phone: 0131 228 1155

#211
Nobles Amusements
Category: Amusement Park
Area: New Town
Address: 140 Princes Street
Edinburgh EH2 4BL

#212
Axo Gallery
Category: Theatre, Art Gallery
Area: Leith
Address: 59 Queen Charlotte St
Edinburgh EH6 7EY

#213
Talbot Rice Gallery
Category: Museum
Area: Old Town, Newington
Address: Old College
Edinburgh EH8 9YL
Phone: 0131 650 2211

#214
Nomads Tent
Category: Art Gallery
Area: Newington
Address: 21 St Leonard's Ln
Edinburgh EH8 9SH
Phone: 0131 662 1612

#215
**British Communists
Party Book Stall**
Category: Amusement Park
Area: Old Town
Address: The Mound
Edinburgh EH2 2EL
Phone: 0141 204 1611

#216
Valvona and Crolla Food Hall
Category: Winery
Area: New Town
Address: 48 Princes St
Edinburgh EH2 2YJ
Phone: 0131 225 2442

#217
**Edinburgh University
Freshers' Week**
Category: Festival, University
Area: Newington
Address: 5/2 Bristo Sq
Edinburgh EH8 9AL
Phone: 0131 650 2656

#218
St Margaret's House
Category: Art Gallery, Venues & Event
Spaces, Local Flavour
Address: 151 London Rd
Edinburgh EH7 6AE

#219
John Murray Archive
Category: Art Gallery
Area: Old Town
Address: National Library of Scotland
Edinburgh EH1 1YH
Phone: 0131 623 3878

#220
Boteco Do Brasil Edinburgh
Category: Music Venues, Brazilian
Area: Old Town, Newington
Address: 45-47 Lothian Street
Edinburgh EH1 1HB
Phone: 0131 220 4287

#221
The Mash House
Category: Music Venues
Area: Old Town, Newington
Address: 37 Guthrie Street
Edinburgh EH1 1JG
Phone: 0131 226 1402

#222
Tron Kirk
Category: Cultural Center,
Music Venues
Area: Old Town, Royal Mile
Address: High St
Edinburgh EH1

#223
The Famous Spiegeltent
Category: Festival
Area: New Town
Address: 54 George Street
Edinburgh EH2 2LR

#224
C Aquila Fringe Venue
Category: Festival
Area: Old Town, Royal Mile
Address: Roman Eagle Lodge Johnston
Terrace, Edinburgh EH1 2PW

#225
Assembly Garden
George Square
Category: Festival, Theatre
Area: Newington, The Meadows
Address: 57 George Square
Edinburgh EH8 9JU

#226
Edinburgh Fencing Club
Category: Sports & Leisure
Address: 2-20 Chalmers Street
Edinburgh EH3 9ES

#227
Xavia supporting Amoriste
Category: Music Venues
Area: Old Town, Royal Mile
Address: Market street
Edinburgh EH1 2NG

#228
Italian Institute
Category: Social Club
Area: Newington
Address: 82 Nicolson Street
Edinburgh EH8 9EW
Phone: 0131 668 2232

#229
Edinburgh Academical
Rugby Club
Category: Sports Club
Area: Stockbridge
Address: Raeburn Place
Edinburgh EH4

#230
Zoo Southside
Category: Music Venues
Area: Newington
Address: 117 Nicholson St
Edinburgh EH8 9ER
Phone: 01432 344885

#231
Festival of Spirituality and Peace
Category: Festival
Area: Old Town
Address: Princes St
Edinburgh EH2 4BJ
Phone: 0131 221 2277

#232
Edinburgh Ski Club
Category: Sports Club
Area: New Town
Address: 2 Howe Street
Edinburgh EH3 6TD
Phone: 0131 220 3121

#233
Peoples Story Museum
Category: Museum, Art Gallery
Area: Old Town, Royal Mile
Address: 163 Canongate
Edinburgh EH8 8BN
Phone: 0131 529 4057

#234
The Torrance Gallery
Category: Art Gallery, Museum
Area: New Town
Address: 36 Dundas Street
Edinburgh EH3 6JN
Phone: 0131 556 6366

#235
Kidding Around Edinburgh
Category: Kids Activities
Area: West End
Address: 12 Alva Street
Edinburgh EH2 4QG

#236
C Central
Category: Theatre
Area: Old Town, Royal Mile
Address: 19 N Bridge
Edinburgh EH1 1SD

#237
C Plaza Fringe Venue
Category: Festival
Area: The Meadows
Address: George Sq
Edinburgh EH8 9LJ

#238
Adam Pottery
Category: Art Gallery
Area: Stockbridge
Address: 76 Henderson Row
Edinburgh EH3 5BJ
Phone: 0131 557 3978

#239
Scots Guard Association Club
Category: Social Club
Area: Haymarket, West End,
Address: 2 Clifton Terrace
Edinburgh EH12 5DR
Phone: 0131 337 1084

#240
Lucie Fenton Gallery
Category: Art Gallery
Area: Stockbridge
Address: 20 Raeburn Place
Edinburgh EH4 1HN
Phone: 0131 332 3999

#241
Winsor & Newton
Category: Art Gallery
Area: Stockbridge
Address: 28A Raeburn Pl
Edinburgh EH4 1HN
Phone: 0131 332 7800

#242
Drummond Tennis Club
Category: Tennis
Area: New Town
Address: East Scotland Street
Edinburgh EH3
Phone: 07828 691181

#243
Palace of Holyroodhouse Shop
Category: Art Gallery
Area: Old Town
Address: Holyrood Palace
Edinburgh EH8 8BA
Phone: 0131 556 5100

#244
Aberglas
Category: Kids Activities
Area: Newington
Address: 140 The Pleasance
Edinburgh EH8 9TL
Phone: 07521 010514

#245
Queen's Gallery
Category: Museum
Area: Old Town
Address: The Palace Of Holyroodhouse
Edinburgh EH8 8DX
Phone: 0131 556 5100

#246
Vietnam House Art Gallery
Category: Art Gallery
Area: Haymarket, West End
Address: Haymarket Terrace
Edinburgh EH12 5JZ

#247
Granada Cinema Edinburgh
Category: Cinema
Address: Newbattle Terrace
Edinburgh EH10 4RJ

#248
Hillside Bowling Club
Category: Sports Club
Address: 9a Brunton Place
Edinburgh EH7 5EG

#249
Outrageous Art
Category: Art Gallery
Area: Bruntsfield, The Meadows
Address: 17-19 Barclay Place
Edinburgh EH10 4HW
Phone: 0131 477 2933

#250
Ingleby Gallery
Category: Art Gallery
Area: Old Town
Address: 6 Carlton Terrace
Edinburgh EH7 5DD
Phone: 0131 556 4441

#251
Royal Lyceum Theatre
Category: Theatre
Address: 29 Roseburn Street
Edinburgh EH12 5PE

#252
Bangholm Recreation Ground
Category: Stadium, Leisure Centre
Area: Leith
Address: Craighall Garden
Edinburgh EH6 4RH
Phone: 0131 552 2749

#253
Vive Le Cabaret
Category: Theatre
Address: 2 Rutland Pl
Edinburgh EH1 2

#254
Me! Me! Me!
Category: Theatre
Address: 2 Rutland Pl
Edinburgh EH1 2

#255
Cabaret Chordelia
Category: Theatre
Address: 2 Rutland Pl
Edinburgh EH1 2

#256
Oktoberfest
Category: Festival
Area: Old Town
Address: Princes Street Garden
Edinburgh EH2 2HG

#257
Toddler Sense
Category: Kids Activities
Area: Leith
Address: 12 Casselbank Street
Edinburgh EH6 5HA
Phone: 07814 448239

#258
**Foodies Festival
@ Holyrood Park**
Category: Festival
Area: Old Town
Address: Holyrood Road
Edinburgh EH8 8BA

#259
Just Scottish Gallery
Category: Art Gallery
Area: Old Town, Royal Mile
Address: 6 North Bank Street
Edinburgh EH1 2LP
Phone: 0131 226 4807

#260
Ladbrokes
Category: Arcade
Area: New Town
Address: 40 Rose St
Edinburgh EH2 2QA
Phone: 0800 022 2454

#261
Zoo Roxy
Category: Music Venues
Area: Newington
Address: 2-3 Roxburgh Pl
Edinburgh EH8 9SU
Phone: 01432 344885

#262
Spectrum Arts
Category: Art Gallery
Area: Old Town, Newington
Address: 317 Cowgate
Edinburgh EH1 1NA
Phone: 0131 556 7740

#263
Cashino
Category: Casino
Area: Newington
Address: 52 Nicholson Street
Edinburgh EH8

#264
No. 27
Category: Art Gallery, Tea Room
Area: New Town
Address: 28 Charlotte Square
Edinburgh EH2 4ET
Phone: 0131 243 9300

#265
Bourne Fine Art
Category: Art Gallery
Area: New Town
Address: 6 Dundas Street
Edinburgh EH3 6HZ
Phone: 0131 557 4050

#266
ShuttleScots Badminton Club
Category: Badminton, Social Club
Address: 139-143 London Road
Edinburgh EH7 6AE

#267
Scottish Gallery
Category: Art Gallery
Area: New Town
Address: 16 Dundas Street
Edinburgh EH3 6HZ
Phone: 0131 558 1200

#268
The Hide
Category: Theatre
Area: Marchmont
Address: 15-17 Argyle Place
Edinburgh EH9 1JJ
Phone: 0131 221 9759

#269
Doggerfisher
Category: Art Gallery
Area: New Town
Address: 11 Gayfield Sq
Edinburgh EH1 3NT
Phone: 0131 558 7110

#270
Scottish Cyclists Union
Category: Sports Club
Address: London Road
Edinburgh EH7 6AD

#271
Traverse Theatre
Category: Theatre
Area: Old Town
Address: 10 Cambridge St
Edinburgh EH1 2ED
Phone: 0131 228 1404

#272
Morningside Park
Category: Park, Playground
Area: Morningside
Address: Morningside Dr
Edinburgh EH10

#273
Wasps Artists Studio
Category: Art Gallery
Address: 78 Albion Road
Edinburgh EH7 5QZ

#274
Leith Dockers Club
Category: Social Club
Area: Leith
Address: 17-17a Academy Street
Edinburgh EH6 7EE
Phone: 0131 467 7879

#275
Subway Cowgate
Category: Music Venues
Area: Old Town
Address: 69 Cowgate
Edinburgh EH1 1JW
Phone: 0131 225 6766

#276
The Third Door
Category: Club, Music Venues
Area: Old Town, Newington
Address: 45 - 47 Lothian Road
Edinburgh EH1 1HB
Phone: 0131 225 6313

#277
Peffermill Playing Fields
Category: Stadium
Address: Peffermill Road
Edinburgh EH16 5LL

#278
**Inch Community
Education Centre**
Category: Social Club
Address: 225 Gilmerton Road
Edinburgh EH16 5UF

#279
Art Shop
Category: Art Gallery
Area: Leith
Address: 19 Haddington Place
Edinburgh EH7 4AF
Phone: 0131 466 3168

#280
Napier University Student Union
Category: Social Club, Bar
Address: Merchiston
Edinburgh EH10 4NS

#281
**The National Museum
Of Scotland**
Category: Museum
Area: Old Town, Newington
Address: Chambers Street
Edinburgh EH1 1JF
Phone: 0131 225 7534

#282
Vue Cinema
Category: Cinema
Area: New Town
Address: Leith Street
Edinburgh EH1 3AT
Phone: 0871 224 0240

#283
Arusha Art Gallery
Category: Art Gallery
Area: West End
Address: 25 Palmerston Place
Edinburgh EH12 5AP
Phone: 07814 189018

#284
Leith Ex Servicemans Club
Category: Social Club
Area: Leith
Address: 7 Smith's Place
Edinburgh EH6 8NT
Phone: 0131 554 4255

#285
Games Hub
Category: Arcade
Area: Old Town
Address: 101 Lauriston Place
Edinburgh EH3 9JB
Phone: 0131 237 2310

#286
Flaubert Gallery
Category: Art Gallery
Area: New Town
Address: 74 St Stephen Street
Edinburgh EH3 5AQ
Phone: 0131 225 5007

#287
Madame Peaches
Category: Theatre
Area: Old Town, Newington
Address: 139 Tailors Hall
Edinburgh EH1 1JS
Phone: 07941 725754

#288
Di Rollo Gallery
Category: Art Gallery
Area: New Town
Address: 18 Dundas Street
Edinburgh EH3 6HZ
Phone: 0131 557 5227

#289
Collective Gallery
Category: Art Gallery
Address: 38 Calton Hill
Edinburgh EH1

#290
The Laurel Gallery
Category: Art Gallery
Area: Stockbridge, New Town
Address: 41 St.Stephen Street
Edinburgh EH3 5AH
Phone: 0131 226 5022

#291
Marginalian Books
Category: Vintage
Area: Bruntsfield
Address: 16 westhall Garden
Edinburgh EH10 4JQ
Phone: 07981 909776

#292
Impro Jam
Category: Comedy Club
Area: New Town
Address: 233 Cowgate Street
Edinburgh EH1

#293
Checkpoint Charlie
Category: Music Venues
Area: Old Town, Newington
Address: 9/3 Brighton Street
Edinburgh EH1 1HD

#294
Assembly Theatre
Category: Theatre
Area: New Town
Address: 50 George Street
Edinburgh EH2 2LE
Phone: 0131 623 3052

#295
Ingleby Gallery
Category: Art Gallery
Area: Old Town
Address: 15 Calton Road
Edinburgh EH8 8DL
Phone: 0131 556 4441

#296
Edinburgh Festival
Category: Festival
Area: Old Town, Royal Mile
Address: 4 East Market Street
Edinburgh EH8 8BG

#297
Open Eye Gallery
Category: Art Gallery
Area: New Town
Address: 34 Abercromby Place
Edinburgh EH3 6QE
Phone: 0131 557 1020

#298
Scottish Building Federation
& District Charitable
Category: Social Club
Area: West End
Address: Trust - Fao Fiona M M Wilson
Exchange Place 3 Semple Street
Edinburgh EH3
Phone: 0131 473 3500

#299
Pheonix 369 Gallery
Category: Art Gallery, Moroccan
Area: New Town
Address: 3 Dundas Street
Edinburgh EH3 6QG
Phone: 0131 556 6497

#300
Murrayfield Indoor Sports Club
Category: Sports Club
Area: New Town
Address: 25 Roseburn Street
Edinburgh EH12 5PE
Phone: 0131 589 6512

#301
Scottish Arts Club
Category: Social Club
Area: West End
Address: 24 Rutland Square
Edinburgh EH1 2BW
Phone: 0131 229 8157

#302
Grand Lodge Of Scotland
Category: Social Club
Area: New Town
Address: 96 George Street
Edinburgh EH2 3DH
Phone: 0131 225 5577

#303
Eyes on Edinburgh Photography
Category: Photographers
Area: Newington
Address: 70 S Clerk St
Edinburgh EH9 1QW
Phone: 07552 470547

#304
Wee Stories Theatre
For Children
Category: Theatre
Area: Old Town, Royal Mile
Address: 5 New Street
Edinburgh EH8 8BH
Phone: 0131 557 6107

#305
The Wind in the Willows
Not Cricket Productions
Category: Theatre
Area: Old Town, Grassmarket
Address: CToo St Columba's by the Castle,
Edinburgh EH1 2JT

#306
Go Reborn
Category: Art Gallery
Area: Leith
Address: 105 Brunswick Street
Edinburgh EH7 5NG

#307
6 Times
Category: Art Gallery
Area: West End
Address: Starts at the Modern Art Gallery,
Edinburgh EH4 3BP

#308
Pilrig St. Paul's Church
Category: Church, Theatre
Area: Leith
Address: 1b Pilrig Street
Edinburgh EH6 8
Phone: 0131 553 1876

#309
Single Connection
Category: Social Club
Address: 100/2 Morningside Road
Edinburgh EH10 4BY

#310
Òr Ceilidh Band
Category: Wedding Planning
Address: 3F2 30 Polwarth Garden
Edinburgh EH11

#311
Alex the Piper
Category: Wedding Planning
Address: 3F2 30 Polwarth Garden
Edinburgh EH11

#312
Africa in Motion
Category: Festival
Area: Leith
Address: Dalmeny Street
Edinburgh EH6 8RA

#313
North Merchiston Club
Category: Social Club, Sports Club
Address: 48 Watson Cresent
Edinburgh EH11 1EP

#314
Columcille Centre
Category: Social Club
Address: 2 Newbattle Ter
Edinburgh EH10 4RT

#315
Forest Fribge
Category: Theatre
Area: Leith
Address: 38 Dalmeny Road
Edinburgh EH6 4QY

#316
Strange Town
Category: Theatre
Area: Leith
Address: 36 Dalmeny Street
Edinburgh EH6 8RG
Phone: 0131 629 0292

#317
Universal Arts
Category: Theatre
Area: Leith
Address: 165 Bonnington Road
Edinburgh EH6 5BQ
Phone: 0131 554 3161

#318
Edinburgh's Got Soul
Category: Specialty School
Area: Leith
Address: 14 Ashley Place
Edinburgh EH6 5PX
Phone: 0131 555 9118

#319
Leitheatre
Category: Theatre
Address: 20-22 Sunnyside Off Easter Road,
Edinburgh EH7 5QG

#320
ShuttleScots Badminton Club
Category: Badminton, Social Club
Address: 139-143 London Road
Edinburgh EH7 6AE

#321
Edinburgh International Science Festival
Category: Theatre, Festival
Area: Leith
Address: Suite 1 Mitchell House 5 Mitchell Street Leith
Edinburgh EH6 7BD
Phone: 0844 557 2686

#322
Ritchie Collins Gallery
Category: Art Gallery
Area: Leith
Address: 83 Henderson Street
Edinburgh EH6 6ED
Phone: 0131 555 3003

#323
Corn Exchange Gallery
Category: Art Gallery
Area: Leith
Address: Constitution Street
Edinburgh EH6 7BS
Phone: 0131 561 7300

#324
Scottish National Portrait Gallery
Category: Art Gallery, Landmark, Historical Building
Area: New Town
Address: 1 Queen St
Edinburgh EH2 1JD
Phone: 0131 624 6200

#325
Superclub Gallery
Category: Art Gallery
Address: 11A Gayfield Square
Edinburgh EH2 2

#326
Tickets Scotland
Category: Local Services, Event Planning & Services, Theatre
Area: New Town
Address: 127 Rose Street
Edinburgh EH2 3DT
Phone: 0131 220 3234

#327
Scottish Tartan Museum
Category: Insurance, Museum
Area: New Town
Address: Princes Street
Edinburgh EH2 2DF

#328
The Ticket Centre
Category: Theatre
Area: Old Town, Royal Mile
Address: 33-34 Market Street
Edinburgh EH1 1QB
Phone: 0131 225 8616

#329
Scottish Pictures
Category: Art Gallery
Area: Old Town, Grassmarket
Address: 64 West Port
Edinburgh EH1 2LD
Phone: 0131 229 5353

#330
Owl & Lion
Category: Art Gallery
Area: Old Town, Grassmarket
Address: 66 West Port
Edinburgh EH1 2LD
Phone: 0131 221 0818

#331
Te Pooka
Category: Theatre
Area: Old Town
Address: 10 Lady Lawson Street
Edinburgh EH3 9DS
Phone: 0131 228 4567

#332
Royal Antediluvian Order Of Buffaloes Club
Category: Social Club
Area: New Town
Address: 5 West Register Street
Edinburgh EH2 2AA
Phone: 0131 556 1131

#333
Royal Scottish Pipers Society
Category: Social Club
Area: New Town
Address: 127 Rose Street
Edinburgh EH2 3DT
Phone: 0131 225 4123

#334
**Scottish International
Childrens Festival Charity**
Category: Theatre
Area: New Town
Address: 45A George St
Edinburgh EH2 2HT
Phone: 0131 225 8050

#335
Cockburn Association
Category: Social Club
Area: Old Town, Royal Mile
Address: 55 High Street
Edinburgh EH1 1SR
Phone: 0131 557 8686

#336
**Lodge Of Edinburgh
Marys Chapel No 1**
Category: Social Club
Area: New Town
Address: 19 Hill Street
Edinburgh EH2 3JP
Phone: 0131 225 7294

#337
Drinkies
Category: Jazz & Blues
Area: New Town
Address: 39A Queen Street
Edinburgh EH2 1
Phone: 0131 226 3417

#338
Meadowbank Jitsu Club
Category: Martial Arts
Area: West End
Address: 139-143 London Road Edinburgh
EH7 6AE

#339
Castle Fine Art
Category: Art Gallery
Area: New Town
Address: 20 Multrees Walk
Edinburgh EH1 3DQ
Phone: 0131 261 9181

#340
National Trust For Scotland
Category: Local Flavour, Art Gallery
Area: New Town
Address: 28 Charlotte Square
Edinburgh EH2 4ET
Phone: 0131 243 9300

#341
Royal Museum
Category: Museum, Art Gallery
Area: Old Town, Newington
Address: Chambers Street
Edinburgh EH1 1JF
Phone: 0131 247 4422

#342
**University Of Edinburgh Graduates
Association**
Category: Social Club
Area: The Meadows
Address: 24 Buccleuch Place
Edinburgh EH8 9LN
Phone: 0131 650 4292

#343
Scottish Volleyball Association
Category: Social Club
Area: Newington
Address: 48 Pleasance
Edinburgh EH8 9TJ
Phone: 0131 556 4633

#344
Art
Category: Art Gallery
Area: West End
Address: 17 Shandwick Place
Edinburgh EH2 4RG
Phone: 0131 229 9032

#345
**Royal Incorporation Of Architects
In Scotland**
Category: Art Gallery
Area: West End
Address: 15 Rutland Square
Edinburgh EH1 2BE
Phone: 0131 229 7205

#346
Anthony Woodd
Category: Art Gallery
Area: New Town
Address: 4 Dundas Street
Edinburgh EH3 6HZ
Phone: 0131 558 9544

#347
Supreme Grand Royal Arch Chapter Of Scotland
Category: Social Club
Area: Old Town, Royal Mile
Address: 23 ST. John Street
Edinburgh EH8 8DG
Phone: 0131 556 6687

#348
Royal Order Of Scotland
Category: Social Club
Area: Old Town, Royal Mile
Address: 23 ST. John Street
Edinburgh EH8 8DG
Phone: 0131 556 1222

#349
Artis
Category: Art Gallery
Area: Tollcross, West End
Address: 58 Home street
Edinburgh EH3 9NA

#350
Wee Stories Theatre For Children
Category: Theatre
Area: Tollcross, The Meadows
Address: 2 Leven Street
Edinburgh EH3 9LQ
Phone: 0131 229 9286

#351
Audience Business
Category: Music Venues
Area: Tollcross, The Meadows
Address: 2 Leven Street
Edinburgh EH3 9LQ
Phone: 0131 622 8100

#352
District
Category: Music Venues
Area: West End
Address: 3 Queensferry Lane
Edinburgh EH2 4PF
Phone: 0131 467 7216

#353
Regular
Category: Theatre
Area: New Town
Address: 42 York Place
Edinburgh EH1 3HU
Phone: 0131 525 6700

#354
Schoolhouse Management
Category: Theatre
Area: New Town
Address: 42 York Place
Edinburgh EH1 3HU
Phone: 0131 557 4242

#355
Kaya Graphics
Category: Art Gallery
Area: Tollcross, West End
Address: 24 Lochrin Buildings
Edinburgh EH3 9NB
Phone: 0131 477 1822

#356
Hanover Fine Arts
Category: Art Gallery
Area: New Town
Address: 22a Dundas Street
Edinburgh EH3 6JN
Phone: 0131 556 2181

#357
Outlook Project
Category: Music Venues
Area: Old Town
Address: Cambridge Street
Edinburgh EH1 2DY
Phone: 0131 228 9076

#358
The Institute For Study Abroad
Category: Art Gallery
Area: New Town
Address: 19 Albany Street
Edinburgh EH1 3QN
Phone: 0131 557 8811

#359
Universal Arts Festival Limited
Category: Theatre
Area: New Town, West End
Address: 18 Queensferry Street
Edinburgh EH2 4QW
Phone: 0131 478 0195

#360
Saltire Society
Category: Social Club
Area: Old Town, Newington, Royal Mile
Address: 9 Fountain Close
Edinburgh EH1 1TF
Phone: 0131 556 1836

#361
The Lambert Agency
Category: Theatre
Area: New Town
Address: 5-7 Northumberland ST. Ln.N.W.
Edinburgh EH3 6JL
Phone: 0131 557 8101

#362
The Palais
Category: Arcade
Area: West End
Address: 125 Fountainbridge
Edinburgh EH3 9QG
Phone: 0131 229 7427

#363
Polish Combatant Association
Category: Social Club
Area: New Town
Address: 11 Drummond Place
Edinburgh EH3 6PJ
Phone: 0131 556 1011

#364
Randolph Gallery
Category: Art Gallery
Area: New Town
Address: 39 Dundas Street
Edinburgh EH3 6QQ
Phone: 0131 556 0808

#365
Royal Engineers Club
Category: Social Club
Area: New Town
Address: 78 Great King Street
Edinburgh EH3 6QU
Phone: 0131 556 4732

#366
Happy Gang
Category: Theatre
Area: The Meadows, Marchmont
Address: 41 Argyle Place
Edinburgh EH9 1JT
Phone: 0131 228 5566

#367
Edinburgh Experience
Category: Museum
Address: Calton Hill
Edinburgh EH7 5AA

#368
Jenny Brown Associates
Category: Theatre
Area: Marchmont
Address: 33 Argyle Place
Edinburgh EH9 1JT
Phone: 0131 229 6695

#369
Fidelo Art Gallery
Category: Art Gallery
Area: New Town
Address: 49a Cumberland Street
Edinburgh EH3 6RA
Phone: 0131 557 2444

#370
Grassmarket Project
Category: Theatre
Area: New Town
Address: 20 Forth Street
Edinburgh EH1 3LH
Phone: 0131 558 3581

#371
Scottish Museum Council
Category: Museum
Area: West End
Address: 20-22 Torphichen Street
Edinburgh EH3 8JB
Phone: 0131 229 7465

#372
One O Clock Gun Design Consultants
Category: Theatre
Area: West End
Address: 18 Torphichen Street
Edinburgh EH3 8JB
Phone: 0131 538 8886

#373
Danish Cultural Institute
Category: Social Club
Area: New Town
Address: 3 Doune Terrace
Edinburgh EH3 6DY
Phone: 0131 225 7189

#374
Whirlie Records & Prods
Category: Theatre
Area: New Town
Address: 14 Broughton Place
Edinburgh EH1 3RX
Phone: 0131 557 9099

#375
Pla
Category: Theatre
Area: New Town
Address: 5 Union Street
Edinburgh EH1 3LT
Phone: 0131 478 7878

#376
St Leonards Gallery
Category: Art Gallery
Area: Newington
Address: 71 ST. Leonards Hill
Edinburgh EH8 9SB
Phone: 0131 667 7997

#377
Zendeh
Category: Theatre
Area: Old Town, Grassmarket
Address: 216 Webster'S Land
Edinburgh EH1 2RU
Phone: 0131 229 9793

#378
Bellevue Gallery
Category: Art Gallery
Area: New Town, Cannonmills
Address: 4 Bellevue Crescent
Edinburgh EH3 6ND
Phone: 0131 558 8368

#379
Living Memory Association
Category: Museum
Area: Newington
Address: 101 St Leonards Street
Edinburgh EH8 9QY
Phone: 0131 667 0761

#380
Calton Gallery
Category: Art Gallery
Address: 6a Regent Terrace
Edinburgh EH7 5BN

#381
Federation Of Scottish Theatre
Category: Theatre
Area: Stockbridge
Address: 34 Hamilton Place
Edinburgh EH3 5AX
Phone: 0131 220 6393

#382
**National Association
Of Youth Orchestras**
Category: Theatre
Area: Tollcross, West End
Address: West Tollcross
Edinburgh EH3 9BP
Phone: 0131 221 1927

#383
Melville Bridge Club
Category: Social Club
Area: West End
Address: 9 Grosvenor Cresent
Edinburgh EH12 5EP
Phone: 0131 337 1102

#384
Royal British Legion
Category: Social Club
Area: Cannonmills
Address: 33 Rodney Street
Edinburgh EH7 4EL
Phone: 0131 557 8164

#385
**Royal Air Forces
Edinburgh Club**
Category: Social Club
Address: 11 Hillside Cresent
Edinburgh EH7 5EA

#386
Jubilee Garden
Category: Theatre
Area: Stockbridge
Address: Saunders Street
Edinburgh EH3 6
Phone: 050 8792 4585

#387
R C A H M S
Category: Museum
Area: Newington
Address: 16 Bernard Terrace
Edinburgh EH8 9NX
Phone: 0131 662 1456

#388
**Workshop & Artists Studio
Provision Scotland**
Category: Art Gallery
Area: Stockbridge
Address: Patriothall
Edinburgh EH3 5AY
Phone: 0131 225 1289

#389
Union Of Communication Workers
Category: Social Club
Area: Leith
Address: 15 Brunswick Street
Edinburgh EH7 5JB
Phone: 0131 556 8974

#390
Art Shop
Category: Art Gallery
Area: Leith
Address: 19 Haddington Place
Edinburgh EH7 4AF
Phone: 0131 466 3168

#391
Morrison & Gibb Social Club
Category: Social Club
Area: Cannonmills
Address: 3a Huntly Street
Edinburgh EH3 5HB
Phone: 0131 556 9453

#392
Grid Iron
Category: Theatre
Area: Cannonmills
Address: 85 East Claremont Street
Edinburgh EH7 4HU
Phone: 0131 558 1879

#393
Pakistan Community Centre
Category: Social Club
Area: Leith, Cannonmills
Address: 43-45 Annandale Street
Edinburgh EH7 4AZ
Phone: 0131 556 1226

#394
Claytara
Category: Theatre
Area: Leith
Address: 61 Brunswick Street
Edinburgh EH7 5HT
Phone: 0131 556 4258

#395
Hostival Festival Accommodation
Category: Festival
Area: New Town
Address: Ocean View Terminal
Edinburgh EH1

#396
Prospective 24
Category: Stadium
Address: 25 Montpelier
Edinburgh EH10 4LY

#397
Gamma
Category: Art Gallery
Area: Stockbridge
Address: 6 Dean Park Street
Edinburgh EH4 1JW
Phone: 0131 332 1777

#398
Gentlemens Club
Category: Social Club
Area: Stockbridge
Address: 43 Comely Bank Place
Edinburgh EH4 1ER
Phone: 0131 332 3247

#399
B M C Austin Section Trust
Category: Social Club
Address: 18 Granville Terrace
Edinburgh EH10 4PQ

#400
**Learmonth Court
Residents Association**
Category: Social Club
Address: 85 Learmonth Court
Edinburgh EH4 1PB

#401
The Art Mart
Category: Art Gallery
Address: 21-22 London Rd
Edinburgh EH7 5AY

#402
Edinburgh Unionist Club
Category: Social Club
Area: Newington
Address: 5 Duncan Street
Edinburgh EH9 1SZ
Phone: 0131 667 7633

#403
Drivers Sports & Social Club
Category: Social Club
Address: 12 Beaverhall Road
Edinburgh EH7 4JE

#404
Lung Ha's
Category: Theatre
Area: Bruntsfield
Address: 15 Morningside Road
Edinburgh EH10 4DP
Phone: 0131 447 8496

#405
Lothian Border Fire Brigade Club
Category: Social Club
Area: Leith
Address: Mcdonald Road
Edinburgh EH7 4NA
Phone: 0131 556 9685

#406
Lodge Waverley
Category: Social Club
Address: 6 Easter Road
Edinburgh EH7 5RG

#407
The Caves
Category: Venues & Event Spaces
Area: Old Town, Newington
Address: 8-12 Niddry Street South
Edinburgh EH1 1NS
Phone: 0131 557 8989

#408
National Gallery Of Scotland
Category: Art Gallery
Area: West End
Address: 72 Belford Road
Edinburgh EH4 3DS
Phone: 0131 624 6200

#409
Hibernian Football
Supporters Club
Category: Social Club
Area: Leith
Address: 11 Sunnyside
Edinburgh EH7 5RA
Phone: 0131 661 3157

#410
Leitheatre
Category: Theatre
Area: Leith
Address: 20 Sunnyside
Edinburgh EH7 5RA
Phone: 0131 661 2626

#411
Dovecot Studio
Category: Art Gallery
Area: Haymarket
Address: West Coates
Edinburgh EH12 5JJ
Phone: 0131 347 5547

#412
Ferranti Sports & Social Club
Category: Social Club
Address: Arboretum Place
Edinburgh EH3 5NY

#413
Cutting Edge Theatre
Category: Theatre
Area: Leith
Address: 6 Albion Terrace
Edinburgh EH7 5QX
Phone: 0131 652 0968

#414
Edinburgh Festival Fringe
Category: Theatre, Festival
Area: Old Town, Newington, Royal Mile
Address: 180 High Street
Edinburgh EH1 1QS
Phone: 0131 226 0026

#415
Framework Gallery
Category: Art Gallery
Area: Morningside
Address: Morningside Road
Edinburgh EH10 4AY
Phone: 0131 447 7881

#416
Merchiston Hearts Social Club
Category: Social Club
Address: 60 Gorgie Road
Edinburgh EH11 2NB

#417
Carlton Club
Category: Social Club
Address: 52-54 Gorgie Road
Edinburgh EH11 2NB

#418
Original Scores
Category: Theatre
Area: Marchmont
Address: 9/8 West Powburn
Edinburgh EH9 3EN
Phone: 0131 668 4907

#419
Mmimi UK
Category: Stadium
Area: Morningside
Address: 31 Canaan Lane
Edinburgh EH10 4SX
Phone: 0131 478 0209

#420
Beechwood Bowling Club
Category: Social Club
Address: 11 Roseburn Street
Edinburgh EH12 5PW

#421
Benchtours Theatre Companies
Category: Theatre
Area: Leith
Address: 72 Newhaven Road
Edinburgh EH6 5QG
Phone: 0131 555 3585

#422
Morningside Club
Category: Social Club
Area: Morningside
Address: 3 Morningside Park
Edinburgh EH10 5HD
Phone: 0131 447 7485

#423
G W Music Services
Category: Theatre
Area: Marchmont
Address: 81 Cluny Garden
Edinburgh EH10 6BW
Phone: 0131 447 8753

#424
B Dirollo
Category: Art Gallery
Area: Leith
Address: 32 Tennant Street
Edinburgh EH6 5NA
Phone: 0131 554 2595

#425
Mecca Social Club
Category: Social Club
Area: Leith
Address: 24 Manderston Street
Edinburgh EH6 8LY
Phone: 0131 554 5017

#426
Lochend Youth FC
Category: Social Club
Address: 4 Lochend Road South
Edinburgh EH7 6BR

#427
Tipperlinn Bowling Club
Category: Social Club
Area: Morningside
Address: Morningside Place
Edinburgh EH10 5HF
Phone: 0131 447 8648

#428
K & M Scenic Productions
Category: Theatre
Area: Leith
Address: 82 Jane Street
Edinburgh EH6 5HG
Phone: 0131 555 0066

#429
Merchant Co
Category: Social Club
Address: 523 Ferry Road
Edinburgh EH5 2DW

#430
The Puppet Lab
Category: Theatre
Area: Leith
Address: 81 Great Junction Street
Edinburgh EH6 5HZ
Phone: 0131 554 8923

#431
Tommy Miah's Curry Club
Category: Social Club
Area: Leith
Address: 87-91 Henderson Street
Edinburgh EH6 6ED
Phone: 0131 538 7900

#432
Fourth Leith Scouts
Category: Social Club
Area: Leith
Address: 34 South Trinity Road
Edinburgh EH5 3NT
Phone: 0131 551 5771

#433
BMC Club
Category: Social Club
Address: Westfield Street
Edinburgh EH11 2QY

#434
Assembly Direct
Category: Theatre
Area: Leith
Address: 89 Giles Street
Edinburgh EH6 6BZ
Phone: 0131 553 4000

#435
Giclee UK
Category: Art Gallery
Area: Leith
Address: 90 Giles Street
Edinburgh EH6 6BZ
Phone: 0131 555 6444

#436
Watsonian Club
Category: Social Club
Address: 79 Myreside Road
Edinburgh EH10 5DB

#437
Unique Events
Category: Arcade
Area: Leith
Address: Gladstone House 6a
Mill Lane, Edinburgh EH6 6TJ

#438
Willowbrae Bowling Club
Category: Social Club
Address: 46 Baronscourt Terrace
Edinburgh EH8 7EP

#439
Waterside Arts
Category: Art Gallery
Area: Leith
Address: 83 Henderson Street
Edinburgh EH6 6ED
Phone: 0131 555 5628

#440
Post Office Sports & Social Club
Category: Social Club
Address: 5 Restalrig Drive
Edinburgh EH7 6JX

#441
S M A S C C
Category: Social Club
Area: Morningside
Address: 116 Comiston Road
Edinburgh EH10 5QN
Phone: 0131 447 6800

#442
Silkcart Art Gallery
Category: Art Gallery
Area: Morningside
Address: 140 Comiston Road
Edinburgh EH10 5QN
Phone: 0131 446 3555

#443
Wardie Residents Club
Category: Social Club
Area: Leith
Address: 125 Granton Road
Edinburgh EH5 3NJ
Phone: 0131 552 2446

#444
Art From Scotland
Category: Print Media, Art Gallery
Area: Leith
Address: 65 Shore
Edinburgh EH6 6RA
Phone: 0131 555 5580

#445
The Leith Gallery
Category: Art Gallery
Area: Leith
Address: 65 The Shore
Edinburgh EH6 6RA
Phone: 0131 553 5255

#446
Feltusfecit
Category: Theatre
Address: Moat Drive
Edinburgh EH14 1NS

#447
Methinks
Category: Theatre
Area: Leith
Address: 60 Constitution Street
Edinburgh EH6 6RR
Phone: 01835 863725

#448
Blink Red
Category: Art Gallery
Area: Leith
Address: 40 Maritime Street
Edinburgh EH6 6JA
Phone: 0131 625 0192

#449
Federation Of Scottish Theatre
Category: Theatre
Area: Leith
Address: 46 Shore
Edinburgh EH6 6QU
Phone: 0131 467 2525

#450
National Museum Of Scotland
Category: Museum
Area: Leith
Address: Commercial St
Edinburgh EH6 6JA
Phone: 0131 553 7679

#451
Leith Franklin Academical Cricket Club
Category: Sports Club, Stadium
Area: Leith
Address: 1 Leith Links
Edinburgh EH6 7QR
Phone: 0131 554 5832

#452
Stills
Category: Art Gallery
Area: Old Town, Royal Mile
Address: 23 Cockburn Street
Edinburgh EH1 1BP
Phone: 0131 622 6200

#453
Granton Centre
Category: Museum
Address: 242 West Granton Road
Edinburgh EH5 1JA

#454
The National Museum Collection Centre
Category: Museum
Address: 242 West Granton Road
Edinburgh EH5 1JA

#455
Cineworld Cinema
Category: Cinema
Address: 130/3 Dundee Street
Edinburgh EH11 1AF

#456
RBS Museum Late Night- National Museum Of Scotland
Category: Museum
Area: Old Town, Newington
Address: Chambers Street
Edinburgh EH1
Phone: 0131 247 4128

#457
B&D's Kitchen
Category: Cantonese,
Art Gallery
Area: Haymarket
Address: 214 dalry road
Edinburgh EH11 2ES
Phone: 0131 261 9248

#458
Art Et Facts
Category: Framing, Art Gallery
Area: Haymarket
Address: 19 Roseburn Terrace
Edinburgh EH12 5NG
Phone: 0131 346 7730

#459
Majestic Wine Warehouse
Category: Winery
Area: Leith
Address: 200 Leith Walk
Edinburgh EH6 5EQ
Phone: 0131 554 0177

#460
The Scotch Malt Whisky Society
Category: Social Club
Area: New Town
Address: 28 Queen Street
Edinburgh EH2 1JX
Phone: 0131 554 3451

#461
Scottish National Portrait Gallery
Category: Art Gallery
Area: New Town
Address: 1 Queen St
Edinburgh EH2 1JD
Phone: 0131 624 6200

#462
The Henderson Gallery
Category: Art Gallery
Area: New Town
Address: 4 Thistle St Ln NW
Edinburgh EH2 1DA
Phone: 0131 225 7464

#463
The Store
Category: Music Venues
Area: Newington
Address: 37 Guthrie St
Edinburgh EH8 9
Phone: 0131 220 2987

#464
Cafe Lucia
Category: Theatre
Area: Newington
Address: 13/29 Nicolson Street
Edinburgh EH8 9FT
Phone: 0131 667 2765

#465
The Edinburgh Philosophy and Psychology Group
Category: Social Club
Area: Newington
Address: 6a Nicolson Street
Edinburgh EH8 9DH

#466
The Crack
Category: Festival, Theatre
Area: Old Town
Address: Assembly at Princes Street Garden, Edinburgh EH2 2AN
Phone: 0131 623 3030

#467
Meow Meow
Category: Theatre, Jazz & Blues
Area: Old Town
Address: Assembley at Princes Street Garden, Edinburgh EH2 2AN
Phone: 0131 623 3030

#468
Saltire Taverns
Category: Club, Music Venues
Area: Old Town
Address: 25 George Iv Bridge
Edinburgh EH1 1EN
Phone: 0131 225 0760

#469
Bedlam Theatre
Category: Theatre
Area: Old Town
Address: 11B Bristo Place
Edinburgh EH1 1EZ
Phone: 0131 629 0430

#470
Warburton Gallery
Category: Art Gallery
Area: Old Town, Grassmarket
Address: 8 Victoria Street
Old Town EH1 2HG

#471
The Red Door Gallery
Category: Art Gallery
Area: Old Town, Royal Mile
Address: 42 Victoria Street
Edinburgh EH1 2JW
Phone: 0131 477 3255

#472
The Fruitmarket Gallery
Category: Art Gallery
Area: Old Town, Royal Mile
Address: 45 Market Street
Edinburgh EH1 1DF
Phone: 0131 225 2383

#473
Edinburgh Art Festival Information Center
Category: Festival
Area: Old Town, Royal Mile
Address: 22-28 Cockburn St
Edinburgh EH1 1NY

#474
Collective Gallery
Category: Art Gallery
Area: Old Town, Royal Mile
Address: 22-28 Cockburn Street
Edinburgh EH1 1NY
Phone: 0131 220 1260

#475
Best of The Fest
Category: Festival, Theatre
Address: Assembly at George Street Music Hall Edinburgh, Midlothian

#476
Alpha Art Gallery
Category: Art Gallery
Area: Stockbridge
Address: 52 Hamilton Place
Edinburgh EH3 5AX
Phone: 0131 226 3066

#477
Scottish National Gallery
of Modern Art
Category: Art Gallery, Museum
Area: West End
Address: 75 Belford Road
Edinburgh EH4 3DR
Phone: 0131 624 6200

#478
Dean Gallery
Category: Art Gallery
Area: West End
Address: 73 Belford Road
Edinburgh EH4 3DS
Phone: 0131 624 6200

#479
Craigmillar Park
Attention: Mr Barry Knowles
Category: Golf
Address: 1 Observatory Road
Edinburgh EH9

#480
McFities
Category: Sports & Leisure
Area: Leith
Address: Newhaven Scout Hut Newhaven
Lane
Edinburgh EH6
Phone: 0131 551 6051

#481
Portobello F P Rugby
Football Club
Category: Sports Club
Address: 129 Duddingston Road West
Edinburgh EH15 3QE

#482
Rainbowlight Yoga
Category: Yoga
Area: Leith
Address: 90/5 Constitution St
Edinburgh EH6 6RP
Phone: 01447 9557 34321

#483
Seafield Bowling Club
Category: Sports Club
Area: Leith
Address: 3 East Links
Edinburgh EH6 7QR
Phone: 0131 554 2372

#484
Victoria Park
Category: Park
Area: Leith
Address: Newhaven Rd
Edinburgh EH6 5PY
Phone: 0131 529 5050

#485
Artroom32
Category: Kids Activities
Area: Leith
Address: 32 Madeira Street
Edinburgh EH6 4AL
Phone: 0131 553 6798

#486
Edinburgh Kettlebell Club
Category: Fitness, Weight Loss Centre
Address: Abercorn Crescent
Edinburgh EH8 7HZ

#487
Tonic Health
Category: Gym
Area: Leith
Address: 41 Commercial Street
Edinburgh EH6 6JD
Phone: 0131 554 6161

#488
GoesWell
Category: Dance Studio
Area: Leith
Address: The Granary
Edinburgh EH6 6QN
Phone: 07940 091638

#489
Bainfield Bowling & Social Club
Category: Sports Club
Address: 34 Hutchison Crossway
Edinburgh EH14 1RU

#490
Zumba Fitness with Laura
Category: Personal Trainers
Address: 28 York Place
Edinburgh EH1 3

#491
Elite Sport Training
Category: Swimming Lessons/School
Address: 17 North Bridge
Edinburgh EH1 1

#492
You Work We Walk
Category: Dog Park, Dog Walkers, Kennels
& Pet Sitting
Address: 19 Hazeldean Terrace
Edinburgh EH16 5RU

#493
Yoga in Edinburgh
Category: Yoga
Address: West Granton Road
Edinburgh EH4 4UP

#494
Edinburgh Golf Shop
Category: Golf
Area: New Town
Address: 3-5 Hanover Street
Edinburgh EH2 2DL
Phone: 0131 225 9494

#495
Discover Swimming
Category: Fitness, Instruction
Area: Old Town
Address: 80 Lauriston Place
Edinburgh EH3 9DE
Phone: 0845 459 1029

#496
Brazilian Soccer
Category: Fitness, Instruction
Area: Old Town, Newington
Address: South Bridge Edinburgh

#497
Evolve Health & Fitness
Category: Leisure Centre
Area: Leith
Address: 21 Pirniefield Bank
Edinburgh EH6 7QQ
Phone: 0131 555 7044

#498
Living Well
Category: Gym
Area: New Town
Address: 4 Princes Street
Edinburgh EH1 2AB
Phone: 0131 222 8836

#499
Lothian Amusements
Category: Amusement Park
Area: Old Town
Address: 23 Bread Street
Edinburgh EH3 9AL
Phone: 0131 228 6997

#500
**The Tone Zone Health
& Fitness Studio**
Category: Gym
Area: Old Town
Address: 22 Bread Street
Edinburgh EH3 9AF
Phone: 0131 228 2427

TOP 500 NIGHTLIFE

The Most Recommended by Locals & Trevelers
(From #1 to #500)

#1
Bramble Bar
Category: Bar
Average price: Expensive
Area: New Town
Address: 16A Queen Street
Edinburgh EH2 1JE
Phone: 0131 226 6343

#2
The Jazz Bar
Category: Pub, Jazz & Blues
Average price: Modest
Area: Old Town, Newington
Address: 1A Chambers Street
Edinburgh EH1 1HR
Phone: 0131 220 4298

#3
The Hanging Bat Beer Cafe
Category: Pub
Average price: Modest
Area: Old Town, West End
Address: 133 Lothian Road
Edinburgh EH3
Phone: 0131 229 0759

#4
BrewDog
Category: Pub, Burgers, Pizza
Average price: Modest
Area: Old Town, Newington
Address: 143 Cowgate
Edinburgh EH1 1JS
Phone: 0131 220 6517

#5
Brass Monkey
Category: Pub, Sandwiches, Lounge
Average price: Modest
Area: Newington
Address: 14 Drummond Street
Edinburgh EH8 9TU
Phone: 0131 556 1961

#6
The Dome
Category: Champagne Bar
Average price: Expensive
Area: New Town
Address: 14 George Street
Edinburgh EH2 2PF
Phone: 0131 624 8624

#7
Thistle Street Bar
Category: Pub
Average price: Modest
Area: New Town
Address: 39 Thistle Street
Edinburgh EH2 1DY
Phone: 0131 478 7029

#8
Dragonfly
Category: Wine Bar, Lounge
Average price: Modest
Area: Old Town
Address: 52 W Port Street
Edinburgh EH1 2LD
Phone: 0131 228 4543

#9
The Last Word Saloon
Category: Bar
Average price: Modest
Area: Stockbridge, New Town
Address: 44 Saint Stephen Street
Edinburgh EH3 5AL
Phone: 0131 225 9009

#10
Stand Comedy Club
Category: Comedy Club
Average price: Modest
Area: New Town
Address: 5 York Place
Edinburgh EH1 3EB
Phone: 0131 558 7373

#11
The Bon Vivant
Category: European, Wine Bar,
Tapas/Small Plates
Average price: Modest
Area: New Town
Address: 55 Thistle Street
Edinburgh EH2 1DY
Phone: 0131 225 3275

#12
Panda & Sons
Category: Cocktail Bar
Average price: Expensive
Area: New Town
Address: 79 Queen Street
Edinburgh EH2 4NF
Phone: 0131 220 0443

#13
The Devil's Advocate
Category: Pub, Gastropub
Average price: Modest
Area: Old Town, Royal Mile
Address: 9 Advocate Close
Edinburgh EH1 1ND
Phone: 0131 225 4465

#14
Victoria
Category: Pub
Average price: Modest
Area: Leith
Address: 265 Leith Walk
Edinburgh EH6 8PD
Phone: 0131 555 1638

#15
Bar Kohl
Category: Pub, Burgers, Cocktail Bar
Average price: Modest
Area: Old Town
Address: 54 George IV Bridge
Edinburgh EH1 1EJ
Phone: 0131 225 6936

#16
Edinburgh Playhouse
Category: Theatre, Music Venues
Average price: Expensive
Area: New Town
Address: 18-22 Greenside Place
Edinburgh EH1 3AA
Phone: 0131 524 3333

#17
Queens Arms
Category: Pub
Average price: Modest
Area: New Town
Address: 49 Frederick Street
Edinburgh EH2 1EP
Phone: 0131 225 1045

#18
Treacle
Category: Bar, Gastropub
Average price: Modest
Area: New Town
Address: 39 Broughton Street
Edinburgh EH1 3JU
Phone: 0131 557 0627

#19
The Bow Bar
Category: Pub
Average price: Modest
Area: Old Town, Grassmarket
Address: 80 West Bow
Edinburgh EH1 2HH
Phone: 0131 226 7667

#20
Scotsman Hotel
Category: Hotel, Bar
Average price: Expensive
Area: Old Town, Royal Mile
Address: 20 N Bridge
Edinburgh EH1 1YT
Phone: 0131 556 5565

#21
The Voodoo Rooms
Category: Lounge, Music Venues
Average price: Expensive
Area: New Town
Address: 19A West Register Street
Edinburgh EH2 2AA
Phone: 0131 556 7060

#22
Cabaret Voltaire
Category: Club, Music Venues
Average price: Modest
Area: Old Town, Newington
Address: 36-38 Blair Street
Edinburgh EH1 1QR
Phone: 0131 247 4704

#23
Blackwood's Bar & Grill
Category: Scottish, Bar
Average price: Expensive
Area: New Town
Address: 10 Gloucester Place
Edinburgh EH3 6EF
Phone: 0131 225 2720

#24
Regent Bar
Category: Pub
Average price: Modest
Area: Old Town
Address: 2 Montrose Terrace
Edinburgh EH7 5DL
Phone: 0131 661 8198

#25
Guildford Arms
Category: Pub, British
Average price: Modest
Area: New Town
Address: 1-5 W Register Street
Edinburgh EH2 2AA
Phone: 0131 556 4312

#26
Sandy Bell's
Category: Pub
Average price: Modest
Area: Old Town
Address: 25 Forrest Road
Edinburgh EH1 2QH
Phone: 0131 225 2751

#27
Secret Arcade
Category: Lounge, British, Cocktail Bar
Average price: Modest
Area: Old Town, Royal Mile
Address: 48 Cockburn Street
Edinburgh EH1 1PB
Phone: 0131 220 1297

#28
The Basement
Category: Pub, British, Mexican
Average price: Expensive
Area: New Town
Address: 10a-12a Broughton Street
Edinburgh EH1 3RH
Phone: 0131 557 0097

#29
Brass Monkey Leith
Category: Pub, British
Average price: Modest
Area: Leith
Address: 362 Leith Walk
Edinburgh EH6 5BR
Phone: 0131 554 5286

#30
Kay's Bar
Category: Pub
Average price: Modest
Area: New Town
Address: 39 Jamaica Street West
Edinburgh EH3 6HF
Phone: 0131 225 1858

#31
Royal Lyceum Theatre
Category: Theatre, Music Venues
Average price: Modest
Area: Old Town
Address: 30b Grindlay Street
Edinburgh EH3 9
Phone: 0131 248 4848

#32
Roseleaf
Category: Pub
Average price: Modest
Area: Leith
Address: 23/24 Sandport Place
Edinburgh EH6 6EW
Phone: 0131 476 5268

#33
Festival Theatre Edinburgh
Category: Music Venues
Average price: Modest
Area: Newington
Address: 13-29 Nicolson Street
Edinburgh EH8 9FT
Phone: 0131 529 6000

#34
Hectors
Category: Pub
Average price: Expensive
Area: Stockbridge
Address: 47-49 Deanhaugh Street
Edinburgh EH4 1LR
Phone: 0131 343 1735

#35
Usher Hall
Category: Music Venues
Average price: Modest
Area: Old Town, West End
Address: Lothian Road
Edinburgh EH1 2EA
Phone: 0131 228 1155

#36
Jekyll & Hyde
Category: Pub
Average price: Modest
Area: New Town
Address: 112 Hanover Street
Edinburgh EH2 1DR
Phone: 0131 225 2022

#37
Under the Stairs
Category: Lounge, Gastropub
Average price: Modest
Area: Old Town
Address: 3A Merchant Street
Edinburgh EH1 2QD
Phone: 0131 466 8550

#38
The Green Mantle
Category: Lounge, Pub, European
Average price: Inexpensive
Area: Newington
Address: 44 W Crosscauseway
Edinburgh EH8 9JP
Phone: 0131 662 8741

#39
Teuchters Landing
Category: Gastropub, Wine Bar
Average price: Modest
Area: Leith
Address: 1a and 1c Dock Place
Edinburgh EH6 6LU
Phone: 0131 5547 4272

#40
No 12 Picardy Place
Category: Hotel, Lounge, European
Average price: Expensive
Area: New Town
Address: 12 Picardy Place
Edinburgh EH1 3JT
Phone: 0131 555 1289

#41
The Vintage
Category: Gastropub, Pub
Average price: Modest
Area: Leith
Address: 60 Henderson Street
Edinburgh EH6
Phone: 0131 563 5293

#42
HMV Picture House
Category: Club, Music Venues
Average price: Modest
Area: Old Town
Address: 31 Lothian Road
Edinburgh EH1 2DJ
Phone: 0131 221 2280

#43
Blue Blazer
Category: Pub
Average price: Modest
Area: Old Town
Address: 2 Spittal Street
Edinburgh EH3 9DX
Phone: 0131 229 5030

#44
Tigerlily
Category: Wine Bar, Hotel
Average price: Expensive
Area: New Town
Address: 125 George St
Edinburgh EH3 5AG
Phone: 0131 225 5005

#45
Oz Bar
Category: Pub, Sports Bar
Average price: Inexpensive
Area: Old Town
Address: 33 Candlemaker Row
Edinburgh EH1 2QG
Phone: 0131 226 7190

#46
Sofi's
Category: Pub
Average price: Modest
Area: Leith
Address: 65 Henderson Street
Edinburgh EH6 6ED
Phone: 0131 555 7019

#47
Tonic
Category: Gastropub, Cocktail Bar
Average price: Expensive
Area: New Town
Address: 34a North Castle Street
Edinburgh EH2 3BN
Phone: 0131 225 6431

#48
Iglu
Category: Pub, Gastropub
Average price: Modest
Area: New Town
Address: 2 Jamaica St
Edinburgh EH3 6HH
Phone: 0131 476 5333

#49
Jake's Place
Category: Pub
Average price: Modest
Area: Old Town, Royal Mile
Address: 9-13 Market Street
Edinburgh EH1 1DE
Phone: 0131 226 1446

#50
The Wee Red Bar
Category: Pub, Club
Average price: Modest
Area: Old Town
Address: 74 Lauriston Place
Edinburgh EH3 9DF
Phone: 0131 651 5859

#51
The Blind Poet
Category: Pub
Average price: Modest
Area: Newington
Address: 32 W Nicolson Street
Edinburgh EH8 9DD
Phone: 0131 667 4268

#52
Opium Nightclub
Category: Club
Average price: Inexpensive
Area: Old Town
Address: 71 Cowgate
Edinburgh EH1 1JW
Phone: 0131 225 8382

#53
Nobles Cafe Bar & Venue
Category: Gastropub, Music Venues
Average price: Modest
Area: Leith
Address: 44a Constitution Street
Edinburgh EH6 6RS
Phone: 0131 629 7215

#54
The Black Rose Tavern
Category: Pub
Average price: Modest
Area: New Town
Address: 49 Rose Street
Edinburgh EH2 2NH
Phone: 0131 220 0414

#55
The Cuckoo's Nest
Category: Pub
Average price: Inexpensive
Area: Tollcross
Address: 69 Home Street
Edinburgh EH3 9JP
Phone: 0131 629 0424

#56
Henry's Cellar Bar
Category: Music Venues
Average price: Modest
Area: West End
Address: 8-16 Morrison Street
Edinburgh EH3 8BJ
Phone: 0131 629 4101

#57
Canny Man's
Category: Pub
Average price: Modest
Area: Morningside
Address: 237 Morningside Road
Edinburgh EH10 4QU
Phone: 0131 447 1484

#58
Browns
Category: Wine Bar, Gastropub
Average price: Modest
Area: New Town
Address: 131-133 George Street
Edinburgh EH2 4JS
Phone: 0131 225 4442

#59
Cloisters Bar
Category: Pub, British
Average price: Modest
Area: Tollcross, The Meadows
Address: 26 Brougham Street
Edinburgh EH3 9JH
Phone: 0131 221 9997

#60
Tourmalet
Category: Pub
Average price: Modest
Area: Leith
Address: 25 Buchanan Street
Edinburgh EH6 8SQ
Phone: 0131 555 4387

#61
Greyfriars Bobby's Bar
Category: Pub, British
Average price: Modest
Area: Old Town
Address: 30-34 Candlemaker Row
Edinburgh EH1 2QE
Phone: 0131 225 8328

#62
The Black Cat
Category: Bar
Average price: Modest
Area: New Town
Address: 168 Rose Street
Edinburgh EH2 4BA
Phone: 0131 225 3349

#63
The Brauhaus
Category: Pub
Average price: Expensive
Area: Old Town
Address: 105 Lauriston Place
Edinburgh EH3 9JG
Phone: 0131 629 5434

#64
The Auld Hoose
Category: Pub, British
Average price: Modest
Area: Newington
Address: 23-25 St Leonard's Street
Edinburgh EH8 9QN
Phone: 0131 668 2934

#65
The Abbotsford
Category: Pub, European
Average price: Modest
Area: New Town
Address: 3-5 Rose Street
Edinburgh EH2 2PR
Phone: 0131 225 5276

#66
Royal Oak
Category: Pub
Average price: Expensive
Area: Old Town, Newington
Address: 1 Infirmary Street
Edinburgh EH1 1LT
Phone: 0131 557 2976

#67
Queen S Hall Edinburgh
Category: Music Venues
Average price: Expensive
Area: Newington
Address: 85-89 Clerk Street
Edinburgh EH8
Phone: 0131 668 3456

#68
Out of the Blue
Category: Music Venues
Average price: Inexpensive
Area: Leith
Address: 36 Dalmeny St
Edinburgh EH6 8RG
Phone: 0131 555 7100

#69
Scotsman's Lounge
Category: Pub, Music Venues
Average price: Modest
Area: Old Town
Address: 73 Cockburn Street
Edinburgh EH1 1BU
Phone: 0131 225 7726

#70
Cask & Barrel
Category: Pub
Average price: Modest
Area: New Town
Address: 115 Broughton Street
Edinburgh EH1 3RZ
Phone: 0131 556 3132

#71
The Southern
Category: Pub, Gastropub
Average price: Modest
Area: Newington
Address: 22-26 South Clerk Street
Edinburgh EH8 9PR
Phone: 0131 662 8926

#72
Red Squirrel
Category: Pub
Average price: Modest
Area: Old Town
Address: 21 Lothian Road
Edinburgh EH1 2
Phone: 0131 229 9933

#73
The Orchard
Category: Bar, British
Average price: Modest
Area: Stockbridge
Address: 1-2 Howard Place
Edinburgh EH3 5JZ
Phone: 0131 550 0850

#74
Thomson's Bar
Category: Pub
Average price: Inexpensive
Area: West End
Address: 182-184 Morrison Street
Edinburgh EH3 8EB
Phone: 0131 228 5700

#75
Teuchters
Category: Pub
Average price: Modest
Area: West End
Address: 26 William Street
Edinburgh EH3 7NH
Phone: 0131 225 2973

#76
GHQ
Category: Gay Bar, Club
Average price: Inexpensive
Area: New Town
Address: 4 Picardy Place
Edinburgh EH1 3JT
Phone: 0845 166 6024

#77
Hotel du Vin & Bistro Edinburgh
Category: Hotel, European,
French, Wine Bar
Average price: Exclusive
Area: Old Town
Address: 11 Bristo Place
Edinburgh EH1 1EZ
Phone: 0131 247 4900

#78
Malones Irish Bar
Category: Pub, Music Venues, Irish
Average price: Modest
Area: Old Town
Address: 14 Forrest Road
Edinburgh EH1 2QN
Phone: 0131 226 5954

#79
Amicus Apple
Category: Pub
Average price: Modest
Area: New Town
Address: 17 Frederick Street
Edinburgh EH2 2EY
Phone: 0131 226 6055

#80
The Meadow Bar
Category: Pub
Average price: Modest
Area: Newington
Address: 42-44 Buccleuch Street
Edinburgh EH8 9LP
Phone: 0131 667 6907

#81
Old Bell Inn
Category: Pub
Average price: Modest
Area: Newington
Address: 233-235 Causewayside
Edinburgh EH9 1PH
Phone: 0131 668 1573

#82
The Royal Dick Bar
Category: Bar
Average price: Modest
Area: Newington
Address: 1 Summerhall
Edinburgh EH9 1PL
Phone: 0131 560 1572

#83
Sygn
Category: Bar, Gastropub
Average price: Modest
Area: New Town
Address: 15 Charlotte Lane
Edinburgh EH2 4QZ
Phone: 0131 225 6060

#84
Liquid Room
Category: Club, Music Venues
Average price: Inexpensive
Area: Old Town, Grassmarket
Address: 9c Victoria Street
Edinburgh EH1 2HE
Phone: 0131 225 2564

#85
The Kenilworth
Category: Pub
Average price: Modest
Area: New Town
Address: 152-154 Rose Street
Edinburgh EH2 3JD
Phone: 0131 226 1773

#86
McEwan Hall
Category: Comedy Club
Average price: Modest
Area: Newington
Address: Bristo Square
Edinburgh EH8 9AL
Phone: 0131 650 4381

#87
Lebowskis
Category: Bar, Gastropub, Burgers
Average price: Modest
Area: West End
Address: 18 Morrison St
Edinburgh EH3 8BJ
Phone: 0131 466 1779

#88
Dirty Dick's
Category: Pub
Average price: Inexpensive
Area: New Town
Address: 159 Rose Street
Edinburgh EH2 4LS
Phone: 0131 260 9920

#89
All Bar One
Category: Wine Bar
Average price: Modest
Area: New Town
Address: 29 George Street
Edinburgh EH2 2PA
Phone: 0131 226 9971

#90
The Huxley
Category: Bar, Gastropub
Average price: Modest
Area: West End
Address: 1 Rutland Street
Edinburgh EH1 2AE
Phone: 0131 229 3402

#91
The Banshee Labyrinth
Category: Pub
Average price: Modest
Area: Old Town, Newington
Address: 29-35 Niddry Street
Edinburgh EH1 1LG
Phone: 0131 558 8209

#92
52 Canoes Tiki Den
Category: Bar, British
Average price: Modest
Area: New Town, West End
Address: 13-14 Melville Place
Edinburgh EH3 8PR
Phone: 0131 226 4732

#93
The Tron
Category: Pub
Average price: Modest
Area: Old Town, Newington, Royal Mile
Address: 9 Hunter Square
Edinburgh EH1 1QW
Phone: 0131 225 3784

#94
Monteiths Restaurant
Category: Wine Bar, European
Average price: Expensive
Area: Old Town, Royal Mile
Address: 61 High Street
Edinburgh EH1 1SR
Phone: 0131 557 0330

#95
**Michael Neave Kitchen
and Whisky Bar**
Category: British, Bar
Average price: Expensive
Area: Old Town, Newington
Address: 21 Old Fishmarket Close
Edinburgh EH1 1RW
Phone: 0131 226 4747

#96
The Cambridge Bar
Category: Pub
Average price: Modest
Area: New Town
Address: 20 Young Street
Edinburgh EH2 4JB
Phone: 0131 226 2120

#97
99 Hanover Street
Category: Wine Bar, Gastropub
Average price: Modest
Area: New Town
Address: 99 Hanover Street
Edinburgh EH2 1DJ
Phone: 0131 226 2872

#98
Electric Circus
Category: Karaoke, Music Venues
Average price: Modest
Area: Old Town, Royal Mile
Address: 36-39 Market Street
Edinburgh EH1 1DF
Phone: 0131 226 4224

#99
Argyle Bar
Category: Pub
Average price: Expensive
Area: Marchmont
Address: 15-17 Argyle Place
Edinburgh EH9 1JJ
Phone: 0131 221 9759

#100
Star Bar
Category: Pub
Average price: Expensive
Area: New Town
Address: 1 Northumberland Place
Edinburgh EH3 6LQ
Phone: 0131 539 8070

#101
Tolbooth Tavern
Category: Pub
Average price: Modest
Area: Old Town, Royal Mile
Address: 167 Canongate
Edinburgh EH8 8BN
Phone: 0131 556 5348

#102
Studio 24
Category: Club, Music Venues
Average price: Modest
Area: Old Town
Address: 24-26 Calton Road
Edinburgh EH8 8
Phone: 0131 558 3758

#103
The Hive
Category: Club
Average price: Inexpensive
Area: Old Town, Newington
Address: 15-17 Niddry Street
Edinburgh EH1 1LG
Phone: 0131 556 0444

#104
Boda Bar
Category: Pub
Average price: Modest
Area: Leith
Address: Leith Walk
Edinburgh EH6 8NX
Phone: 0131 554 5880

#105
Malt & Hops
Category: Pub
Average price: Modest
Area: Leith
Address: 45 Shore
Edinburgh EH6 6QU
Phone: 0131 555 0083

#106
Boda
Category: Bar
Average price: Modest
Area: Leith
Address: 229 Leith Walk
Edinburgh EH6 8NY
Phone: 0131 553 5900

#107
Whistle Binkies
Category: Pub
Average price: Expensive
Area: Old Town, Newington, Royal Mile
Address: 4-6 S Bridge
Edinburgh EH1 1LL
Phone: 0131 557 5114

#108
Ghillie Dhu
Category: Wine Bar, British, Pub
Average price: Expensive
Area: West End
Address: 2-6 Rutland Place
Edinburgh EH1 2AD
Phone: 0131 222 9930

#109
Henrick's Bar
Category: Bar
Average price: Modest
Area: Bruntsfield, The Meadows
Address: 1-3 Barclay Place
Edinburgh EH10 4HW
Phone: 0131 229 2442

#110
Conan Doyle
Category: Pub
Average price: Modest
Area: New Town
Address: 71-73 York Place
Edinburgh EH1 3JD
Phone: 0131 557 9539

#111
The Doric
Category: Pub
Average price: Expensive
Area: Old Town, Royal Mile
Address: 15-16 Market Street
Edinburgh EH1 1DE
Phone: 0131 225 1084

#112
Negociants
Category: Pub, Gastropub
Average price: Modest
Area: Old Town, Newington
Address: 45-47 Lothian Street
Edinburgh EH11 1HB
Phone: 0131 225 6313

#113
Deacon Brodies Tavern
Category: Pub
Average price: Modest
Area: Old Town, Royal Mile
Address: 435 Lawnmarket
Edinburgh EH1 2NT
Phone: 0131 225 6531

#114
La Garrigue
Category: French, Wine Bar
Average price: Modest
Area: Old Town, Royal Mile
Address: 31 Jeffrey Street
Edinburgh EH1 1DH
Phone: 0131 557 3032

#115
Earl Of Marchmont
Category: Pub
Average price: Modest
Area: Marchmont
Address: 22 Marchmont Cresent
Edinburgh EH9 1HG
Phone: 0131 662 1877

#116
Kilderkin
Category: Pub
Average price: Modest
Area: Old Town, Royal Mile
Address: 65/67 Canongate
Edinburgh EH8 8BT
Phone: 0131 556 2101

#117
Whighams Wine Cellars
Category: Wine Bar
Average price: Modest
Area: New Town
Address: 13 Hope Street
Edinburgh EH2 4EL
Phone: 0131 225 8674

#118
Bar Missoni
Category: Lounge
Average price: Expensive
Area: Old Town, Royal Mile
Address: 1 George IV Bridge
Edinburgh EH1 1AD
Phone: 0131 220 6666

#119
The Queens Hall
Category: Music Venues
Average price: Modest
Area: Newington
Address: 85-89 Clerk Street
Edinburgh EH8 9JG
Phone: 0131 668 2019

#120
Bennets Bar
Category: Pub
Average price: Modest
Area: Bruntsfield, The Meadows
Address: 8 Leven Street
Edinburgh EH3 9LG
Phone: 0131 229 5143

#121
The Cocktail Emporium
Category: Bar
Average price: Expensive
Area: New Town
Address: 44 Broughton Street
Edinburgh EH1 3SA
Phone: 0131 557 6819

#122
The Bongo Club
Category: Club, Music Venues
Average price: Inexpensive
Area: Old Town
Address: 66 Cowgate
Edinburgh EH1 1JX
Phone: 0131 558 8844

#123
Malt Shovel
Category: Pub, Local Flavour
Average price: Modest
Area: Old Town, Royal Mile
Address: 11-15 Cockburn Street
Edinburgh EH1 1BP
Phone: 0131 225 6843

#124
The Cumberland Bar
Category: Pub
Average price: Modest
Area: New Town
Address: 1 - 3 Cumberland Street
Edinburgh EH3 6RT
Phone: 0131 558 3134

#125
The Mitre
Category: Pub
Average price: Modest
Area: Old Town, Royal Mile
Address: 133 High Street
Edinburgh EH1 1SG
Phone: 0131 652 3902

#126
Mithas
Category: Indian, Cocktail Bar
Average price: Exclusive
Area: Leith
Address: 7 Dock Place
Edinburgh EH6 6LU
Phone: 0131 554 0008

#127
The Newsroom
Category: Wine Bar, Pub
Average price: Modest
Area: New Town
Address: 5 Leith Street
Edinburgh EH1 3AT
Phone: 0131 557 5830

#128
Frankenstein
Category: Pub
Average price: Inexpensive
Area: Old Town
Address: 26 George IV Bridge
Edinburgh EH1 1EN
Phone: 0131 622 1818

#129
Castle Arms
Category: Pub
Average price: Expensive
Area: Old Town
Address: 6 Johnston Terrace
Edinburgh EH1 2PW
Phone: 0131 225 7432

#130
Milne's Bar
Category: Wine Bar, Pub
Average price: Modest
Area: New Town
Address: 35 Hanover Street
Edinburgh EH2 2PJ
Phone: 0131 225 6738

#131
The Advocate
Category: Pub, Gastropub
Average price: Inexpensive
Area: Old Town, Newington
Address: 7 Hunter Square
Edinburgh EH1 1QW
Phone: 0131 226 2749

#132
Belushi's
Category: Sports Bar, Pub
Average price: Modest
Area: Old Town, Royal Mile
Address: 9-13 Market Street
Edinburgh EH1 1DE
Phone: 0131 226 1446

#133
Assembly Roxy
Category: Music Venues, Theatre
Average price: Modest
Area: Newington
Address: 2 Roxburgh Place
Edinburgh EH8 9SU
Phone: 0871 750 0077

#134
The Chanter
Category: Pub
Average price: Expensive
Area: Old Town
Address: 30 - 32 Bread Street
Edinburgh EH3 9AF
Phone: 0131 221 0575

#135
John Leslie
Category: Pub
Average price: Modest
Area: Newington
Address: 45 Ratcliffe Terrace
Edinburgh EH9 1SU
Phone: 0131 667 7205

#136
Element
Category: Pub, Lounge
Average price: Modest
Area: New Town
Address: 110-114 Rose Street
Edinburgh EH2 3JF
Phone: 0131 225 3297

#137
Captains Bar
Category: Pub
Average price: Modest
Area: Old Town, Newington
Address: 4 S College St
Edinburgh EH8 9AA
Phone: 0131 668 2312

#138
Room at 34
Category: Lounge
Average price: Modest
Area: Newington
Address: 32 Potterrow
Edinburgh EH8 9BT
Phone: 0131 662 9960

#139
Candy Bar
Category: Pub, Wine Bar
Average price: Modest
Area: New Town
Address: 113-115 George St
Edinburgh EH2 4JN
Phone: 0131 225 9179

#140
The Magnum
Category: Pub, British
Average price: Expensive
Area: New Town
Address: 1 Albany Street
Edinburgh EH1 3PY
Phone: 0131 557 4366

#141
The Lioness of Leith
Category: Lounge, British, Cocktail Bar
Average price: Modest
Area: Leith
Address: 21-25 Duke Street
Edinburgh EH6 8HH
Phone: 0131 629 0580

#142
Compass Bar
Category: Pub, British
Average price: Modest
Area: Leith
Address: 44 Queen Charlotte Street
Edinburgh EH6 7EX
Phone: 0131 554 1979

#143
Medina
Category: Bar, Music Venues
Average price: Inexpensive
Area: Old Town, Newington
Address: 45-47 Lothian Street
Edinburgh EH1 1HB
Phone: 0131 220 4287

#144
The Potting Shed
Category: Pub
Average price: Modest
Area: Newington
Address: 32 Potterow
Edinburgh EH8 9BT
Phone: 0131 668 2810

#145
Drouthy Neebors
Category: Pub
Average price: Modest
Area: Newington
Address: 1-2 West Preston Street
Edinburgh EH8 9PX
Phone: 0131 662 9617

#146
Oxford Bar
Category: Pub
Average price: Inexpensive
Area: New Town
Address: 8 Young Street
Edinburgh EH2 4JB
Phone: 0131 539 7119

#147
Walkabout Inn/Jongleurs
Category: Comedy Club
Average price: Expensive
Area: New Town
Address: Unit 6/7 Omni Leisure Developme
Greenside Place
Edinburgh EH1 3AA
Phone: 0870 428 9617

#148
Canon's Gait
Category: Pub
Average price: Modest
Area: Old Town, Royal Mile
Address: 232 Canongate
Edinburgh EH8 8DQ
Phone: 0131 556 4481

#149
The Antiquary
Category: Bar
Average price: Modest
Area: Stockbridge, New Town
Address: 72-78 St Stephen Street
Edinburgh EH3 5AQ
Phone: 0131 225 2858

#150
Lock 25
Category: Pub
Average price: Modest
Area: West End
Address: 85-87 Fountainbridge
Edinburgh EH3 9QA
Phone: 0131 228 8831

#151
The Peartree House
Category: Pub
Average price: Expensive
Area: Newington
Address: 38 West Nicolson Street
Edinburgh EH8 9DD
Phone: 0131 667 7533

#152
Shakespeare's Bar
Category: Pub
Average price: Inexpensive
Area: Old Town
Address: 65 Lothian Road
Edinburgh EH1 2DJ
Phone: 0131 228 8400

#153
The Standing Order
Category: Pub
Average price: Inexpensive
Area: New Town
Address: 62-66 George Street
Edinburgh EH2 2LR
Phone: 0131 225 4460

#154
Frankenstein
Category: Pub, Karaoke
Average price: Modest
Area: Old Town
Address: 26 George IV Bridge
Edinburgh EH1 1EN
Phone: 0131 622 1818

#155
Bierex Public House
Category: Pub
Average price: Modest
Area: Newington
Address: 1 Grange Road
Edinburgh EH9 1UH
Phone: 0131 667 2335

#156
The Other Place
Category: Pub, Scottish
Average price: Modest
Area: Cannonmills
Address: 2-4 Broughton Road
Edinburgh EH7 4EB
Phone: 0131 556 1024

#157
Doctors
Category: Gastropub, Pub
Average price: Inexpensive
Area: Old Town
Address: 32 Forrest Rd
Edinburgh EH1 2QN
Phone: 0131 225 1819

#158
Jam House
Category: British, Jazz & Blues
Average price: Modest
Area: New Town
Address: 5 Queen Street
Edinburgh EH2 1JE
Phone: 0131 226 4380

#159
56 North
Category: Wine Bar
Average price: Modest
Area: Newington
Address: 2 West Crosscauseway
Edinburgh EH8 9JW
Phone: 0131 662 8860

#160
Blackfriars
Category: Bar, British
Average price: Inexpensive
Area: Old Town, Newington
Address: 57-61 Blackfriars Street
Edinburgh EH1 1NB
Phone: 0131 558 8684

#161
Forth Floor Restaurant
Category: Bar, British
Average price: Expensive
Area: New Town
Address: 30-34 St Andrew Square
Edinburgh EH2 2AD
Phone: 0131 524 8350

#162
Ryan's Bar
Category: Pub, Wine Bar
Average price: Modest
Area: New Town
Address: 2 - 4 Hope St
Edinburgh EH2 4DB
Phone: 0131 226 6669

#163
The Caley Bar
Category: Bar
Average price: Modest
Area: West End
Address: Princes Street
Edinburgh EH1 2AB
Phone: 0131 222 8888

#164
Montpelliers
Category: Pub
Average price: Modest
Area: Old Town, Newington
Address: 41 Lothian Street
Edinburgh EH1 1HB
Phone: 0131 220 4288

#165
Dropkick Murphys
Category: Pub
Average price: Modest
Area: Old Town
Address: 7 Merchant Street
Edinburgh EH1 2QD
Phone: 0131 225 2002

#166
Le Di-Vin
Category: Wine Bar, French
Average price: Expensive
Area: New Town
Address: 9 Randolph Pl
Edinburgh EH3 7TE
Phone: 0131 538 1815

#167
Virgin Lounge
Category: Lounge
Average price: Inexpensive
Area: New Town
Address: 28 St Andrew Square
Edinburgh EH2 1AF
Phone: 07712 848300

#168
White Horse Bar
Category: Pub
Average price: Modest
Area: Old Town, Royal Mile
Address: 266 Canongate
Edinburgh EH8 8AA
Phone: 0131 557 3512

#169
Cafe Habana
Category: Pub, Gay Bar, Karaoke
Average price: Modest
Area: New Town
Address: 18-22 Greenside Place
Edinburgh EH1 3AA
Phone: 0131 558 1270

#170
Jeremiah's Taproom
Category: Pub
Average price: Inexpensive
Area: New Town
Address: 7-8 Elm Row
Edinburgh EH7 4AA
Phone: 0131 556 8201

#171
Bennet's of Morningside
Category: Pub
Average price: Modest
Area: Morningside
Address: 1 Maxwell Street
Edinburgh EH10 5HT
Phone: 0131 447 1903

#172
The Southsider
Category: Pub
Average price: Modest
Area: Newington
Address: 3-7 W Richmond Street
Edinburgh EH8 9EF
Phone: 0131 667 2003

#173
Ryrie's Bar
Category: Pub, British
Average price: Inexpensive
Area: Haymarket, West End
Address: 1 Haymarket Terrace
Edinburgh EH12 5EY
Phone: 0131 337 0550

#174
Grand Cru
Category: Bar, Gastropub
Average price: Modest
Area: New Town
Address: 79 Hanover St
Edinburgh EH2 1EE
Phone: 0131 226 6427

#175
The Albanach
Category: Pub, Gastropub
Average price: Modest
Area: Old Town, Royal Mile
Address: 197 High Street
Edinburgh EH1 1PE
Phone: 0131 220 5277

#176
Revolution
Category: Pub
Average price: Modest
Area: Old Town
Address: 30a Chambers Street
Edinburgh EH1 1HU
Phone: 0131 220 5679

#177
The Three Sisters
Category: Bar, British
Average price: Expensive
Area: Old Town, Newington
Address: 139 Cowgate
Edinburgh EH1 1JS
Phone: 0131 622 6802

#178
Lulu
Category: Club
Average price: Expensive
Area: New Town
Address: 125a George St
Edinburgh EH2 4JN
Phone: 0131 225 5005

#179
Vegas in the Gardens
Category: Club
Average price: Modest
Area: New Town
Address: Princes Street
Edinburgh EH2 3AA
Phone: 0131 529 4068

#180
Hebrides Bar
Category: Pub
Average price: Modest
Area: Old Town, Royal Mile
Address: 17 Market St
Edinburgh EH1 1DE
Phone: 0131 220 4213

#181
The Grv
Category: Bar
Average price: Modest
Area: Old Town, Newington
Address: 37 Guthrie Street
Edinburgh EH1 1JG
Phone: 0131 220 0885

#182
Clarks Bar
Category: Pub
Average price: Modest
Area: Stockbridge
Address: 142 Dundas Street
Edinburgh EH3 5DQ
Phone: 0131 556 1067

#183
The Links Bar
Category: Hotel, Pub
Average price: Modest
Area: Bruntsfield, The Meadows
Address: 4-6 Alvanley Terrace
Edinburgh EH9 1DU
Phone: 0131 229 3834

#184
Au Bar
Category: Pub
Average price: Modest
Area: West End
Address: 101 Shandwick Place
Edinburgh EH2 4SD
Phone: 0131 228 2648

#185
Pleasance Theatre
Category: Theatre, Music Venues
Average price: Modest
Area: Newington
Address: 60 Pleasance
Edinburgh EH8 9TJ
Phone: 0131 556 1513

#186
The Outhouse
Category: Pub
Average price: Modest
Area: New Town
Address: 12a Broughton Street Lane
Edinburgh EH1 3LY
Phone: 0131 557 6668

#187
The Village
Category: Pub
Average price: Modest
Area: Leith
Address: 16 S Fort Street
Edinburgh EH6 4DN
Phone: 0131 478 7810

#188
Biblos
Category: Pub, Gastropub
Average price: Modest
Area: Old Town, Newington
Address: 1a Chambers Street
Edinburgh EH1 1HR
Phone: 0131 226 7177

#189
Smithie's Ale House
Category: Pub
Average price: Modest
Area: Cannonmills
Address: 49-51 Eyre Place
Edinburgh EH3 5EY
Phone: 0131 556 9805

#190
Cameo Bar
Category: Bar
Average price: Modest
Area: Leith
Address: 23 Commercial Street
Edinburgh EH6 6JA
Phone: 0131 554 9999

#191
The Cafe Royal
Category: Seafood, Bar, British
Average price: Modest
Area: New Town
Address: 19 W Register Street
Edinburgh EH2 2AA
Phone: 0131 556 1884

#192
The Globe Bar
Category: Pub
Average price: Inexpensive
Area: Old Town, Newington
Address: 30 Niddry Street
Edinburgh EH1 1LG
Phone: 0131 557 4670

#193
Sneaky Pete's
Category: Club, Music Venues
Average price: Inexpensive
Area: Old Town
Address: 73 Cowgate
Edinburgh EH1 1JW
Phone: 0131 225 1757

#194
Finnegan's Wake
Category: Irish, Pub, Music Venues
Average price: Modest
Area: Old Town, Grassmarket
Address: 9B Victoria Street
Edinburgh EH1 2HE
Phone: 0131 225 9348

#195
Cargo Bar
Category: Pub, Lounge
Average price: Modest
Area: West End
Address: 129 Fountainbridge
Edinburgh EH3 9QG
Phone: 0131 659 7880

#196
Port O'Leith
Category: Pub
Average price: Inexpensive
Area: Leith
Address: 58 Constitution Street
Edinburgh EH6 6RS
Phone: 0131 554 3568

#197
The Meadows Hotel
Category: Lounge, American
Average price: Modest
Area: Newington
Address: 72 Causewayside
Edinburgh EH9 1PY
Phone: 0131 667 5250

#198
The Amber Rose
Category: Pub
Average price: Modest
Area: New Town
Address: 22 Castle Street
Edinburgh EH2 3HT
Phone: 0131 226 1224

#199
1780
Category: Pub
Average price: Modest
Area: New Town
Address: 167 Rose St
Edinburgh EH2 4
Phone: 0131 225 1446

#200
Rose Street Brewery
Category: Pub
Average price: Inexpensive
Area: New Town
Address: 55-57 Rose Street
Edinburgh EH2 2NH
Phone: 0131 220 1227

#201
The Rat Pack
Category: Club
Average price: Modest
Area: West End
Address: 9 Shandwick Place
Edinburgh EH2 4RG
Phone: 0131 228 9147

#202
Arcade Bar
Category: Pub
Average price: Modest
Area: Old Town, Royal Mile
Address: 48 Cockburn Street
Edinburgh EH1 1PB
Phone: 0131 220 1297

#203
The Granary
Category: Pub
Average price: Modest
Area: Leith
Address: 32 The Shore
Edinburgh EH6 6QN
Phone: 0845 166 6005

#204
Auld Hundred
Category: Pub
Average price: Modest
Area: New Town
Address: 100-102 Rose St
Edinburgh EH2 2NN
Phone: 0131 225 1809

#205
Bees
Category: Bar, Cafe
Average price: Inexpensive
Area: Old Town
Address: 21 Candlemaker Row
Edinburgh EH1 2QG
Phone: 0131 225 9996

#206
Mean Fiddler Picture House
Purchase Ledger
Category: Music Venues
Average price: Modest
Area: Old Town
Address: 31 Lothian Road
Edinburgh EH1 2DJ
Phone: 0131 221 2282

#207
Ivory Lounge
Category: Pub
Average price: Inexpensive
Area: New Town
Address: 126-128 George Street
Edinburgh EH2 4JN
Phone: 0131 220 6180

#208
The Parlour
Category: Bar
Average price: Modest
Area: Leith
Address: 142 Duke Street
Edinburgh EH6 8HR
Phone: 0131 555 3848

#209
New Town Bar
Category: Pub, Club, Gay Bar
Average price: Modest
Area: New Town
Address: 26b Dublin Street
Edinburgh EH3 6NN
Phone: 0131 538 7775

#210
Opal Lounge
Category: Champagne Bar, Club
Average price: Expensive
Area: New Town
Address: 51a George St
Edinburgh EH2 2
Phone: 0131 226 2275

#211
Diane's Pool Hall
Category: Snooker & Pool Hall
Average price: Modest
Area: West End
Address: 242 Morrison Street
Edinburgh EH3 8DT
Phone: 0131 228 1156

#212
Barony Bar
Category: Pub
Average price: Modest
Area: New Town
Address: 81-85 Broughton Street
Edinburgh EH1 3RJ
Phone: 0131 558 2874

#213
The Stockbridge Tap
Category: British, Pub, Gastropub
Average price: Modest
Area: Stockbridge
Address: 2-4 Raeburn Pl
Edinburgh EH4 1HN
Phone: 0131 343 3000

#214
The Maltings
Category: Pub
Average price: Inexpensive
Area: Newington
Address: 85 St Leonards Street
Edinburgh EH8 9QY
Phone: 0131 667 5946

#215
Bank Hotel
Category: Hotel, Pub
Average price: Modest
Area: Old Town, Newington
Address: 1-3 S Bridge
Edinburgh EH1 1LL
Phone: 0131 556 9940

#216
Tailors Hall Hotel Festival Inns
Category: Pub, Hotel
Average price: Modest
Area: Old Town, Newington
Address: 139 Cowgate
Edinburgh EH1 1JS
Phone: 0131 622 6823

#217
Slug & Lettuce
Category: Pub, Gastropub
Average price: Modest
Area: New Town
Address: Unit 8 Omni Ctr
Edinburgh EH1 3BN
Phone: 0131 524 7700

#218
CC Blooms
Category: Wine Bar, Club
Average price: Modest
Area: New Town
Address: 23 Greenside Place
Edinburgh EH1 3AA
Phone: 0131 556 9331

#219
The Black Bull
Category: Pub
Average price: Modest
Area: Old Town, Grassmarket
Address: 12 Grassmarket
Edinburgh EH1 2JU
Phone: 0131 225 6636

#220
Cameo Cinema Bar
Category: Bar
Average price: Modest
Area: Tollcross, West End
Address: 38 Home Street
Edinburgh EH3 9LZ
Phone: 0131 228 4141

#221
The Pond
Category: Pub
Average price: Modest
Area: Leith
Address: 2-4 Bath Road
Edinburgh EH6 7JT
Phone: 0131 553 0639

#222
One Square
Category: Wine Bar, British
Average price: Expensive
Area: West End
Address: 1 Festival Square
Edinburgh EH3 9SR
Phone: 0131 221 6422

#223
Cross & Corner
Category: Gastropub, Pub
Average price: Modest
Area: Cannonmills
Address: 1 Canonmills Edinburgh
Edinburgh EH3 5HA
Phone: 0131 558 7080

#224
Waiting Room
Category: Pub, Gastropub
Average price: Modest
Area: Morningside
Address: 7 Belhaven Terrace
Edinburgh EH10 5HZ
Phone: 0131 452 9707

#225
Sportsters
Category: Sports Bar, American
Average price: Inexpensive
Area: Old Town, Royal Mile
Address: 1A Market St
Edinburgh EH1 1DE
Phone: 0131 226 9560

#226
Tiles
Category: Pub, Lounge, Gastropub
Average price: Modest
Area: New Town
Address: 1 St Andrew's Square
Edinburgh EH2 2BD
Phone: 0131 558 1507

#227
Woodland Creatures
Category: Bar, Cafe
Average price: Modest
Area: Leith
Address: 260 - 262 Leith Walk
Edinburgh EH6 5EL
Phone: 0131 629 5509

#228
Hudsons Bar
Category: Bar, Gastropub
Average price: Modest
Area: New Town
Address: 7-11 Hope Street
Edinburgh EH2 4EL
Phone: 0131 247 7000

#229
The Store
Category: Club, Music Venues
Average price: Inexpensive
Area: Newington
Address: 37 Guthrie St
Edinburgh EH8 9
Phone: 0131 220 2987

#230
The Abbey
Category: Pub
Average price: Modest
Area: Newington
Address: 65 South Clerk Street
Edinburgh EH8 9PP
Phone: 0131 668 4862

#231
The Phoenix
Category: Pub
Average price: Modest
Area: New Town
Address: 46-48a Broughton Street
Edinburgh EH1 3SA
Phone: 0131 557 0234

#232
Bar Soba
Category: Bar, Asian Fusion
Average price: Modest
Area: New Town
Address: 104 Hanover Street
Edinburgh EH2 1DR
Phone: 0131 225 6220

#233
Carriers Quarters
Category: Pub
Average price: Modest
Area: Leith
Address: 42 Bernard Street
Edinburgh EH6 6PR
Phone: 0131 554 4122

#234
Guilty Lily
Category: Pub
Average price: Modest
Area: Leith
Address: 284 Bonnington Road
Edinburgh EH6 5BE
Phone: 0131 554 5824

#235
Supercube
Category: Karaoke
Average price: Modest
Area: New Town
Address: 58A George Street
Edinburgh EH2 2LR
Phone: 0131 226 4218

#236
Bar 50
Category: Bar
Average price: Inexpensive
Area: Old Town, Newington
Address: 50 Blackfriars Street
Edinburgh EH1 1NE
Phone: 0131 524 1989

#237
All Bar One
Category: Wine Bar, Pub
Average price: Expensive
Area: West End
Address: 50 Lothian Road
Edinburgh EH3 9BY
Phone: 0131 221 7951

#238
Bar Salsa
Category: Pub, Dive Bar
Average price: Inexpensive
Area: Old Town, Grassmarket
Address: 3 Cowgatehead
Edinburgh EH1 1JY
Phone: 0131 629 8431

#239
St Vincent
Category: Pub, Gastropub
Average price: Modest
Area: Stockbridge, New Town
Address: 11 St Vincent Street
Edinburgh EH3 6SW
Phone: 0131 226 6861

#240
Henry J Beans
Category: American, Bar
Average price: Modest
Area: West End
Address: Rutland Pl
Edinburgh EH1 2AD
Phone: 0131 222 8844

#241
The Foot Of The Walk
Category: Pub
Average price: Inexpensive
Area: Leith
Address: 183 Constitution Street
Edinburgh EH6 7AA
Phone: 0131 553 0120

#242
Divino Enoteca
Category: Wine Bar, Italian
Average price: Expensive
Area: Old Town
Address: 5 Merchant St
Edinburgh EH1 2QD
Phone: 0131 225 1770

#243
The Clubhouse
Category: Golf, Bar
Average price: Modest
Area: West End
Address: Fountainbridge
Edinburgh EH3 9QG
Phone: 0131 228 3894

#244
The Merlin
Category: Pub
Average price: Modest
Area: Morningside
Address: 168 Morningside Road
Edinburgh EH10 4PU
Phone: 0131 447 4329

#245
Sala Cafe Bar
Category: Gay Bar
Average price: Modest
Area: New Town
Address: 58a Broughton Street
Edinburgh EH1 3SA
Phone: 0131 556 5758

#246
Royal Mile Tavern
Category: Pub
Average price: Modest
Area: Old Town, Royal Mile
Address: 127 High Street
Edinburgh EH1 1SG
Phone: 0131 557 9681

#247
Pearce's Bar
Category: Pub
Average price: Modest
Area: New Town
Address: 23 Elm Row
Edinburgh EH7 4AA
Phone: 0131 556 1310

#248
Harry's Bar
Category: Pub, Italian
Average price: Inexpensive
Area: New Town
Address: 7b Randolph Place
Edinburgh EH3 7TH
Phone: 0131 539 8100

#249
Mathers
Category: Pub
Average price: Inexpensive
Area: New Town
Address: 25 Broughton Street
Edinburgh EH1 3JU
Phone: 0131 556 6754

#250
Robbie's
Category: Pub
Average price: Inexpensive
Area: Leith
Address: 367 Leith Walk
Edinburgh EH6 8SE
Phone: 0131 554 6850

#251
Windsor Buffet
Category: Pub
Average price: Modest
Area: Leith
Address: 45 Elm Row
Edinburgh EH7 4AH
Phone: 0131 556 4558

#252
The Grosvenor
Category: Pub
Average price: Modest
Area: West End
Address: 26-28 Shandwick Place
Edinburgh EH2 4RT
Phone: 0131 226 4579

#253
Beanscene
Category: Music Venues
Average price: Modest
Area: West End
Address: 2 Grosvenor St
Edinburgh EH12 5EG
Phone: 0131 346 8043

#254
City Limits
Category: Pub
Average price: Modest
Area: Leith
Address: 379 Leith Walk
Edinburgh EH6 8SE
Phone: 0131 554 1515

#255
No 1 High Street Bar
Category: Pub
Average price: Modest
Area: Old Town, Royal Mile
Address: 1 High Street
Edinburgh EH1 1SW
Phone: 0131 556 5758

#256
Biddy Mulligans
Category: Irish, Pub
Average price: Modest
Area: Old Town, Grassmarket
Address: 94-96 Grassmarket
Edinburgh EH1 2JR
Phone: 0131 220 1246

#257
Espionage
Category: Club, Bar
Average price: Modest
Area: Old Town, Grassmarket
Address: 4 India Buildings
Edinburgh EH1 2EX
Phone: 0131 477 7007

#258
Citrus Club
Category: Club
Average price: Modest
Area: Old Town
Address: 40-42 Grindlay Street
Edinburgh EH3 9AP
Phone: 0131 622 7086

#259
Morningside Glory
Category: Pub, Gastropub
Average price: Modest
Area: Morningside
Address: 1 Comiston Road
Edinburgh EH10 6AA
Phone: 0131 447 1205

#260
The Melville Bar
Category: Pub
Average price: Modest
Area: West End
Address: 23-25 William Street
Edinburgh EH3 7NG
Phone: 0131 226 0920

#261
The Courtyard Bar & Brasserie
Category: Pub
Average price: Modest
Area: Leith
Address: 2 Bonnington Road Lane
Edinburgh EH6 5BJ
Phone: 0131 554 1314

#262
Planet Bar
Category: Pub
Average price: Inexpensive
Area: New Town
Address: 6 Baxter's Place
Edinburgh EH1 3AF
Phone: 0131 556 5551

#263
Walkabout
Category: Theatre, Pub
Average price: Modest
Area: Old Town, Royal Mile
Address: Unit 6 Omni Leisure Development
Edinburgh EH1 3AA
Phone: 0131 524 9300

#264
Lava and Ignite
Category: Bar
Average price: Inexpensive
Area: Tollcross, West End
Address: 3 W Tollcross
Edinburgh EH3 9BP
Phone: 0131 228 3252

#265
The Bon Vivant Stockbridge
Category: Gastropub, Lounge
Average price: Modest
Area: Stockbridge
Address: Dean Street
Edinburgh EH4 1LW
Phone: 0131 315 3311

#266
Bert's Bar
Category: Pub
Average price: Modest
Area: West End
Address: 29-31 William Street
Edinburgh EH3 7NG
Phone: 0131 225 5748

#267
The Priory Bar & Kitchen
Category: Bar, British
Average price: Modest
Area: West End
Address: 192-194 Morrison St
Edinburgh EH3 8EB
Phone: 0131 229 5676

#268
Carters Bar
Category: Pub
Average price: Modest
Area: West End
Address: 185 Morrison Street
Edinburgh EH3 8DZ
Phone: 0131 228 9149

#269
The Alexander Graham Bell
Category: Pub
Average price: Inexpensive
Area: New Town
Address: 128 George Street
Edinburgh EH2 4JZ
Phone: 0131 240 8220

#270
Elm Bar
Category: Pub
Average price: Expensive
Area: New Town
Address: 7-8 Elm Row
Edinburgh EH7 4AA
Phone: 0131 558 8624

#271
Why Not?
Category: Club, Bar
Average price: Modest
Area: New Town
Address: 14 George Street
Edinburgh EH2 2PF
Phone: 0131 624 8633

#272
Shanghai
Category: Bar
Average price: Expensive
Area: New Town
Address: 16 George Street
Edinburgh EH2 2PF
Phone: 0131 270 3900

#273
Lord Bodos
Category: Pub
Average price: Modest
Area: New Town
Address: 3 Dublin Street
Edinburgh EH1 3PG
Phone: 0131 477 2563

#274
El Bar
Category: Tapas Bar, Theatre
Average price: Inexpensive
Area: Newington
Address: 6-8 Howden Street
Edinburgh EH8 9HQ
Phone: 0131 667 3600

#275
Wayside
Category: Pub
Average price: Modest
Area: Newington
Address: 114 Causewayside
Edinburgh EH9 1PU
Phone: 0131 629 0935

#276
Mathers
Category: Pub
Average price: Modest
Area: West End
Address: 1 Queensferry Street
Edinburgh EH2 4PA
Phone: 0131 225 3549

#277
The Balmoral Bar
Category: Bar, Hotel
Average price: Exclusive
Area: Old Town
Address: 1 Princes Street
Edinburgh EH2 2EQ
Phone: 0131 556 2414

#278
The Breakfast Club
Category: Bar
Average price: Inexpensive
Area: Old Town, Newington
Address: 45-47 Lothian Street
Edinburgh EH1 1HB
Phone: 0131 220 4287

#279
Cafe Voltaire
Category: Cocktail Bar
Average price: Modest
Area: Old Town, Newington
Address: 36-38 Blair Street
Edinburgh EH1 1QR
Phone: 0131 247 4707

#280
Traverse Bar Café
Category: Bar, British, Burgers
Average price: Modest
Area: Old Town
Address: 10 Cambridge Street
Edinburgh EH1 2ED
Phone: 0131 228 1404

#281
Bar Alba
Category: Pub, Lounge
Average price: Modest
Area: Old Town, Grassmarket
Address: 11-13 Grassmarket
Edinburgh EH1 2HY
Phone: 0131 229 2665

#282
Smirnoff Underbelly
Category: Bar
Average price: Modest
Area: Old Town, Grassmarket
Address: Stage Door George 1V Bridge
Victoria Street
Edinburgh EH1 1EE
Phone: 0131 624 1503

#283
Filament Coffee
Category: Wine Bar
Average price: Inexpensive
Area: Old Town, Grassmarket
Address: 5 India Buildings
Edinburgh EH1 2EX
Phone: 07914 189590

#284
Soco
Category: Bar
Average price: Modest
Area: Old Town, Newington
Address: cowgate
Edinburgh EH1 1JG
Phone: 0131 558 7682

#285
Henry J Beans Bar & Grill
Category: Pub
Average price: Modest
Area: Old Town
Address: 4 Princes Street
Edinburgh EH1 2AB
Phone: 0131 222 8844

#286
Finnegans Sandwich Bar
Category: Bar
Average price: Modest
Area: New Town
Address: 28 Queensferry Street
Edinburgh EH2 4QS
Phone: 0131 226 5005

#287
Baroque
Category: Pub
Average price: Modest
Area: New Town
Address: 39-41 Broughton Street
Edinburgh EH3 3JU
Phone: 0131 557 0627

#288
Lothain & Border Police Association Club
Category: Sports Club, Club
Average price: Modest
Area: New Town
Address: 28 York Place
Edinburgh EH1 3EP
Phone: 0131 524 0110

#289
The Wash Bar
Category: Pub
Average price: Modest
Area: Old Town, Royal Mile
Address: 11-13 N Bank Street
Edinburgh EH1 2LP
Phone: 0131 225 6193

#290
Wally Gug The Public House
Category: Pub
Average price: Modest
Area: New Town
Address: 32 Northumberland Street
Edinburgh EH3 6LS
Phone: 0131 558 1593

#291
Voodoo Bar
Category: Bar
Average price: Modest
Area: West End
Address: 8 Torphichen Place
Edinburgh EH3
Phone: 07988 760030

#292
Theatre Workshop Edinburgh
Category: Theatre, Music Venues
Average price: Modest
Area: Stockbridge
Address: 34 Hamilton Place
Edinburgh EH3 5AX
Phone: 0131 226 4366

#293
The Constitution Bar
Category: Bar
Average price: Modest
Area: Leith
Address: 48 Constitution St
Edinburgh EH6 6RS
Phone: 0131 538 9374

#294
Nor Loch Bar
Category: Pub, British
Average price: Expensive
Area: Old Town
Address: Waverley Railway Station
Edinburgh EH1 1BB
Phone: 0131 557 9124

#295
Siglo Nightclub
Category: Club, Dive Bar
Average price: Modest
Area: Old Town, Newington
Address: 184 Cowgate
Edinburgh EH1 1JJ
Phone: 0131 220 1228

#296
The Lane
Category: Club
Average price: Modest
Area: West End
Address: 3 Queensferry St Lane
Edinburgh EH2 4PF
Phone: 0131 629 9891

#297
Ensign Ewart
Category: Pub
Average price: Modest
Area: Old Town, Royal Mile
Address: 521 Lawnmarket
Edinburgh EH1 2PE
Phone: 0131 225 7440

#298
Aspen Bar and Grill
Category: Pub
Average price: Inexpensive
Area: Old Town, Newington
Address: 66 South Bridge
Edinburgh EH1 1LS
Phone: 0131 556 0200

#299
Subway
Category: Club
Average price: Inexpensive
Area: Old Town
Address: 23 Lothian Road
Edinburgh EH1 2DJ
Phone: 0131 229 9056

#300
Reverie
Category: Wine Bar, Lounge
Average price: Modest
Area: Newington
Address: 1-5 Newington Road
Edinburgh EH9 1QR
Phone: 0131 667 8870

#301
The Ale House
Category: Pub, Music Venues
Average price:
Area: Newington
Address: 18-22 Clerk Street
Edinburgh EH8 9HX
Phone: 0131 629 0275

#302
Edinburgh Jazz and Blues
Category: Jazz & Blues
Average price: Modest
Area: Leith
Address: 89 Giles St
Edinburgh EH6 6BZ
Phone: 0131 473 2000

#303
Lola Lo
Category: Bar, Club
Average price: Expensive
Area: New Town
Address: 43B Frederick Street
Edinburgh EH2 1EP
Phone: 0131 226 2224

#304
Edinburgh Famous Burke & Hare
Category: Adult Entertainment
Average price: Exclusive
Area: Old Town
Address: 1 High Riggs
Edinburgh EH3 9BX
Phone: 0131 466 2567

#305
Monboddo
Category: Mediterranean, Bar
Average price: Modest
Area: Old Town
Address: 34 Bread St
Edinburgh EH3 9AF
Phone: 0131 221 5555

#306
Isobar
Category: Bar
Average price: Modest
Area: Leith
Address: 7 Bernard Street
Edinburgh EH6 6PW
Phone: 0131 467 8904

#307
Banter
Category: Pub
Average price: Modest
Area: Tollcross, West End
Address: 85 Fountainbridge
Edinburgh EH3 9PU
Phone: 0131 228 8793

#308
Footlights Bar & Grill
Category: Sports Bar, Comedy Club
Average price: Modest
Area: Old Town
Address: 7-11 Spittal Street
Edinburgh EH3 9DY
Phone: 0131 229 6466

#309
Rose & Crown
Category: Pub
Average price: Modest
Area: New Town
Address: 170 Rose Street
Edinburgh EH2 4BA
Phone: 0131 225 4039

#310
Anderson's Bar
Category: Pub
Average price: Modest
Area: Leith
Address: 1-2 Yardheads
Edinburgh EH6 6BU
Phone: 0131 467 7109

#311
Gladstone's Bar
Category: Pub
Average price: Modest
Area: Leith
Address: 1-2 Mill Lane
Edinburgh EH6 6TJ
Phone: 0131 554 5586

#312
Ripping Records
Category: Music Venues
Average price: Modest
Area: Old Town, Newington
Address: 91 South Bridge
Edinburgh EH1 1HN
Phone: 0131 226 7010

#313
City Nightclub
Category: Club
Average price: Modest
Area: Old Town, Royal Mile
Address: 1a Market St
Edinburgh EH1 1DE
Phone: 0131 226 9560

#314
The Strathie
Category: Pub
Average price: Modest
Area: Leith
Address: 17 Iona Street
Edinburgh EH6 8SG
Phone: 0131 554 8717

#315
The Harp and Castle
Category: Pub
Average price: Inexpensive
Area: Leith
Address: 298 Leith Walk
Edinburgh EH6 5BU
Phone: 0131 555 2238

#316
Swanys Lounge Bar
Category: Pub, Lounge
Average price: Modest
Area: Newington
Address: 1 Ratcliffe Terrace
Edinburgh EH9 1SX
Phone: 0131 667 8023

#317
Priscillas Bar
Category: Gay Bar, Karaoke
Average price: Modest
Area: Leith
Address: 17 Albert Place
Edinburgh EH7 5HN
Phone: 0131 554 8962

#318
Hermitage Bar
Category: Pub
Average price: Modest
Area: Morningside
Address: 1-5 Comiston Road
Edinburgh EH10 6AA
Phone: 0131 447 1205

#319
Middleton Bar
Category: Pub
Average price: Modest
Area: Leith
Address: 69 Easter Road
Edinburgh EH7 5PW
Phone: 0131 661 4463

#320
The Jinglin' Geordie
Category: Pub
Average price: Modest
Area: Old Town, Newington, Royal Mile
Address: 22 Fleshmarket Close
Edinburgh EH1 1DY
Phone: 0131 225 2803

#321
The Hogshead
Category: Pub
Average price: Modest
Area: New Town
Address: 133 Rose Street
Edinburgh EH2 4LS
Phone: 0131 226 1224

#322
Vat and Fiddle
Category: Pub
Average price: Inexpensive
Area: Old Town
Address: 21 Lothian Road
Edinburgh EH1 2DJ
Phone: 0131 229 9933

#323
Festival Tavern
Category: Pub
Average price: Modest
Area: West End
Address: 16-20A Morrison Street
Edinburgh EH3 8BJ
Phone: 0131 229 3303

#324
Spey Lounge
Category: Pub
Average price: Inexpensive
Area: Leith
Address: 39 Leith Walk
Edinburgh EH6 8LS
Phone: 0131 554 9442

#325
The Fiddler's Arms
Category: Bar
Average price: Inexpensive
Area: Old Town, Grassmarket
Address: 11-13 Grassmarket
Edinburgh EH1 2HY
Phone: 0131 228 6113

#326
Po Na Na Souk Bar
Category: Club
Average price: Modest
Area: New Town
Address: 43b Frederick St
Edinburgh EH2 1EP
Phone: 0131 226 2224

#327
The One Below
Category: Club
Average price: Modest
Area: New Town, West End
Address: 1 - 3 Rutland St
Edinburgh EH1 2AE
Phone: 0131 229 3402

#328
The Edinburgh Corn Exchange
Category: Club
Average price: Modest
Area: Old Town, Royal Mile
Address: 9 Newmarket Road
Edinburgh EH14 1RJ
Phone: 0131 477 3500

#329
The City Cafe
Category: Bar, American
Average price: Modest
Area: Old Town, Newington
Address: 19 Blair Street
Edinburgh EH1 1QR
Phone: 0131 220 0125

#330
The Office
Category: Pub
Average price: Modest
Area: Leith
Address: 180 Albert Street
Edinburgh EH7 5NA
Phone: 0131 554 3828

#331
Madogs Night Club
Category: Club
Average price: Expensive
Area: New Town
Address: 38a George Street
Edinburgh EH2 2LE
Phone: 0131 225 3408

#332
Edwards Bar
Category: Pub
Average price: Modest
Area: New Town
Address: 4 South Charlotte Street
Edinburgh EH2 4AW
Phone: 0131 226 5526

#333
Shanghai Club
Category: Club
Average price: Expensive
Area: New Town
Address: 16a George Street
Edinburgh EH2 2PF
Phone: 0131 270 3914

#334
The World's End
Category: Pub
Average price: Modest
Area: Old Town, Newington, Royal Mile
Address: 4 High St
Edinburgh EH1 1TB
Phone: 0131 556 3628

#335
Base Nightclub
Category: Club
Average price: Inexpensive
Area: Old Town
Address: 69 The Cowgate
Edinburgh EH1 1JW
Phone: 0131 225 7377

#336
Dagda Bar
Category: Pub
Average price: Modest
Area: Newington
Address: 93-95 Buccleuch Street
Edinburgh EH8 9NG
Phone: 0131 667 9773

#337
Faith
Category: Hotel, Club
Average price: Modest
Area: Old Town, Newington
Address: Wilkie Ho Theatre Cowgate
Edinburgh EH1 1RP
Phone: 0131 225 9764

#338
Boteco Do Brasil Edinburgh
Category: Cocktail Bar, Brazilian
Average price: Modest
Area: Old Town, Newington
Address: 45-47 Lothian Street
Edinburgh EH1 1HB
Phone: 0131 220 4287

#339
The Mash House
Category: Bar, Club, Music Venues
Average price: Modest
Area: Old Town, Newington
Address: 37 Guthrie Street
Edinburgh EH1 1JG
Phone: 0131 226 1402

#340
Blair Street Sauna
Category: Adult Entertainment
Average price: Modest
Area: Old Town, Newington
Address: Blair Street
Edinburgh EH1 1QR
Phone: 0131 226 2114

#341
Zoo Southside
Category: Music Venues
Average price: Modest
Area: Newington
Address: 117 Nicholson St
Edinburgh EH8 9ER
Phone: 01432 344885

#342
International Vodka & Beer Bar
Category: Bar
Average price: Modest
Area: New Town
Address: 89 Rose Street North Lane
Edinburgh EH2 3DX
Phone: 07958 198173

#343
Panda Inn
Category: Pub, Chinese
Average price: Inexpensive
Area: Bruntsfield, The Meadows
Address: 36 Leven Street
Edinburgh EH3 9LJ
Phone: 0131 228 8293

#344
Fingers Piano Bar
Category: Pub, Lounge
Average price: Expensive
Area: New Town
Address: 61a Frederick Street
Edinburgh EH2 1LH
Phone: 0131 225 3026

#345
Pepper
Category: Lounge
Average price: Modest
Area: New Town
Address: 14 Picardy Place
Edinburgh EH1 3JT
Phone: 0131 557 0952

#346
The New Gentle Touch
Category: Massage, Adult Entertainment
Average price: Modest
Area: Marchmont
Address: 40 Argyle Place
Edinburgh EH9 1JT
Phone: 0131 477 2648

#347
The 1/4 Gill
Category: Pub
Average price: Modest
Area: Newington
Address: 77 Clerk Street
Edinburgh EH8 9JG
Phone: 0131 622 7000

#348
Brunswick Bar
Category: Pub
Average price: Inexpensive
Area: Leith
Address: 71 Elm Row
Edinburgh EH7 4AQ
Phone: 0131 556 3274

#349
St Bernard
Category: Pub
Average price: Modest
Area: Stockbridge
Address: 10 Raeburn Place
Edinburgh EH4 1HN
Phone: 0131 332 2655

#350
The Halfway House
Category: Pub
Average price: Modest
Area: Old Town, Royal Mile
Address: 24 Fleshmarket Close
Edinburgh EH1 1BX
Phone: 0131 225 7101

#351
The Inn on the Mile
Category: Bar
Average price: Modest
Area: Old Town, Royal Mile
Address: 82 High Street
Edinburgh EH1 1LL
Phone: 0131 556 9940

#352
Royal Nip
Category: Pub
Average price: Modest
Area: Leith
Address: 180 Albert Street
Edinburgh EH7 5NA
Phone: 0131 554 3828

#353
Melville Lounge Bar
Category: Pub
Average price: Modest
Area: West End
Address: 23 William Street
Edinburgh EH3 7NG
Phone: 0131 225 1358

#354
Dickens Lounge Bar
Category: Pub
Average price: Modest
Area: Haymarket, West End
Address: 88 Dalry Road
Edinburgh EH11 2AX
Phone: 0131 346 3286

#355
Pond Bar
Category: Pub
Average price: Modest
Area: Leith
Address: 2-4 Bath Road
Edinburgh EH6 7JT
Phone: 0131 467 3825

#356
The Horseshoe Bar
Category: Pub
Average price: Inexpensive
Area: Leith
Address: 362 Leith Walk
Edinburgh EH6 5BR
Phone: 0131 554 5286

#357
The Persevere Bar
Category: Pub
Average price: Inexpensive
Area: Leith
Address: 398 Easter Road
Edinburgh EH6 8HT
Phone: 0131 554 0271

#358
Lona Bar
Category: Pub
Average price: Modest
Area: Leith
Address: 203 Easter Road
Edinburgh EH6 8LF
Phone: 0131 554 5180

#359
Victoria Bar
Category: Pub, Dive Bar
Average price: Inexpensive
Area: Newington
Address: 25 Causewayside
Edinburgh EH9 1QF
Phone: 0131 667 1145

#360
Mood
Category: Club
Average price: Modest
Area: New Town
Address: 1 Greenside Place
Edinburgh EH1 3AA
Phone: 0131 550 1640

#361
Filthy McNasty's
Category: Pub
Average price: Inexpensive
Area: New Town
Address: 168 Rose Street
Edinburgh EH2 4BA
Phone: 0131 226 2990

#362
The Grape
Category: Pub
Average price: Modest
Area: New Town
Address: St Andrews Square George
Street, Edinburgh EH2 2BH
Phone: 0131 557 4522

#363
Alan Breck Lounge
Category: Pub
Average price: Modest
Area: Leith
Address: 159 Constitution Street
Edinburgh EH6 7AD
Phone: 0131 467 2581

#364
The Grapes
Category: Pub, Dive Bar
Average price: Modest
Area: Newington
Address: 77 Clerk Street
Edinburgh EH8 9LF
Phone: 0131 557 4522

#365
The Montague
Category: Pub
Average price: Modest
Area: Newington
Address: 81-85 St Leonards Street
Edinburgh EH8 9QY
Phone: 0131 667 5946

#366
Villager
Category: Bar, Burgers
Average price: Modest
Area: Old Town
Address: 49 George IV Bridge
Edinburgh EH1 1EJ
Phone: 0131 226 2781

#367
Montpeliers
Category: Wine Bar
Average price: Modest
Area: Bruntsfield
Address: 159-161 Bruntsfield Pl
Edinburgh EH10 4DG
Phone: 0131 229 3115

#368
Mr Bird's Myo
Takeaway Food Bar
Category: Bar
Average price: Modest
Area: New Town, West End
Address: 40 Queensferry Street
Edinburgh EH2 4RA
Phone: 0131 226 6667

#369
University Of Edinburgh Students
Association
Category: Club
Average price: Modest
Area: Newington
Address: Bristo Square
Edinburgh EH8 9AL
Phone: 0131 650 2656

#370
Abbotsford Bar
Category: Bar, British
Average price: Modest
Area: New Town
Address: 43 Princes Street
Edinburgh EH2 2BY
Phone: 0131 556 4648

#371
The Wee Red Bar
Category: Bar
Average price: Modest
Area: Old Town
Address: Edinburgh College of Art
Edinburgh EH3 9DF
Phone: 0131 229 1003

#372
Ambassador Sauna
Category: Adult Entertainment
Average price: Modest
Area: Old Town
Address: 91 Lothian Road
Edinburgh EH3 9AW
Phone: 0131 229 3260

#373
Zoo Roxy
Category: Music Venues
Average price: Modest
Area: Newington
Address: 2-3 Roxburgh Pl
Edinburgh EH8 9SU
Phone: 01432 344885

#374
Waterloo Buffet
Category: Pub
Average price: Modest
Area: New Town
Address: 3-7 Waterloo Place
Edinburgh EH1 3BG
Phone: 0131 556 7597

#375
Liquorice Club Edinburgh
Category: Adult Entertainment
Average price: Modest
Area: Tollcross, West End
Address: 16 Home St
Edinburgh EH3 9LY
Phone: 0131 228 9330

#376
The Scotch Of St James
Category: Pub
Average price: Expensive
Area: West End
Address: 192 Morrison Street
Edinburgh EH3 8EB
Phone: 0131 221 0499

#377
Thistle Hotel
Category: Hotel, Bar
Average price: Modest
Area: West End
Address: 59 Manor Place
Edinburgh EH3 7EG
Phone: 0131 225 6144

#378
Platform 5
Category: Wine Bar
Average price: Modest
Area: Haymarket, West End
Address: 8 Clifton Terrace
Edinburgh EH12 5DR
Phone: 0131 347 1616

#379
El Barrio Latino Bar & Club
Category: Bar, Club, Mexican
Average price: Modest
Area: New Town
Address: 47 Hanover Street
Edinburgh EH2 2PJ
Phone: 0131 220 6818

#380
Stags Head
Category: Pub
Average price: Modest
Area: Cannonmills
Address: 2-4 Broughton Road
Edinburgh EH7 4EB
Phone: 0131 556 2911

#381
Dalmeny Bar
Category: Pub
Average price: Modest
Area: Leith
Address: 297 Leith Walk
Edinburgh EH6 8SA
Phone: 0131 554 3482

#382
Volunteer Arms Public House
Category: Pub
Average price: Modest
Area: Leith
Address: 180 Leith Walk
Edinburgh EH6 5EA
Phone: 0131 538 8383

#383
Hotel Missoni
Category: Hotel, European, Bar
Average price: Exclusive
Area: Old Town, Royal Mile
Address: 1 George IV Bridge
Edinburgh EH1 1AD
Phone: 0131 220 6666

#384
Four In Hand
Category: Pub
Average price: Modest
Area: Leith
Address: 218 Easter Road
Edinburgh EH7 5QH
Phone: 0131 538 9911

#385
The Albion Bar
Category: Pub
Average price: Modest
Area: Leith
Address: 49 Albion Road
Edinburgh EH7 5QP
Phone: 0131 661 2946

#386
Subway Cowgate
Category: Music Venues
Average price: Modest
Area: Old Town
Address: 69 Cowgate
Edinburgh EH1 1JW
Phone: 0131 225 6766

#387
The Gordon Arms
Category: Pub
Average price: Modest
Area: New Town
Address: 133 Rose Street
Edinburgh EH2 4LS
Phone: 0131 225 8492

#388
Andersons
Category: Pub
Average price: Inexpensive
Area: Old Town, West End
Address: 161 Lothian Road
Edinburgh EH3 9AA
Phone: 0131 629 0751

#389
Spiers Bar
Category: Pub
Average price: Modest
Area: Leith
Address: 10 Bowhill Terrace
Edinburgh EH3 5QY
Phone: 0131 552 4849

#390
Bar Seinne
Category: Pub
Average price: Modest
Area: Leith
Address: 96-98 Leith Walk
Edinburgh EH6 5HB
Phone: 0131 553 3665

#391
Foxs Bar
Category: Pub
Average price: Modest
Area: Leith
Address: 8 Bonnington Road
Edinburgh EH6 5JD
Phone: 0131 467 7640

#392
Norries Bar
Category: Pub
Average price: Modest
Area: Leith
Address: 159 Constitution Street
Edinburgh EH6 7AD
Phone: 0131 467 2578

#393
Flying Dog
Category: Bar
Average price: Modest
Area: Leith
Address: 24 Henderson Street
Edinburgh EH6 6ED
Phone: 0131 467 7712

#394
Cav
Category: Club
Average price: Modest
Area: Tollcross, West End
Address: 3 West Tollcross
Edinburgh EH3 9BP
Phone: 0131 228 3252

#395
Swanny's Bar
Category: Bar
Average price: Modest
Area: Leith
Address: 32 North Junction Street
Edinburgh EH6 6HP
Phone: 0131 467 7717

#396
The Third Door
Category: Club, Music Venues
Average price: Modest
Area: Old Town, Newington
Address: 45 - 47 Lothian Road
Edinburgh EH1 1HB
Phone: 0131 225 6313

#397
Western Bar
Category: Adult Entertainment
Average price: Modest
Area: Old Town
Address: 157 West Port
Edinburgh EH3 9DP
Phone: 0131 229 7983

#398
The Burgh
Category: Bar
Average price: Expensive
Area: New Town
Address: 7 South St Andrew Street
Edinburgh EH2 2AU
Phone: 0131 524 0041

#399
Olivers Pub
Category: Pub
Average price: Inexpensive
Area: New Town
Address: 178 Rose Street
Edinburgh EH2 4BA
Phone: 0131 220 3933

#400
Scotts Bar
Category: Pub
Average price: Modest
Area: New Town
Address: 202 Rose St
Edinburgh EH2 4AZ
Phone: 0131 225 7401

#401
The Stage Door
Category: Bar
Average price: Modest
Area: Tollcross, West End
Address: 69 Home Street
Edinburgh EH3 9JP
Phone: 0131 229 6232

#402
Apero
Category: Champagne Bar
Average price: Modest
Area: West End
Address: 34 Alva Street
Edinburgh EH3 7
Phone: 0131 220 6105

#403
Randolph Bar
Category: Lounge
Average price: Modest
Area: New Town, West End
Address: 13a-14 Melville Pl
Edinburgh EH3 7PR
Phone: 0131 226 3404

#404
Thirty Seven Bar
Category: Pub
Average price: Modest
Area: New Town
Address: 37 Rose Street
Edinburgh EH2 2NH
Phone: 0131 226 5402

#405
Angels with Bagpipes
Category: Bar, British
Average price: Expensive
Area: Old Town, Newington, Royal Mile
Address: 343 High St
Edinburgh EH1 1PW
Phone: 0131 220 1111

#406
Alhambra Bar
Category: Pub
Average price: Modest
Area: Leith
Address: 227 Leith Walk
Edinburgh EH6 5
Phone: 0131 554 4868

#407
Kings Arms
Category: Pub
Average price: Modest
Area: Tollcross
Address: 45 Home Street
Edinburgh EH3 9JP
Phone: 0131 229 6085

#408
The Broadsheet Bistro
Category: British, Bar
Average price: Modest
Area: Old Town, Royal Mile
Address: 26 St Giles Street
Edinburgh EH1 1PT
Phone: 0131 221 7211

#409
Balfours Bar
Category: Pub
Average price: Modest
Area: Leith
Address: 260 Leith Walk
Edinburgh EH6 5EL
Phone: 0131 467 7054

#410
The Central Bar
Category: Pub
Average price: Exclusive
Area: Leith
Address: 7-9 Leith Walk
Edinburgh EH7 4
Phone: 0131 467 3925

#411
Grassmarket Bar
Category: Pub
Average price: Expensive
Area: Old Town, Grassmarket
Address: 7 West Port
Edinburgh EH1 2JA
Phone: 0131 221 1448

#412
Dockers Tavern
Category: Pub
Average price: Modest
Area: Leith
Address: 18 -Salamander Street
Edinburgh EH6 7HR
Phone: 0131 553 4100

#413
Clouds & Soil
Category: Cocktail Bar
Average price: Modest
Area: New Town
Address: 4 Picardy Pl
Edinburgh EH1 3JT
Phone: 0131 629 2728

#414
Bar Sirius
Category: Pub
Average price: Inexpensive
Area: Leith
Address: 7-10 Dock Place
Edinburgh EH6 6LU
Phone: 0131 555 3344

#415
Tam 'O' Shanter
Category: Pub
Average price: Modest
Area: Leith
Address: 39 Great Junction Street
Edinburgh EH6 5HX
Phone: 0131 554 0897

#416
Marksman Bar
Category: Pub
Average price: Inexpensive
Area: Leith
Address: 13 Duke Street
Edinburgh EH6 8HG
Phone: 0131 467 7632

#417
Cranston's Restaurant
Category: Bar, British
Average price: Modest
Area: New Town
Address: 43 Princes Street
Edinburgh EH2 2BY
Phone: 0131 556 4648

#418
Scotsman Hotel
Category: Hotel, Bar
Average price: Expensive
Area: Old Town, Royal Mile
Address: 20 North Bridge
Edinburgh EH1 1YT
Phone: 0131 556 5565

#419
Athletic Arms
Category: Pub
Average price: Modest
Area: Old Town
Address: 1 Angle Park Terrace
Edinburgh EH11 2JT
Phone: 0131 337 3822

#420
Jongleurs
Category: Comedy Club
Average price: Modest
Area: Tollcross, West End
Address: 3 West Tollcross
Edinburgh EH3 9
Phone: 0131 228 3252

#421
Home's Bar
Category: Pub
Average price: Inexpensive
Area: Leith
Address: 102 Constitution Street
Edinburgh EH6 6AW
Phone: 0131 553 7710

#422
Sin Club & Lounge
Category: Lounge
Average price: Expensive
Area: Old Town, Newington
Address: 207 Cowgate
Edinburgh EH1 1JQ
Phone: 0131 558 3332

#423
**Gravity Club Edinburgh
at The Store**
Category: Club
Average price: Modest
Area: Old Town, Newington
Address: 37 Guthrie Street
Edinburgh EH1 1JG
Phone: 07814 878815

#424
Frenchies
Category: Pub
Average price: Modest
Area: New Town
Address: 87-89 Rose St Ln N
Edinburgh EH2 3DT
Phone: 0131 225 7651

#425
Omni Taverns
Category: Pub, British
Average price: Expensive
Area: Old Town, Royal Mile
Address: 119 High Street
Edinburgh EH1 1SG
Phone: 0131 556 3095

#426
Brass Monkey
Category: Pub
Average price: Modest
Area: Newington
Address: 14 Drummond Street
Edinburgh EH8 9TU
Phone: 0131 556 1961

#427
Scott's Bar
Category: Pub
Average price: Modest
Area: New Town
Address: 202 Rose Street
Edinburgh EH2 4AZ
Phone: 0131 225 7401

#428
Punchline
Category: Comedy Club
Average price: Modest
Area: Old Town, West End
Address: Lothian Road Edinburgh
Phone: 0131 228 1155

#429
An Evening of Bollywood Magic
Category: Bar
Average price: Modest
Area: New Town
Address: Roxburghe Hotel Charlotte
Square, Edinburgh EH2 4HQ
Phone: 07909 226506

#430
Fantasy Palace Lapdancing Bar
Category: Wine Bar, Adult Entertainment
Average price: Modest
Area: West End
Address: 12 Shandwick Place
Edinburgh EH2 4RN
Phone: 0131 538 3000

#431
Timber Bush Bar
Category: Pub
Average price: Expensive
Area: Leith
Address: 28 Bernard Street
Edinburgh EH6 6PP
Phone: 0131 553 6400

#432
The Meadow Bar & Kitchen
Category: British, Pub
Average price: Modest
Area: Newington
Address: 44 Buccleuch Street
Edinburgh EH8 9
Phone: 0131 667 6907

#433
Hemma
Category: Bar, British
Average price: Modest
Area: Old Town
Address: 75 Holyrood Road
Edinburgh EH8 8AJ
Phone: 0131 629 3327

#434
The Golf Tavern
Category: Pub
Average price: Inexpensive
Area: Bruntsfield, The Meadows
Address: 30-31 Wrights Houses
Edinburgh EH10 4HR
Phone: 0131 221 5221

#435
ENZO Bar Restaurant
Category: Cocktail Bar, Italian
Average price: Modest
Area: The Meadows
Address: 8 Lister Square
Edinburgh EH3 9GL
Phone: 07881 366620

#436
The King's Wark
Category: Pub, Gastropub
Average price: Modest
Area: Leith
Address: 36 The Shore
Edinburgh EH6 6QU
Phone: 0131 554 9260

#437
The Eric Alexander Quartet
Category: Bar
Average price: Modest
Area: Newington
Address: Bf1 5 Dalkeith Road
Edinburgh EH16
Phone: 0131 667 0684

#438
**Greene King Finance
Shared Services**
Category: Pub
Average price: Modest
Area: New Town
Address: Belhaven Brewery
Edinburgh EH1
Phone: 07791 263090

#439
Queen Charlotte Rooms
Category: Pub
Average price: Modest
Area: Leith
Address: 56A Queen Charlotte Street
Edinburgh EH6 7ET
Phone: 0131 555 6660

#440
Siamsior
Category: Bar
Average price: Modest
Area: Leith
Address: 81-85 Portland Street Leith Eh6
4ay, Edinburgh EH6
Phone: 07886 537597

#441
The Beehive Inn
Category: Pub, Gastropub
Average price: Modest
Area: Old Town, Grassmarket
Address: 18-20 Grassmarket
Edinburgh EH1 2JU
Phone: 0131 225 7171

#442
Burlington Bertie
Category: Pub
Average price: Inexpensive
Area: Tollcross, The Meadows
Address: 11-13 Tarvit Street
Edinburgh EH3 9LB
Phone: 0131 229 8659

#443
Wally Dug
Category: Pub
Average price: Expensive
Area: New Town
Address: 32 Northumberland Street
Edinburgh EH3 6LS
Phone: 0131 557 6825

#444
Berties
Category: Pub
Average price: Modest
Area: Old Town
Address: 7 Merchant Street
Edinburgh EH1 2QD
Phone: 0131 225 2002

#445
Saltyre Taverns
Category: Pub
Average price: Modest
Area: Old Town
Address: 23 George Iv Bridge
Edinburgh EH1 1EN
Phone: 0131 622 1820

#446
Chasers Bar
Category: Pub
Average price: Modest
Area: Old Town, Newington
Address: 139 Cowgate
Edinburgh EH1 1JS
Phone: 0131 225 5995

#447
Massa Discos
Category: Club
Average price: Modest
Area: Old Town, Royal Mile
Address: 36-39 Market Street
Edinburgh EH1 1DF
Phone: 0131 226 4224

#448
Three Tuns Wine Vaults
Category: Pub
Average price: Modest
Area: New Town
Address: 7-11 Hanover Street
Edinburgh EH2 2DL
Phone: 0131 225 8998

#449
The Coconut Groove Company
Category: Pub, Club
Average price: Modest
Area: New Town
Address: 47 Hanover Street
Edinburgh EH2 2PJ
Phone: 0131 220 6818

#450
Morrison Bro's
Category: Pub
Average price: Modest
Area: New Town
Address: 49 Rose Street
Edinburgh EH2 2NH
Phone: 0131 220 0414

#451
D M Stewart
Category: Pub
Average price: Modest
Area: New Town
Address: 34 Rose St North Lane
Edinburgh EH2 2NP
Phone: 0131 220 1122

#452
Brecks Bar
Category: Pub
Average price: Modest
Area: New Town
Address: 110-114 Rose Street
Edinburgh EH2 3JF
Phone: 0131 225 3297

#453
Cellar N O 1
Category: Pub
Average price: Modest
Area: Old Town, Newington
Address: 1A Chambers St
Edinburgh EH1 1HR
Phone: 0131 220 4298

#454
Peppermint Lounge
Category: Wine Bar
Average price: Modest
Area: Old Town, Newington
Address: 1a Chambers Street
Edinburgh EH1 1HR
Phone: 0131 220 4298

#455
The Burgh
Category: Bar
Average price: Modest
Area: New Town
Address: South St Andrew Street
Edinburgh EH2 2AU
Phone: 0131 478 4554

#456
Bruce Taverns
Category: Pub
Average price: Modest
Area: New Town
Address: 17 West Register Street
Edinburgh EH2 2AA
Phone: 0131 556 1106

#457
The Gordon Arms
Category: Pub
Average price: Modest
Area: New Town
Address: 133 Rose Street
Edinburgh EH2 4LS
Phone: 0131 225 8492

#458
Hogshead
Category: Pub
Average price: Modest
Area: Old Town
Address: 30-32 Bread Street
Edinburgh EH3 9AF
Phone: 0131 221 0575

#459
The World
Category: Pub
Average price: Modest
Area: New Town
Address: 55 Thistle Street
Edinburgh EH2 1DY
Phone: 0131 225 3275

#460
Tipplers
Category: Pub
Average price: Modest
Area: Old Town
Address: 17-19 Bread Street
Edinburgh EH3 9AL
Phone: 0131 228 2690

#461
Signature Pub
Category: Pub
Average price: Modest
Area: Old Town
Address: 51 Lothian Road
Edinburgh EH1 2DJ
Phone: 0131 228 4981

#462
Saphire Rooms
Category: Wine Bar, Adult Entertainment
Average price: Modest
Area: Old Town
Address: 81-83 Lothian Road
Edinburgh EH3 9AW
Phone: 0131 229 6391

#463
Revolution
Category: Bar
Average price: Modest
Area: Old Town
Address: 31 Lothian Road
Edinburgh EH1 2DJ
Phone: 0131 228 1681

#464
Fish Tank
Category: Pub
Average price: Modest
Area: New Town
Address: 16a Queen Street
Edinburgh EH2 1JE
Phone: 0131 226 5959

#465
Bottoms Up Showbar
Category: Pub, Adult Entertainment
Average price: Modest
Area: Old Town
Address: 93 Lothian Road
Edinburgh EH3 9AW
Phone: 0131 229 1599

#466
Drinkies
Category: Jazz & Blues
Average price: Modest
Area: New Town
Address: 39A Queen Street
Edinburgh EH2 1
Phone: 0131 226 3417

#467
Doric Bar
Category: Pub
Average price: Modest
Area: Old Town, Royal Mile
Address: Market Street
Edinburgh EH1 1DE
Phone: 0131 225 5243

#468
Fiscal & Firkin Public House
Category: Pub
Average price: Modest
Area: Old Town, Newington, Royal Mile
Address: Hunter Square
Edinburgh EH1 1QW
Phone: 0131 226 6958

#469
The Granary
Category: Pub
Average price: Modest
Area: New Town
Address: 42-43 Queensferry Street
Edinburgh EH2 4RA
Phone: 0131 226 7903

#470
Tapis Productions
Category: Pub
Average price: Modest
Area: Newington
Address: 2/8 West Crosscauseway
Edinburgh EH8 9JP
Phone: 0131 662 8860

#471
Audience Business
Category: Music Venues
Average price: Modest
Area: Tollcross, The Meadows
Address: 2 Leven Street
Edinburgh EH3 9LQ
Phone: 0131 622 8100

#472
Kildares Public House
Category: Pub
Average price: Modest
Area: Newington
Address: 33 West Crosscauseway
Edinburgh EH8 9JP
Phone: 0131 667 3749

#473
District
Category: Music Venues
Average price: Modest
Area: West End
Address: 3 Queensferry Lane
Edinburgh EH2 4PF
Phone: 0131 467 7216

#474
The Grovener
Category: Pub
Average price: Modest
Area: West End
Address: 26-28 Shandwick Place
Edinburgh EH2 4RT
Phone: 0131 226 4579

#475
Montpeliers Edinburgh
Category: Pub
Average price: Modest
Area: New Town
Address: 29 Queensferry Street
Edinburgh EH2 4QS
Phone: 0131 226 1370

#476
Hazel Carr
Category: Pub
Average price: Modest
Area: New Town
Address: 1 ST. Colme Street
Edinburgh EH3 6AA
Phone: 0131 220 8247

#477
Outlook Project
Category: Music Venues
Average price: Modest
Area: Old Town
Address: Cambridge Street
Edinburgh EH1 2DY
Phone: 0131 228 9076

#478
Steamworks
Category: Adult Entertainment
Average price: Modest
Area: New Town
Address: 5 Broughton Market
Edinburgh EH3 6NU
Phone: 0131 477 3567

#479
Cafe Provencal
Category: Wine Bar
Average price: Modest
Area: West End
Address: 34 Alva Street
Edinburgh EH2 4PY
Phone: 0131 220 6105

#480
Clouds & Soil
Category: Wine Bar, British
Average price: Modest
Area: New Town
Address: 4 Picardy Pl
Edinburgh EH1 3JT
Phone: 0131 629 2728

#481
William Mcewens
Category: Pub
Average price: Modest
Area: Newington
Address: 18-22 Clerk Street
Edinburgh EH8 9HX
Phone: 0131 668 4786

#482
Proctors Bar
Category: Wine Bar, Lounge
Average price: Modest
Area: Newington
Address: 93 Buccleuch Street
Edinburgh EH8 9NG
Phone: 0131 667 9773

#483
Harley's Cellar Bar
Category: Pub
Average price: Modest
Area: New Town
Address: 46-48a Broughton Street
Edinburgh EH1 3SA
Phone: 0131 558 8001

#484
Offian's Bar
Category: Pub
Average price: Modest
Area: West End
Address: 185 Morrison Street
Edinburgh EH3 8DZ
Phone: 0131 228 9149

#485
Ceroc Scotland
Category: Club
Average price: Modest
Area: Stockbridge, New Town
Address: St Stephens Street
Edinburgh EH3 5AB
Phone: 07528 694901

#486
Grouchos Bar
Category: Wine Bar
Average price: Modest
Area: West End
Address: 8 Torphichen Place
Edinburgh EH3 8DU
Phone: 0131 625 3702

#487
Renegade Communications
Category: Club
Average price: Modest
Area: New Town
Address: 5-6 Broughton Place Lane
Edinburgh EH1 3RS
Phone: 0131 558 3824

#488
Edinburgh Society Of Musicians
Category: Pub
Average price: Modest
Area: West End
Address: 3 Belford Road
Edinburgh EH4 3BL
Phone: 0131 220 5528

#489
Junction Bar
Category: Pub
Average price: Modest
Area: Newington
Address: 24-26 West Preston Street
Edinburgh EH8 9PZ
Phone: 0131 667 3010

#490
Berts Bar
Category: Pub
Average price: Modest
Area: Stockbridge
Address: 2 Raeburn Place
Edinburgh EH4 1HN
Phone: 0131 332 6345

#491
Minders Public House
Category: Pub
Average price: Modest
Area: Newington
Address: 114 Causewayside
Edinburgh EH9 1PU
Phone: 0131 667 9479

#492
Maclay
Category: Pub
Average price: Modest
Area: Leith
Address: 8 Mcdonald Road
Edinburgh EH7 4LZ
Phone: 0131 558 3523

#493
Gentlemens Club
Category: Social Club,
Adult Entertainment
Average price: Modest
Area: Stockbridge
Address: 43 Comely Bank Place
Edinburgh EH4 1ER
Phone: 0131 332 3247

#494
Blind Beggar
Category: Pub
Average price: Modest
Area: Cannonmills
Address: 97-99 Broughton Road
Edinburgh EH7 4EG
Phone: 0131 557 3130

#495
Ceroc Scotland
Category: Club
Average price: Modest
Area: Leith
Address: 1 Shrub Place Lane
Edinburgh EH7 4PB
Phone: 07528 694901

#496
Old Salt
Category: Pub
Average price: Modest
Area: Leith
Address: 17 Albert Place
Edinburgh EH7 5HN
Phone: 0131 554 9522

#497
Pilmeny Youth Centre
Category: Bar
Average price: Modest
Area: Leith
Address: 44 Buchanan Street
Edinburgh EH6 8RF
Phone: 0131 554 0953

#498
Jaynes
Category: Pub
Average price: Modest
Area: Leith
Address: 298-300 Leith Walk
Edinburgh EH6 5BU
Phone: 0131 555 2238

#499
Tempus
Category: Wine Bar, French, Scottish
Average price: Modest
Area: New Town
Address: 25 George Street
Edinburgh EH2 2PB
Phone: 0131 240 7197

#500
Tamson's Bar
Category: Pub
Average price: Modest
Area: Leith
Address: 280 Easter Road
Edinburgh EH6 8JU
Phone: 0131 554 4692

Made in the USA
San Bernardino, CA
06 April 2015